Digital Direct Selling Success
Handbook for Students and Distributors

Index

Part 1: Foundation

Chapter 1: Introduction to Digital Direct Selling

- Definition of digital direct selling
- Benefits of digital direct selling (increased reach, cost-effectiveness, personalized engagement)
- Overview of the Indian direct selling industry
- Setting goals and expectations for digital direct selling success

Chapter 2: Setting Up Your Digital Presence

- Creating a professional website (domain registration, web hosting, website design)
- Website Builders and CMS
- Establishing social media profiles (Facebook, Instagram, Twitter, LinkedIn)
- Claiming Google My Business listing
- Setting up email marketing system (Mailchimp, Constant Contact)
- Choosing CRM software (HubSpot, Zoho)

Chapter 3: Understanding Your Target Audience

- Identifying customer segments
  - Demographics (age, location, income)
  - Psychographics (interests, values, lifestyle)
  - Pain points and needs
- Analyzing customer behavior (buying habits, preferences)
- Creating buyer personas
- Developing a customer-centric approach

Chapter 4: Content Creation Strategy

- Types of content (blog posts, videos, infographics, podcasts)
- Content creation tools (Canva, Adobe Creative Cloud)
- Content calendar planning
- Repurposing and upcycling content
- Measuring content effectiveness

Part 2: Social Media Marketing

Chapter 5: Facebook Marketing

- What is Facebook and how does it work for you?

- Creating engaging Facebook content (posts, stories, reels)
- Facebook advertising (targeting, budgeting, ad creative)
- Facebook groups and community building (Join and participate in relevant groups)
- Facebook Messenger marketing
- Facebook analytics and tracking
- Facebook advertising approximate cast in India and international

Chapter 6: Instagram Marketing

- What is Instagram and how it's useful to the peoples in the world?
- Creating visually appealing Instagram content
- Instagram hashtags and tagging
- Instagram Stories and Reels
- Instagram Influencer marketing
- Instagram shopping and ecommerce integration
- Instatram advertising costs internationally and in India

Chapter 7: X (Formally Twitter) Marketing (x.com)

- What is X (formally Twitter) and how to use it?
- Crafting compelling tweets
- Twitter Chats and hashtag participation
- Twitter Polls and surveys
- Twitter advertising
- Twitter analytics and tracking
- Twitter Advertising cost India and International

Chapter 8: WhatsApp Business Marketing

- What is WhatsApp and WhatsApp business?
- Setting up WhatsApp Business
- Creating and sending broadcasts
- Using WhatsApp groups
- Customer support and response
- Integrating WhatsApp with other channels

Chapter 9: YouTube Marketing

- What is YouTube and YouTube Marketing?
- Creating engaging video content
- YouTube SEO optimization or Channel Optimization
- Advanced YouTube SEO techniques
- Video optimization strategies
- YouTube algorithm updates
- SEO audit and analysis
- YouTube marketing case studies
- SEO-friendly title and description writing
- SEO optimization for live streams
- YouTube advertising strategies

- Influencer marketing on YouTube
- YouTube Analytics and tracking
- YouTube marketing case studies
- YouTube marketing tools and software
- YouTube marketing best practices
- YouTube marketing trends
- YouTube SEO certifications, YouTube marketing certifications and courses
- YouTube Analytics and tracking
- Collaborations sponsorships and partnerships
- Live streaming on YouTube
- Live streaming equipment and software
- Podcasting on YouTube
- Engaging thumbnail design
- Animated explainer videos
- Content calendar planning
- Video editing software

Chapter 10: LinkedIn Marketing

- What is LinkedIn and how it is works for you?
- Creating a professional LinkedIn profile
- Participating in LinkedIn groups
- Building connections and networking
- Sharing content and engaging (Publishing articles and posts)
- Job searching and recruitment
- LinkedIn advertising and marketing
- LinkedIn Marketing advertising cost in India and international
- LinkedIn premium features
- Optimizing LinkedIn profile
- LinkedIn algorithms
- Advanced LinkedIn strategies
- Networking and connections
- LinkedIn certifications and courses

Part 3: Content Creation and Funnel Building

Chapter 11: Content Creation Strategy

- Blogging
- Video creation
- Infographics
- Podcasting

Chapter 12: Building Sales Funnels

- What is funnel and how it is work for me in my business
- Understanding sales funnel stages (awareness, interest, desire, and action)
- Creating landing pages
- Lead magnets and opt-in forms
- Email nurturing sequences
- Conversion rate optimization

- Free and paid tools for creating funnels with Email nurturing sequences and WhatsApp auto-messages

Chapter 13: Email Marketing

- What is Email Marketing and how it's works?
- Building an email list
- Crafting effective email campaigns
- Email automation and sequencing
- Email Automation Cost in India
- Personalization and segmentation
- Tracking and analytics

Chapter 14: Webinar and Zoom Meeting Strategy

- What is Webinar and Zoom Meeting?
- What is Webinar and Zoom Meeting Strategy and how I can use it?
- Choosing Topics for Webinars and Zoom Meetings
- Hosting webinars and Zoom meeting
- Promoting webinars and Zoom meeting
- Engaging attendees
- Follow-up and conversion
- Recording and repurposing
- Webinar and Zoom Meeting cost in India and International

Part 4: Advertising and Lead Generation

Chapter 15: Google Ads

- What is Google Ads and how to configure and monetize it?
- Google Ads account setup and configuration
- Google Ads campaign optimization
- Google Ads bidding strategies
- Ad copywriting and creative
- Landing page optimization
- Ad extensions and formats
- Keyword research and targeting

Chapter 16: Facebook and Instagram Ads

- Creating ad campaigns
- Facebook Ads and Instagram Ads setup and structure
- Facebook Ads and Instagram Ads automation
- Facebook Ads and Instagram Ads for e-commerce
- Target audience selection
- Ad creative and copy
- Budgeting and bidding
- Optimizing ad performance and Tracking

Chapter 17: Lead Generation

- What is Lead Generation?
- Strategies for generating leads (webinars, free resources, referrals)
- Creating lead magnets
- Using opt-in forms and landing pages
- Lead scoring and qualification
- Referrals and word-of-mouth
- Paid advertising
- Follow-up and conversion

Chapter 18: AI Tools for Lead Generation

- What is AI?
- AI Tools for Direct Selling Marketing
- Chatbots and conversational marketing
- Predictive analytics and scoring
- Personalization and recommendation
- Automated email and messaging
- Social media monitoring

Part 5: Advanced Strategies and Tools

Chapter 19: Podcasting for Direct Sales

- What is Podcasting
- Choosing a niche and format
- Creating engaging podcast content
- Guest selection and interviewing
- Promotion and distribution
- Monetization and sponsorship

Chapter 20: Utilizing Quora and Blogger

- What is Quora and Blogger?
- Creating informative content
- Building authority and credibility
- Engaging with audiences
- Driving traffic and sales
- Measuring success

Chapter 21: Pinterest and Printrest Marketing

- What is Pinterest and Printrest Marketing?
- Creating boards and pins
- Optimizing images and descriptions
- Using hashtags and keywords
- Engaging with audience
- Running Pinterest Ads
- Pinterest Ads cost in India and International

Chapter 22: White Labeling tools or Software's

- What is White Labeling tools or software's and how to use it for Direct Selling Marketing?
- What is White Labeling tools or software's cost in India and International and contact details and support.

Chapter 23: Measuring Success and Tracking Performance

- Measuring Success and Tracking Performance of direct selling marketing
- Key metrics for digital direct selling (website traffic, social media engagement, lead generation)
- Tools for tracking (Google Analytics, social media insights, Email marketing metrics, Sales funnel analysis)
- CRM software and sales funnel analysis (Sales Revenue)
- Adjusting strategies based on data

Chapter 24: Overview of video editing software's and keyword research tools and techniques
- Overview of video editing software's
- Overview of keyword research tools and techniques

Welcome to "Digital Direct Selling Success": Handbook for Students and Distributors

The direct selling industry has evolved significantly in the digital age. With the internet and social media, students and distributors can reach new customers, build relationships, and grow their businesses.

Designed to help students and direct sellers thrive in a rapidly changing industry, this comprehensive handbook equips them with skills, knowledge, and strategies.

You can discover the following information through these pages:

1. Digital direct selling fundamentals
2. Effective social media marketing strategies
3. Proven content creation and funnel building techniques
4. Strategies for lead generation and advertising
5. Metrics that measure success

This book offers useful advice and actionable insights to help you reach your objectives, whether you're just starting out or trying to grow your current workplace.

About the Author

This handbook has been created by Goverdhan Goud V, a skilled professional in direct selling as well as other online marketing from Hyderabad, India, to convey essential knowledge experience to distributors and students.

Acknowledgments

Special thanks to Co-Direct Selling Distributors to encourage me to write this book.
Now, let's move on to the next step.

******

Part 1: Foundation

Chapter 1: Introduction to Digital Direct Selling

Digital Direct Selling:

Let's say you own a clothing store and sell online from your computer or phone rather than in person.

Digital direct selling is the practice of selling goods or services to clients directly via online platforms such as

1. Social Media (Facebook, Instagram, WhatsApp)
2. Online Marketplaces (Amazon, eBay)
3. Messaging Apps (WhatsApp, Telegram)
4. Email
5. Websites

Example:

Assume that Vennela, your friend, is a huge fan of the skincare line "Glowing Skin." Vennela joins Glowing Skin as a distributor and uses WhatsApp to share products with her loved ones.

You receive a message from Vennela: "Hey! Glowing Skin has a fantastic face cream that I use. Do you want to give it a try? Just Rs. 40.

"Yes, I'll take one!" is your response.

Vennela receives payment for the sale after delivering the item to you.

Important points:

1. Vennela sells to you directly; no stores are involved.
2. Vennela sells through digital platforms like WhatsApp.
3. Every sale brings in money for Vennela.

Benefits of digital direct selling

1. Convenience (ability to shop remotely)
2. Expanded reach (sell to people all over the world)
3. Reduced expenses (no need for a physical store)
4. Adaptability (sell whenever you want)

Kids, imagine you can sell:

1. Online handmade crafts
2. Your social media artwork
3. Using messaging apps to send friends cookies or treats

☐ Benefits of digital direct selling (increased reach, cost-effectiveness, personalized engagement)

Here are the benefits of digital direct selling, explained step-by-step with examples:

Benefit 1: Increased Reach

Digital direct selling allows you to reach a wider audience beyond geographical limitations.

Step-by-Step:

1. Create a social media presence (e.g., Facebook, Instagram).
2. Share product information, images, and videos.
3. Utilize hashtags to increase visibility.
4. Engage with potential customers through comments and messaging.

Example:

Vennela sells jewelry through her Facebook page. She shares high-quality product images, descriptions, and prices. Vennela uses relevant hashtags (#jewelrylover, #handmadejewelry) to reach a broader audience.

Benefit 2: Cost-Effectiveness

Digital direct selling reduces costs associated with traditional sales methods.

Step-by-Step:

1. Eliminate physical store rental or maintenance costs.
2. Reduce inventory storage and shipping costs.
3. Leverage free or low-cost digital marketing tools (social media, email).
4. Automate sales and payment processes.

Example:

Karthik sells eBooks through his website. He eliminates printing and storage costs. Karthik uses email marketing and social media to promote his eBooks, reducing advertising expenses.

Benefit 3: Personalized Engagement

Digital direct selling enables personalized interactions with customers.

Step-by-Step:

1. Use customer data to tailor recommendations.
2. Engage through social media comments and messaging.
3. Offer personalized promotions and discounts.

4. Utilize email marketing automation.

Example:

Vennela sells skincare products through her website. She uses customer purchase history to suggest relevant products. Vennela responds to customer inquiries through social media, offering personalized advice.

Additional Benefits:

1. Flexibility: Sell 24/7, anywhere, anytime.
2. Measurable Results: Track sales, website analytics, and customer engagement.
3. Competitive Advantage: Differentiate through unique digital experiences.
4. Scalability: Easily expand your business with digital tools.

Digital Direct Selling Platforms:

1. Social Media (Facebook, Instagram, Twitter)
2. E-commerce Websites (Shopify, WooCommerce)
3. Online Marketplaces (Amazon, eBay)
4. Messaging Apps (WhatsApp, Telegram)
5. Email Marketing Tools (Mailchimp, Constant Contact)

Getting Started:

1. Choose a platform or combination of platforms.
2. Set up your digital storefront.
3. Develop a marketing strategy.
4. Engage with customers.

☐ Overview of the Indian direct selling industry

Here's an overview of the Indian direct selling industry:

Industry Size:

- Estimated size: ₹15,000 crores (approximately $2 billion USD) (2022)
- Growth rate: 10-15% annually

Key Players:

1. Herbalife International India
2. Oriflame India
3. Tupperware India
4. Avon Beauty Products India
5. Modicare

6. Vestige Marketing
7. Mi Lifestyle Marketing
8. Sun Edge Marketing

Product Categories:

1. Wellness and Nutrition (35-40% market share)
2. Beauty and Personal Care (25-30% market share)
3. Home Care (15-20% market share)
4. Fashion and Apparel (10-15% market share)
5. Electronics and Durables (5-10% market share)

Distribution Channels:

1. Online (30-40% sales)
2. Offline (60-70% sales)
3. Social Media (10-20% sales)

Regulatory Framework:

1. Ministry of Consumer Affairs
2. Direct Selling Guidelines (2016)
3. Consumer Protection Act (2019)

Challenges:

1. Lack of regulatory clarity
2. Pyramid scheme concerns
3. Competition from e-commerce platforms
4. Quality control issues
5. Public perception and awareness

Opportunities:

1. Growing middle class
2. Increasing internet penetration
3. Rising demand for wellness and nutrition products
4. Expanding rural market
5. Government initiatives (e.g., Digital India)

Trends:

1. Digitalization and online sales
2. Social selling and influencer marketing
3. Health and wellness focus
4. Sustainable and eco-friendly products
5. Personalized and customized products

Statistics:

1. 5.7 million direct sellers in India (2020)
2. 70% of direct sellers are women
3. 60% of direct sellers are from rural areas
4. Average annual spending per direct seller: ₹50,000-₹1 lakh

Associations:

1. Indian Direct Selling Association (IDSA)
2. Federation of Indian Chambers of Commerce and Industry (FICCI) - Direct Selling Committee

Reports and Studies:

1. "Direct Selling in India" by KPMG (2020)
2. "India Direct Selling Market" by Research and Markets (2022)
3. "Direct Selling Industry in India" by IDSA (2020)

☐ Setting goals and expectations for digital direct selling success

Setting clear goals and expectations is crucial for digital direct selling success. Here's a comprehensive guide to help you set achievable goals and expectations:

Goal Setting:

1. Define your why: Identify your purpose and motivation for starting a digital direct selling business.
2. Set SMART goals:
   - **Specific** (e.g., sell 10 products per week)
   - **Measurable** (track sales, revenue, and customer engagement)
   - **Achievable** (consider resources, skills, and market conditions)
   - **Relevant** (align goals with your "why")
   - **Time-bound** (set deadlines, e.g., monthly, quarterly)
3. Break down big goals into smaller, manageable tasks.

Short-Term Goals (0-3 months):

1. Build a social media presence (e.g., 100 followers on Instagram)
2. Develop a content calendar (posting schedule)
3. Engage with 10 potential customers daily
4. Sell X products per week
5. Reach ₹X revenue per month

Mid-Term Goals (3-6 months):

1. Grow social media following to 1,000
2. Launch email marketing campaigns
3. Collaborate with influencers or other sellers
4. Increase sales by 20% monthly
5. Expand product offerings

Long-Term Goals (6-12 months):

1. Establish a strong brand identity
2. Develop a loyal customer base (100+ repeat customers)
3. Achieve ₹X monthly revenue
4. Expand team (hire/mentor other sellers)
5. Explore new markets or product lines

Expectations:

1. Time commitment: 5-10 hours/week (initially)
2. Financial investment: ₹X (initial inventory, marketing)
3. Learning curve: 1-3 months (product knowledge, digital marketing)
4. Customer acquisition: 1-5 customers/week
5. Sales conversion rate: 10-20%

Key Performance Indicators (KPIs):

1. Website traffic
1. 2.Social media engagement (likes, comments, shares)
2. Email open rates
3. Sales conversion rate
4. Customer retention rate

Tracking Progress:

1. Use analytics tools (Google Analytics, social media insights)
2. Monitor sales and revenue
3. Track customer engagement and feedback
4. Adjust strategies based on data

Staying Motivated:

1. Celebrate small wins
2. Join a community or support group
3. Continuously learn and improve skills
4. Set achievable milestones
5. Reward yourself for reaching goals

By setting clear goals and expectations, you'll be better equipped to measure progress, stay motivated, and achieve success in digital direct selling.

Example:

Here's a comprehensive goal-setting guide for digital direct selling of Sun Edge Marketing products:

Short-Term Goals (0-3 months)

1. **Product Knowledge:**
    a. Complete Sun Edge Marketing's online training programs.
    b. Familiarize yourself with 5-10 key products.
2. **Social Media Presence:**
    c. Create profiles on Facebook, Instagram, and Twitter.
    d. Post 3 times a week, focusing on product benefits and testimonials.
    e. Reach 100 followers on each platform.
3. **Customer Acquisition:**
    f. Engage with 10 potential customers daily.
    g. Sell 5-10 products per week.
    h. Achieve ₹10,000 monthly revenue.
4. **Team Building:**
    i. Sponsor 2-3 new distributors.
    j. Conduct 2-3 training sessions for team members.

Mid-Term Goals (3-6 months)

1. **Sales Growth:**
    a. Increase sales by 20% monthly.
    b. Achieve ₹25,000 monthly revenue.
2. **Customer Retention:**
    c. Maintain a 50% customer retention rate.
    d. Conduct regular customer surveys.
3. **Digital Marketing:**
    e. Launch email marketing campaigns.
    f. Utilize Sun Edge Marketing's digital marketing tools.
4. **Leadership Development:**
    g. Attend Sun Edge Marketing's leadership training events.
    h. Mentor 2-3 team members.

Long-Term Goals (6-12 months)

1. **Business Expansion:**
    a. Establish a strong online presence.
    b. Expand product offerings.
    c. Achieve ₹50,000 monthly revenue.
2. **Team Leadership:**
    a. Develop a team of 10+ distributors.
    b. Conduct regular team meetings.

3. **Customer Loyalty:**
    a. Achieve a 75% customer retention rate.
    b. Implement loyalty programs.
4. **Personal Development:**
    a. Attend industry conferences.
    b. Continuously update product knowledge.

Key Performance Indicators (KPIs)

1. Sales revenue
2. Customer acquisition and retention rates
3. Social media engagement (likes, comments, shares)
4. Email open rates
5. Team growth and leadership development

Action Plan

1. Week 1-4: Set up social media profiles, complete product training.
2. Week 5-8: Launch email marketing campaigns, engage with potential customers.
3. Week 9-12: Analyze sales data, adjust strategies.

Sun Edge Marketing-Specific Resources

1. Sun Edge Marketing University (online training)
2. Sun Edge Marketing's Digital Marketing Platform
3. Sun Edge Marketing's Social Media Guidelines
4. Sun Edge Marketing's Leadership Development Programs

Tracking Progress

1. Use Sun Edge Marketing's sales tracking tools.
2. Monitor social media analytics.
3. Track email open rates.
4. Conduct regular team meetings.

By setting these goals and tracking progress, you'll be well on your way to achieving success in digital direct selling with Sun Edge Marketing.

Chapter 2: Setting Up Your Digital Presence

☐ **Creating a professional website (domain registration, web hosting, website design)**

Setting up your digital presence involves creating and managing your online identity, including various digital platforms, tools, and content, to establish a strong and professional online reputation.

Key Components:

1. **Website or Blog:** Central hub for your online presence.
2. **Social Media Profiles:** Facebook, Instagram, Twitter, LinkedIn, etc.
3. **Email Marketing:** Newsletters, promotional emails, and automated sequences.
4. **Online Directories:** Google My Business, Yelp, etc.
5. **Content Creation:** Blog posts, videos, podcasts, infographics, etc.
6. **Search Engine Optimization (SEO):** Improve visibility on search engines.
7. **Digital Networking:** Engage with influencers, peers, and customers online.

Benefits:

1. Increased visibility and credibility
2. Improved brand awareness and recognition
3. Enhanced customer engagement and communication
4. Increased website traffic and sales
5. Better competition differentiation
6. Data-driven decision-making

Digital Presence Setup Checklist:

Phase 1: Research and Planning

1. Define target audience and goals
2. Conduct competitor analysis
3. Choose digital platforms and tools
4. Develop content strategy

Phase 2: Setup and Configuration

1. Register domain name and web hosting
2. Create website or blog
3. Set up social media profiles
4. Configure email marketing tools
5. Claim online directories

Phase 3: Content Creation and Optimization

1. Develop content calendar
2. Create high-quality content
3. Optimize website for SEO
4. Implement analytics and tracking

Phase 4: Launch and Promotion

1. Launch website and social media profiles
2. Promote digital presence through advertising
3. Engage with audience through content and social media
4. Monitor analytics and adjust strategy

Tools and Resources:

1. Website builders (WordPress, Wix, Squarespace)
2. Social media management tools (Hootsuite, Buffer)
3. Email marketing software (Mailchimp, Constant Contact)
4. SEO tools (Google Analytics, Ahrefs)

5. Content creation tools (Canva, Adobe Creative Cloud)

Best Practices:

1. Consistency across all digital platforms
2. Regular content updates and engagement
3. Responsive design for mobile devices
4. Secure and reliable hosting
5. Continuous monitoring and improvement

Creating a professional website involves several steps:

Step 1: Domain Registration

1. Choose a domain name (e.g., [yourbusiness].com)
2. Check availability using tools like GoDaddy or Namecheap
3. Register domain name (typically $10-$35/year)

Step 2: Web Hosting

1. Select a web hosting service (e.g., Bluehost, SiteGround)
2. Choose a hosting plan (shared, VPS, dedicated)
3. Consider factors: storage, bandwidth, security, support

Step 3: Website Design

1. Determine website purpose (e.g., informational, e-commerce)
2. Choose a website builder (e.g., WordPress, Wix, and Squarespace)
3. Select a template or theme
4. Customize design and content

Website Building Options:

1. Website builders (e.g., Wix, Squarespace)
2. Content Management Systems (CMS) (e.g., WordPress, Joomla)
3. Custom development (hire a developer)

Key Website Elements:

1. Home page
2. About page
3. Products/Services page
4. Contact page
5. Blog (optional)

Design Considerations:

1. Responsive design (mobile-friendly)
2. Clear navigation
3. Compelling content
4. Visual hierarchy
5. Brand consistency

Web Hosting Types:

1. Shared hosting
2. Virtual Private Server (VPS)
3. Dedicated hosting
4. Cloud hosting

Web Hosting Features:

1. Storage space
2. Bandwidth
3. Email accounts
4. Security features (e.g., SSL, firewall)
5. Customer support

Recommended Web Hosting Services:

1. Bluehost
2. SiteGround
3. HostGator
4. InMotion Hosting
5. WP Engine (WordPress-specific)

Recommended Website Builders:

1. WordPress
2. Wix
3. Squarespace
4. Weebly
5. Shopify (e-commerce specific)

Costs:

1. Domain registration: $10-$35/year
2. Web hosting: $5-$50/month

3. Website design: $500-$5,000 (dependent on complexity)

Estimated costs in India:

Domain Registration:

1. .com domain: ₹799 - ₹1,499/year (approximately $11-$21 USD)
2. .in domain: ₹499 - ₹999/year (approximately $7-$14 USD)
3. Other domains (e.g., .co.in, .net.in): ₹499 - ₹1,499/year

Web Hosting:

1. Shared Hosting:
    a. Basic: ₹99 - ₹299/month (approximately $1.40-$4.20 USD)
    b. Premium: ₹299 - ₹499/month (approximately $4.20-$7 USD)
2. Virtual Private Server (VPS):
    a. Basic: ₹499 - ₹999/month (approximately $7-$14 USD)
    b. Premium: ₹999 - ₹2,499/month (approximately $14-$35 USD)
3. Dedicated Hosting:
    a. Basic: ₹2,499 - ₹4,999/month (approximately $35-$70 USD)
    b. Premium: ₹4,999 - ₹9,999/month (approximately $70-$140 USD)

Website Design:

1. Basic Website (5-10 pages): ₹10,000 - ₹30,000 (approximately $140-$420 USD)
2. Custom Website (10-50 pages): ₹30,000 - ₹1,00,000 (approximately $420-$1,400 USD)
3. E-commerce Website: ₹50,000 - ₹2,50,000 (approximately $700-$3,500 USD)
4. Complex Website (e.g., custom development): ₹1,00,000 - ₹5,00,000 (approximately $1,400-$7,000 USD)

Other Costs:

1. Content Creation (writing, images, and videos): ₹5,000 - ₹50,000
2. SEO Services: ₹5,000 - ₹50,000
3. Website Maintenance: ₹2,000 - ₹10,000/year

Popular Web Hosting Providers in India:

1. HostGator India
2. Bluehost India
3. GoDaddy India
4. BigRock
5. ZNetLive

Popular Website Design Companies in India:

1. Wipro
2. Infosys
3. TCS
4. HCL
5. Local web design agencies

Note: Please note that these estimates may vary depending on the specific requirements and complexity of your project.

Timeline:

1. Domain registration: immediate
2. Web hosting setup: 1-2 days
3. Website design: 1-4 weeks (dependent on complexity)

Website Builders and CMS

Website builders and Content Management Systems (CMS) are tools that help create and manage websites. Popular options include:

Website Builders:

1. Wix: Drag-and-drop builder, easy to use.
2. Squarespace: Sleek designs, user-friendly interface.
3. Weebly: Simple, intuitive builder.
4. Shopify: E-commerce focused, scalable.

Content Management Systems (CMS):

1. WordPress: Flexible, customizable, vast community.
2. Joomla: Robust, feature-rich, user-friendly.
3. Drupal: Advanced, secure, scalable.

Key Features:

1. Drag-and-drop editors
2. Responsive designs
3. Customizable templates
4. E-commerce integration
5. SEO optimization
6. Security features

Choosing the Right Option:

1. Consider your needs (blog, e-commerce, portfolio)
2. Evaluate ease of use and customization
3. Assess scalability and security
4. Research community support and resources

E-commerce Solutions

E-commerce solutions enable online sales and payment processing. Popular options include:

E-commerce Platforms:

1. Shopify: User-friendly, scalable, integrations.
2. WooCommerce (WordPress): Flexible, customizable.
3. BigCommerce: Robust, feature-rich, scalable.
4. Magento: Advanced, customizable, enterprise-level.

Key Features:

1. Product management
2. Payment gateways (e.g., PayPal, Stripe)
3. Shipping integrations
4. Inventory management
5. Order tracking
6. Analytics and reporting

Here are popular payment gateways in India:

Domestic Payment Gateways:

1. Paytm Payment Gateway
2. Razorpay
3. PayU India
4. CC Avenue
5. EBS (E-Billing Solutions)
6. HDFC Payment Gateway
7. ICICI Payment Gateway
8. SBI Payment Gateway
9. Axis Payment Gateway
10. Yes Bank Payment Gateway

International Payment Gateways:

1. PayPal
2. Stripe
3. 2Checkout

4. (link unavailable)
5. CyberSource
6. WorldPay
7. First Data
8. Global Payments
9. Elavon
10. Wirecard

Government-Approved Payment Gateways:

1. Bharat Interface for Money (BHIM)
2. Unified Payments Interface (UPI)
3. National Electronic Funds Transfer (NEFT)
4. Real-Time Gross Settlement (RTGS)
5. Immediate Payment Service (IMPS)

Payment Methods Supported:

1. Credit/Debit Cards (Visa, Mastercard, Amex, etc.)
2. Net Banking (all major Indian banks)
3. UPI
4. Wallets (Paytm, Mobikwik, etc.)
5. Cash Cards
6. Mobile Payments (e.g., Google Pay, PhonePe)

Transaction Fees:

1. Domestic transactions: 1.5% - 3.5% + GST
2. International transactions: 3.5% - 5.5% + GST

Integration Fees:

1. One-time setup fees: ₹5,000 - ₹50,000
2. Annual maintenance fees: ₹5,000 - ₹20,000

Security Features:

1. PCI-DSS compliance
2. SSL encryption
3. 2-Factor Authentication
4. Tokenization
5. Risk management tools

Popular E-commerce Platforms with Integrated Payment Gateways:

1. Shopify
2. WooCommerce
3. Magento
4. OpenCart
5. PrestaShop

When selecting a payment gateway, consider factors such as:

1. Transaction fees
2. Integration complexity
3. Security features
4. Customer support
5. Scalability

Choosing the Right Option:

1. Consider your business needs (products, services)
2. Evaluate ease of use and customization
3. Assess scalability and security
4. Research integrations and compatibility

- Establishing social media profiles (Facebook, Instagram, Twitter, LinkedIn)

Establishing social media profiles involves creating and optimizing profiles on various platforms to showcase your brand, engage with your audience, and drive business results.
Profile Creation Checklist:

1. Facebook:
   - Profile name
   - Profile picture (logo)
   - Cover photo
   - About section
   - Contact information
2. Instagram:
   - Username
   - Profile picture (logo)
   - Bio
   - Profile link
   - Contact information
3. Twitter:
   - Handle (username)
   - Profile picture (logo)
   - Header image
   - Bio
   - Contact information
4. LinkedIn:
   - Company name
   - Logo
   - Description
   - Industry
   - Contact information

Optimization Tips:

1. Consistency: Use the same branding across all platforms.
2. Completeness: Fill out all profile sections.
3. High-quality visuals: Use professional images and logos.
4. Keywords: Include relevant keywords in your profiles.
5. Engagement: Respond to comments and messages promptly.

Content Strategy:

1. Content types: Posts, stories, reels, tweets, articles.
2. Content calendar: Plan and schedule content.
3. Hashtags: Research and use relevant hashtags.
4. Engagement: Encourage interactions and conversations.
5. Analytics: Track performance using built-in analytics tools.

Best Practices:

1. Post regularly.
2. Use visual content.
3. Engage with your audience.
4. Monitor and respond to comments.
5. Run social media ads.

Platform-Specific Tips:

1. Facebook:
   - Use Facebook Groups.
   - Create Facebook Events.
   - Utilize Facebook Live.
2. Instagram:
   - Use Instagram Stories.
   - Leverage hashtags.
   - Collaborate with influencers.
3. Twitter:
   - Use Twitter Chats.
   - Share breaking news.
   - Utilize Twitter Polls.
4. LinkedIn:
   - Share industry insights.
   - Participate in LinkedIn Groups.
   - Publish LinkedIn Articles.

Time-Saving Tools:

1. Hootsuite
2. Buffer
3. Sprout Social
4. SocialPilot
5. Canva

Common Mistakes to Avoid:

1. Inconsistency.
2. Lack of engagement.
3. Poor content quality.
4. Insufficient analytics tracking.
5. Ignoring customer service.

By establishing a strong social media presence, you'll be able to:

1. Increase brand awareness.
2. Drive website traffic.
3. Generate leads.
4. Boost sales.
5. Enhance customer engagement

Claiming Google My Business listing

Claiming your Google My Business (GMB) listing is essential for local businesses. Here's a step-by-step guide:

Why Claim Your GMB Listing?

1. Verify your business existence
2. Improve local search visibility
3. Manage online reputation
4. Provide customers with essential info
5. Enhance Google Maps presence

Claiming Your GMB Listing:

Step 1: Check Eligibility

1. Ensure your business has a physical location.
2. Verify your business category (e.g., retail, service).

Step 2: Find Your Listing

1. Search for your business on Google Maps.
2. Click "Add your business" if not listed.

Step 3: Claim Your Listing

1. Sign in to Google My Business.
2. Enter business name, address, and category.
3. Verify your business (phone, email, or postcard).

Verification Methods:

1. Phone Verification: Receive a call with verification code.
2. Email Verification: Receive an email with verification link.
3. Postcard Verification: Receive a postcard with verification code.

Step 4: Complete Profile

1. Business name
2. Address
3. Hours of operation
4. Contact info (phone, email, website)
5. Description
6. Categories
7. Photos and videos

Step 5: Optimize Profile

1. Add high-quality photos.
2. Respond to customer reviews.
3. Use keywords in description.
4. Set up Google Posts.
5. Monitor insights and analytics.

GMB Features:

1. Google Posts
2. Reviews
3. Photos
4. Videos
5. Q&A
6. Booking and appointments
7. Messaging

Tips and Best Practices:

1. Keep profile up-to-date.
2. Respond promptly to reviews.
3. Use relevant categories.
4. Add high-quality photos.

5. Utilize Google Posts.

Common Issues:

1. Verification issues
2. Duplicate listings
3. Incorrect information

4. Suspended listings

Google My Business Support:

1. Google My Business Help Center
2. Google My Business Community Forum
3. Google Support Phone: +1 866-246-6453

By claiming and optimizing your Google My Business listing, you'll improve your local online presence and attract more customers.

Optimizing Your Google My Business Listing

Optimization helps your business appear in relevant search results and attracts more customers.

Key Optimization Factors:

1. Accuracy: Ensure name, address, and hours are up-to-date.
2. Completeness: Fill out all profile sections.
3. Relevance: Use relevant categories and keywords.
4. Visuals: Add high-quality photos and videos.
5. Reviews: Encourage and respond to customer reviews.

Optimization Tips:

1. Use keywords in your business description.
2. Add photos of your business, products, and services.
3. Respond promptly to customer reviews.
4. Use Google Posts to share updates and offers.
5. Monitor insights and analytics.

3. Resolving Verification Issues

Verification issues can prevent you from managing your Google My Business listing.

Common Verification Issues:

1. Failed phone verification
2. Invalid address
3. Duplicate listings
4. Verification code not received

Troubleshooting Steps:

1. Check your phone number and address.
2. Ensure you're using the correct verification method.
3. Contact Google My Business support.
4. Try alternative verification methods (e.g., email or postcard).

Google My Business Support:

1. Google My Business Help Center
2. Google My Business Community Forum
3. Google Support Phone: +1 866-246-6453

☐ Setting up email marketing system (Mailchimp, Constant Contact)

Setting up an email marketing system involves choosing an email service provider (ESP), creating an account, and configuring settings for optimal performance.

Email Service Providers (ESPs):

1. Mailchimp
2. Constant Contact
3. Sendinblue
4. ConvertKit
5. AWeber

Setup Process:
Step 1: Choose an ESP

1. Consider features (e.g., automation, analytics)
2. Evaluate pricing plans
3. Assess customer support

Step 2: Create an Account

1. Sign up for the chosen ESP
2. Verify email address
3. Set up password and security questions

Step 3: Configure Settings

1. Set up sender name and email address
2. Configure email templates
3. Define subscriber lists and segments
4. Establish automated email sequences (e.g., welcome emails)

Step 4: Design Email Templates

1. Choose pre-designed templates or create custom ones
2. Customize templates with branding and content
3. Ensure mobile-friendliness

Step 5: Set up Subscription Forms

1. Create subscription forms for website integration
2. Configure form fields (e.g., name, email)
3. Set up confirmation emails and welcome messages

Step 6: Integrate with Website

1. Add subscription forms to website
2. Use ESP-provided plugins or APIs for integration
3. Test integration for seamless functionality

Mailchimp Setup:

1. Sign up for Mailchimp
2. Create a list and set up sender information
3. Design email templates
4. Configure automation and RSS campaigns
5. Integrate with website using Mailchimp plugins or APIs

Constant Contact Setup:

1. Sign up for Constant Contact
2. Create a list and set up sender information
3. Design email templates
4. Configure automated email sequences
5. Integrate with website using Constant Contact plugins or APIs

Best Practices:

1. Segment subscriber lists for targeted campaigns
2. Use clear, concise subject lines and content
3. Optimize email templates for mobile devices
4. Use automation to streamline email workflows
5. Monitor analytics for campaign performance

Costs:

1. Mailchimp: Free (up to 2,000 subscribers), then $10-$299/month

2. Constant Contact: $20-$45/month (depending on features and subscribers)

1. Here are the costs in India for Mailchimp and Constant Contact:

Mailchimp:

1. Free plan: Up to 2,000 subscribers, 12,000 emails/month (approximately ₹0)
2. Essential plan: ₹745 - ₹2,995/month (up to 50,000 subscribers)
3. Pro plan: ₹2,995 - ₹5,995/month (up to 100,000 subscribers)
4. Business plan: ₹5,995 - ₹11,995/month (up to 200,000 subscribers)

Constant Contact:

1. Email plan: ₹1,449 - ₹2,899/month (up to 500 subscribers)
2. Email Plus plan: ₹2,899 - ₹4,499/month (up to 1,000 subscribers)
3. Ecommerce plan: ₹4,499 - ₹6,999/month (up to 2,000 subscribers)

Other Email Marketing Services in India:

1. Sendinblue: ₹1,499 - ₹4,999/month (up to 10,000 subscribers)
2. Zoho Campaigns: ₹1,200 - ₹3,600/month (up to 10,000 subscribers)
3. SendGrid: ₹1,499 - ₹4,999/month (up to 10,000 subscribers)
4. MailerLite: ₹1,200 - ₹3,600/month (up to 10,000 subscribers)

Payment Gateways:

1. PayPal
2. Stripe
3. Razorpay
4. PayU India
5. CCAvenue

Taxes:

1. GST (18%): Applicable on all email marketing services
2. Income Tax: Applicable on business income generated from email marketing

Discounts:

1. Annual payment discounts
2. Non-profit organization discounts
3. Student discounts

Free Trials:

1. Mailchimp: 30-day free trial
2. Constant Contact: 60-day free trial
3. Sendinblue: 30-day free trial
4. Zoho Campaigns: 30-day free trial

Please note that prices may vary depending on the specific plan and features chosen.

☐ Choosing CRM software (HubSpot, Zoho)

Choosing the right CRM software for your business can be overwhelming, especially with popular options like HubSpot and Zoho. Let's break down the costs and features to help you make an informed decision.

Zoho CRM Pricing

- Standard: ₹800/user/month (billed annually), ideal for streamlining sales operations and workflows
- Professional: ₹1,400/user/month (billed annually), accelerates customer acquisition and growth

- Enterprise: ₹2,400/user/month (billed annually), leverages deep AI and customization
- Ultimate: ₹2,600/user/month (billed annually), unlocks exponential growth and BI capabilities

HubSpot CRM Pricing

Unfortunately, I couldn't find the exact pricing for HubSpot CRM. However, I can suggest checking out Techjockey or HubSpot's official website for the latest pricing information.

Key Features to Consider
When choosing between Zoho and HubSpot, consider the following key features:

- Sales Automation: Zoho's workflow automation and Blueprint feature simplify sales processes
- Marketing Automation: HubSpot's marketing automation tools help with lead generation and nurturing
- Customer Support: Zoho's Omni channel helpdesk solution provides excellent customer support
- Integration: Both Zoho and HubSpot offer seamless integration with other business apps

Other CRM Options
If you're not set on Zoho or HubSpot, here are some alternative CRM options:

- Salesforce CRM: $25/user/year, known for its comprehensive sales and marketing tools
- Leadhooper: ₹499/user/month, offers AI-powered CRM features
- Kylas CRM: ₹12,999/month (unlimited users), provides sales CRM solutions for growing businesses

Remember to evaluate your business needs and compare features before making a final decision.

Chapter 3: Understanding Your Target Audience

◻ Identifying customer segments

Identifying customer segments involves dividing your target audience into distinct groups based on shared characteristics, needs, or behaviors.

Types of Customer Segments:

1. Demographic Segments: Age, gender, income, education, occupation
2. Psychographic Segments: Interests, values, lifestyle, personality
3. Behavioral Segments: Purchase history, frequency, loyalty
4. Firmographic Segments: Company size, industry, job function
5. Geographic Segments: Location, region, climate

Methods to Identify Customer Segments:

1. Surveys and feedback forms
2. Market research reports
3. Social media analytics
4. Customer interviews
5. Data mining and analytics
6. CRM (Customer Relationship Management) software

Tools for Customer Segmentation:

1. Google Analytics
2. HubSpot
3. Salesforce
4. Marketo
5. SurveyMonkey
6. Excel and statistical software (e.g., SPSS, R)

Benefits of Customer Segmentation:

1. Personalized marketing and messaging
2. Targeted product development
3. Efficient resource allocation
4. Improved customer satisfaction
5. Increased loyalty and retention
6. Enhanced competitiveness

Common Customer Segmentation Mistakes:

1. Over-segmentation
2. Under-segmentation
3. Lack of data-driven insights
4. Failure to update segments
5. Insufficient resources for segmentation

Best Practices:

1. Start with clear objectives
2. Use multiple segmentation methods
3. Analyze customer feedback
4. Continuously refine segments
5. Integrate segmentation with marketing strategies

Example of Customer Segmentation:

E-commerce Company:

- Demographic Segment: Young adults (18-35)
- Psychographic Segment: Fashion-conscious, environmentally aware

- Behavioral Segment: Frequent online shoppers
- Geographic Segment: Urban areas

By identifying and understanding customer segments, businesses can tailor their marketing efforts, products, and services to meet specific needs, increasing customer satisfaction and loyalty.

✔ Demographics (age, location, income)

Demographics are statistical characteristics of a population, including:

Age:

1. Generation Z (18-24)
2. Millennials (25-34)
3. Generation X (35-44)
4. Baby Boomers (45-64)
5. Silent Generation (65+)

Location:

1. Urban
2. Rural
3. Suburban
4. Metropolitan
5. Regional (e.g., North, South, East, West)

Income:

1. Low-income (< ₹2,50,000/year)
2. Middle-income (₹2,50,000 - ₹10,00,000/year)
3. Upper-middle-income (₹10,00,000 - ₹25,00,000/year)
4. High-income (₹25,00,000+/year)

Other Demographics:

1. Education (e.g., high school, college, graduate)
2. Occupation (e.g., student, working professional, entrepreneur)
3. Marital Status (e.g., single, married, divorced)
4. Family Size (e.g., single, couple, family with children)
5. Ethnicity (e.g., Indian, Asian, European)

Indian Demographics:

1. Age: 65% of population is below 35 years
2. Location: 34% urban, 66% rural
3. Income: Median household income ₹2,50,000 - ₹5,00,000/year
4. Education: 74% literacy rate
5. Occupation: 55% working in agriculture, 25% in services

Tools for Demographic Analysis:

1. Government census data
2. Market research reports
3. Social media analytics
4. Customer surveys
5. CRM software

Benefits of Demographic Analysis:

1. Targeted marketing
2. Product development
3. Customer segmentation
4. Market research
5. Business strategy development

Common Demographic Analysis Mistakes:

1. Over-reliance on assumptions
2. Lack of data accuracy
3. Failure to update demographics
4. Insufficient consideration of diversity
5. Overemphasis on single demographics

✔ Psychographics (interests, values, lifestyle)

Psychographics involves understanding a person's:

Interests:

1. Hobbies (e.g., reading, traveling, sports)
2. Entertainment preferences (e.g., movies, music, gaming)
3. Leisure activities (e.g., exercise, cooking, volunteering)

Values:

1. Personal values (e.g., honesty, creativity, ambition)
2. Social values (e.g., environmentalism, social justice, community)
3. Cultural values (e.g., tradition, innovation, diversity)

Lifestyle:

1. Lifestyle stage (e.g., student, working professional, retiree)
2. Living situation (e.g., urban, rural, suburban)
3. Health and wellness habits (e.g., fitness, nutrition, mindfulness)

Other Psychographic Factors:

1. Personality traits (e.g., extraversion, introversion, optimism)
2. Attitudes (e.g., toward technology, sustainability, fashion)
3. Opinions (e.g., on politics, social issues, consumerism)
4. Behavioral patterns (e.g., shopping habits, travel frequency)

Psychographic Segmentation Tools:

1. Surveys and focus groups
2. Social media listening
3. Customer interviews
4. Psychographic profiling software (e.g., PRIZM, VALS)
5. Market research reports

Benefits of Psychographic Analysis:

1. Deeper customer understanding
2. Targeted marketing and messaging
3. Product development and innovation
4. Brand loyalty and engagement
5. Competitive advantage

Psychographic Segmentation Examples:

1. Outdoor enthusiasts
2. Health-conscious individuals
3. Foodies
4. Tech-savvy professionals
5. Environmentally aware consumers

Indian Psychographics:

1. 70% of Indians consider family important
2. 60% prioritize traditional values
3. 55% are interested in technology
4. 45% value sustainability
5. 40% prioritize health and wellness

Psychographic Analysis Challenges:

1. Data accuracy and reliability
2. Complexity of human behavior
3. Constantly evolving values and interests
4. Difficulty in measuring attitudes and opinions

5. Ensuring representation and diversity

✔ Pain points and needs

Identifying pain points and needs involves understanding the challenges, frustrations, and aspirations of your target audience.

Pain Points:

1. Financial struggles (e.g., budget constraints)
2. Time management issues (e.g., lack of productivity)
3. Emotional distress (e.g., stress, anxiety)
4. Physical discomfort (e.g., health issues)
5. Technical difficulties (e.g., software complexity)

Needs:

1. Convenience (e.g., easy-to-use solutions)
2. Cost-effectiveness (e.g., affordable options)
3. Efficiency (e.g., time-saving tools)
4. Support (e.g., customer service)
5. Personal growth (e.g., skills development)

Customer Needs Framework:

1. Functional needs (e.g., product features)
2. Emotional needs (e.g., feeling valued)
3. Social needs (e.g., community connection)
4. Psychological needs (e.g., self-expression)

Identifying Pain Points and Needs:

1. Customer surveys
2. Focus groups
3. Interviews
4. Social media listening
5. Online reviews
6. Competitor analysis

Tools for Pain Point and Needs Analysis:

1. Empathy maps
2. Customer journey mapping
3. Pain point analysis templates
4. SWOT analysis
5. Market research reports

Benefits of Pain Point and Needs Analysis:

1. Targeted solutions
2. Improved customer satisfaction
3. Increased loyalty
4. Competitive advantage
5. Revenue growth

Common Mistakes:

1. Assuming customer needs
2. Lack of customer feedback
3. Focusing on features rather than benefits
4. Ignoring emotional needs
5. Not validating assumptions

Best Practices:

1. Continuously gather customer feedback
2. Validate assumptions
3. Prioritize customer needs
4. Develop solutions addressing pain points
5. Monitor customer satisfaction

Example:

E-commerce Company:

Pain Points:

- Difficulty finding products
- Long shipping times
- Poor customer support

- Easy product search
- Fast shipping
- Reliable customer support

Needs:

By understanding pain points and needs, businesses can develop targeted solutions, improve customer satisfaction, and drive growth.

☐ Analyzing customer behavior (buying habits, preferences)

Analyzing customer behavior involves studying buying habits, preferences, and decision-making processes to understand customer needs and optimize business strategies.

Types of Customer Behavior:

1. Buying habits: Frequency, timing, and volume of purchases.
2. Purchase decisions: Influencing factors, such as price, quality, and convenience.
3. Product interactions: Usage patterns, feedback, and returns.
4. Channel preferences: Online, offline, mobile, or social media.
5. Loyalty and retention: Repeat business and customer churn.

Methods for Analyzing Customer Behavior:

1. Data mining and analytics
2. Customer surveys and feedback
3. Market research reports
4. Social media listening
5. Customer journey mapping
6. A/B testing and experimentation

Tools for Analyzing Customer Behavior:

1. Google Analytics
2. CRM software (e.g., Salesforce)
3. Customer feedback platforms (e.g., SurveyMonkey)
4. Social media analytics tools (e.g., Hootsuite)
5. Data visualization tools (e.g., Tableau)
6. Machine learning and AI-powered analytics

Benefits of Analyzing Customer Behavior:

1. Personalized marketing and recommendations
2. Improved customer satisfaction and loyalty
3. Enhanced product development and innovation
4. Optimized pricing and revenue strategies
5. Better customer retention and acquisition

Common Metrics for Analyzing Customer Behavior:

1. Customer lifetime value (CLV)
2. Customer acquisition cost (CAC)
3. Conversion rates
4. Average order value (AOV)
5. Net promoter score (NPS)
6. Customer churn rate

Best Practices:

1. Continuously collect and analyze customer data
2. Integrate multiple data sources
3. Use data visualization techniques
4. Segment customers based on behavior
5. Test and refine hypotheses

Example:

E-commerce Company:

Analysis:
1. 60% of customers purchase during sales
2. 40% prefer mobile checkout
3. 30% return products due to size issues

Action:
1. Offer targeted promotions during sales
7. Optimize mobile checkout process
8. Improve product sizing and fit guidance

By analyzing customer behavior, businesses can gain valuable insights to inform marketing, product, and customer experience strategies.

☐ Creating buyer personas

Creating buyer personas involves developing detailed profiles of ideal customers, including their characteristics, needs, and behaviors.

Benefits of Buyer Personas:

1. Improved marketing targeting
2. Enhanced customer understanding
3. Personalized content creation
4. Better product development
5. Increased sales and revenue

Components of a Buyer Persona:

1. Demographics: Age, location, occupation, education
2. Psychographics: Values, interests, lifestyle
9. Goals and challenges: Professional and personal objectives
10. Behavior patterns: Buying habits, online activities
11. Pain points: Problems or frustrations
12. Preferred communication channels: Social media, email, phone

Steps to Create Buyer Personas:

1. Conduct customer research: Surveys, interviews, focus groups
2. Analyze customer data: Sales history, website analytics
3. Identify patterns and trends: Demographic, behavioral, psychographic
4. Develop persona profiles: Document characteristics, goals, challenges
5. Refine and iterate: Continuously update personas based on new data

Example Buyer Persona:

Name: Emma, Marketing Manager

Demographics: 28-35, urban, college-educated

Psychographics: Values innovation, interested in technology

Goals: Increase brand awareness, improve social media engagement

Challenges: Limited budget, measuring campaign effectiveness

Behavior: Active on LinkedIn, attends industry events

Pain Points: Difficulty finding relevant content, measuring ROI

Preferred Communication: Email, LinkedIn messaging

Tools for Creating Buyer Personas:

1. HubSpot's Make My Persona
2. Xtensio's Persona Template
3. Canva's Persona Creator
4. Google Forms for surveys
5. Customer feedback software (e.g., SurveyMonkey)

Best Practices:

1. Create multiple personas for different customer segments
2. Continuously update personas based on new data
3. Use personas to inform marketing and sales strategies
4. Share personas across departments for alignment
5. Use storytelling to bring personas to life

☐ Developing a customer-centric approach

1. **Developing a customer-centric approach involves prioritizing customer needs, preferences, and experiences throughout the organization.**

Key Principles:

1. Customer focus: Prioritize customer needs and goals.
2. Empathy: Understand customer perspectives and emotions.
3. Personalization: Tailor experiences to individual customers.
4. Responsiveness: Promptly address customer inquiries and concerns.
5. Continuous improvement: Gather feedback and iterate.

Customer-Centric Strategies:

1. Map customer journeys to identify pain points.
2. Implement customer feedback mechanisms.
3. Develop customer personas to guide decision-making.
4. Invest in employee training and empowerment.
5. Foster a culture of customer obsession.

Benefits:

1. Increased customer satisfaction and loyalty.
2. Improved customer retention and acquisition.
3. Enhanced brand reputation and advocacy.
4. Increased revenue and growth.
5. Competitive differentiation.

Customer-Centric Metrics:

1. Net Promoter Score (NPS).
2. Customer Satisfaction (CSAT).
3. Customer Effort Score (CES).
4. Customer Lifetime Value (CLV).
5. Customer Retention Rate.

Tools and Technologies:

1. CRM software (e.g., Salesforce).
2. Customer feedback platforms (e.g., SurveyMonkey).
3. Social media listening tools (e.g., Hootsuite).
4. Customer journey mapping software (e.g., SmartDraw).
5. Personalization engines (e.g., Adobe Target).

Best Practices:

1. Establish a customer-centric vision and mission.
2. Align organization-wide goals and objectives.
3. Empower employees to make customer-centric decisions.
4. Continuously gather and act on customer feedback.
5. Monitor and measure customer-centric metrics.

Challenges:

1. Cultural transformation.
2. Siloed organizations.
3. Limited customer data.
4. Inadequate resources.
5. Balancing customer needs with business goals.

Example Companies:

1. Amazon (customer obsession).
2. Apple (customer experience).
3. Zappos (customer service).
4. Netflix (personalization).
5. Starbucks (customer engagement).

2. Implementing Customer Feedback Mechanisms

Implementing customer feedback mechanisms involves:

- Surveys: Online, email, or in-app surveys to collect structured feedback.
- Social Media Listening: Monitoring social media for customer comments and concerns.
- Customer Reviews: Analyzing customer reviews on websites, apps, or social media.
- Focus Groups: Organized discussions with customers to gather qualitative feedback.
- Net Promoter Score (NPS): Measuring customer loyalty through a single-question survey.

Best Practices:

- Make feedback easy to provide.
- Respond promptly to feedback.
- Analyze and act on feedback.
- Close the feedback loop.
- Continuously collect feedback.

Tools:

- SurveyMonkey
- Medallia
- Freshdesk
- Hootsuite
- AskNIcely

3. Employee Training and Empowerment

Employee training and empowerment involve:

- Training Objectives: Understanding customer needs, empathy, communication, problem-solving, and customer-centric mindset.
- Empowerment Strategies: Autonomy, access to customer data, recognition, continuous feedback, and cross-functional collaboration.

Training Methods:

- Workshops and role-playing.
- Online courses and webinars.
- Mentorship programs.
- Customer interaction simulations.
- Gamification.

4. Tools and Technologies for Customer-Centricity

Tools and technologies for customer-centricity include:

- Customer Relationship Management (CRM): Salesforce, HubSpot, Zoho CRM, Freshsales, Pipedrive.
- Customer Feedback and Survey Tools: SurveyMonkey, Medallia, AskNicely, Freshdesk, Hootsuite.
- Customer Analytics and Insights: Google Analytics, Mixpanel, Segment, Clearbit.

5. Creating a Customer Journey Map

Creating a customer journey map involves:

- Identifying Customer Personas: Understanding customer demographics, needs, and goals.
- Defining Customer Goals and Pain Points: Identifying customer objectives and challenges.
- Mapping Customer Interactions: Visualizing customer touchpoints and channels.
- Identifying Touchpoints and Channels: Pinpointing customer interaction points.
- Prioritizing and Refining the Map: Focusing on key areas for improvement.

Tools:

- SmartDraw
- Lucidchart
- Gliffy
- Customer Journey Map template
- Sticky notes and whiteboard

Chapter 4: Content Creation Strategy

☐ Types of content (blog posts, videos, infographics, podcasts)

Here are various types of content:

Written Content:

1. Blog posts
2. Articles
3. Case studies
4. E-books
5. Whitepapers
6. Newsletters
7. Press releases
8. Guest posts
9. Product descriptions
10. FAQs

Visual Content:

1. Infographics
2. Videos (explainers, tutorials, testimonials)
3. Images (photographs, illustrations, graphics)
4. Webinars
5. Animated GIFs
6. Podcast thumbnails
7. Social media graphics
8. Presentations (SlideShare)
9. Charts and graphs
10. Data visualizations

Audio Content:

1. Podcasts
2. Audiobooks
3. Interviews (audio)
4. Voiceovers
5. Audio testimonials

Interactive Content:

1. Quizzes
2. Polls
3. Surveys
4. Contests
5. Games
6. Webinars (live)
7. Chatbots
8. Interactive videos
9. Simulations
10. Virtual reality experiences

Video Content:

1. Explainer videos
2. Tutorial videos
3. Testimonial videos
4. Product demos
5. Brand stories
6. Event coverage
7. Live streaming
8. 360-degree videos
9. Animated videos
10. Vlogs

Social Media Content:

1. Facebook posts
2. Twitter tweets
3. Instagram posts
4. LinkedIn posts

5. TikTok videos
6. Snapchat stories
7. Pinterest pins
8. Reddit posts
9. YouTube videos
10. Podcast promotions

Repurposed Content:

1. Turning blog posts into videos
2. Creating infographics from articles
3. Converting webinars into podcasts
4. Making eBooks from blog series
5. Developing courses from expert interviews

Content Formats:

1. PDFs
2. MP3s
3. MP4s
4. JPEGs
5. PNGs
6. GIFs
7. HTML
8. CSV
9. Excel files
10. PowerPoint presentations

Content Distribution Channels:

1. Website
2. Social media platforms
3. Email newsletters
4. Podcast platforms
5. Video sharing sites
6. Blogging platforms
7. Online communities
8. Forums
9. Guest blogging
10. Influencer marketing

☐ Content creation tools (Canva, Adobe Creative Cloud and many more...)

Here are some popular content creation tools:

Graphic Design Tools:

1. Canva (graphic design, templates)
2. Adobe Creative Cloud (Photoshop, Illustrator, InDesign)
3. Sketch (digital design)
4. Figma (collaborative design)
5. GIMP (free alternative to Photoshop)

Video Editing Tools:

1. Adobe Premiere Pro (video editing)
2. Final Cut Pro (video editing)
3. DaVinci Resolve (video editing)
4. iMovie (free video editing)
5. WeVideo (cloud-based video editing)

Writing and Editing Tools:

1. Grammarly (writing assistant)
2. Hemingway Editor (writing simplicity)
3. ProWritingAid (writing analysis)
4. Microsoft Word (word processing)
5. Google Docs (cloud-based word processing)

Audio Editing Tools:

1. Adobe Audition (audio editing)
2. Audacity (free audio editing)
3. GarageBand (music creation)
4. Logic Pro X (professional audio editing)
5. Anchor (podcast editing)

Content Management Tools:

1. WordPress (content management system)
2. Medium (blogging platform)
3. Ghost (blogging platform)
4. Contentful (headless CMS)
5. Drupal (enterprise CMS)

Social Media Management Tools:

1. Hootsuite (social media scheduling)
2. Buffer (social media scheduling)
3. Sprout Social (social media management)
4. SocialPilot (social media scheduling)
5. Sendible (social media management)

Other Tools:

1. Unsplash (free stock photos)
2. Pexels (free stock photos)
3. Pixabay (free stock photos)
4. Animoto (video creation)
5. Powtoon (animated video creation)

Benefits of Content Creation Tools:

1. Improved productivity
2. Enhanced creativity
3. Increased efficiency
4. Better collaboration
5. Professional-grade content

Best Practices:

1. Choose tools that fit your needs
2. Learn tool basics and advanced features
3. Experiment with different tools
4. Collaborate with team members
5. Continuously evaluate and improve tool usage

▢ Content calendar planning

Content calendar planning involves organizing and scheduling content in advance to ensure consistency and efficiency.

Benefits of Content Calendar Planning:

1. Improved content organization
2. Reduced last-minute scrambles
3. Increased productivity
4. Enhanced team collaboration
5. Better content alignment with goals

Steps to Create a Content Calendar:

1. Define content goals and objectives
2. Identify target audience and personas
3. Determine content types and channels
4. Plan content themes and topics
5. Assign content creation tasks and deadlines
6. Schedule content publication dates
7. Review and revise the calendar regularly

Content Calendar Templates:

1. Google Sheets
2. Microsoft Excel
3. Trello
4. Asana
5. CoSchedule
6. Hootsuite Content Calendar
7. Content Calendar Template (PDF)

Content Calendar Columns:

1. Date
2. Content Type (blog, social, video, etc.)
3. Title/Headline
4. Description
5. Keywords
6. Target Audience
7. Channel (website, social, email, etc.)
8. Status (draft, pending, published)
9. Author/Creator
10. Notes

Content Calendar Tools:

1. CoSchedule
2. Hootsuite
3. Buffer
4. Sprout Social
5. Trello
6. Asana

7. Google Calendar
8. Microsoft Outlook
9. Content Calendar Plugin (WordPress)
10. Planoly (Instagram planning)

Best Practices:

1. Plan content 3-6 months in advance
2. Review and revise the calendar regularly
3. Involve team members in planning
4. Consider holidays and events
5. Leave room for flexibility
6. Use analytics to inform content decisions

7. Ensure consistency across channels
8. Use automation tools to streamline publishing

Common Content Calendar Mistakes:

1. Lack of planning
2. Inconsistent scheduling
3. Insufficient team collaboration
4. Failure to review and revise
5. Overlooking analytics
6. Ignoring audience feedback
7. Not considering SEO
8. Inadequate content diversity

Repurposing and upcycling content

Repurposing and upcycling content involves transforming existing content into new formats to maximize its value and reach.

Repurposing Content:

1. Turning blog posts into videos
2. Converting webinars into podcasts
3. Creating infographics from data
4. Developing email courses from blog series
5. Making eBooks from whitepapers
6. Transforming case studies into testimonials
7. Creating social media posts from blog summaries
8. Developing online courses from expert interviews
9. Turning podcasts into transcripts
10. Creating animations from static images

Upcycling Content:

1. Updating outdated content with fresh insights
2. Expanding brief content into comprehensive guides
3. Combining related content into anthologies
4. Creating interactive content from static content
5. Developing personalized content from generic content
6. Transforming text-based content into visual stories
7. Creating immersive experiences from existing content
8. Developing micro-content from long-form content
9. Turning complex content into simple, bite-sized pieces
10. Creating evergreen content from timely content

Benefits:

1. Increased content ROI
2. Improved content efficiency
3. Enhanced content reach and engagement
4. Reduced content creation time and cost
5. Better content organization and management
6. Improved SEO and search rankings
7. Increased audience engagement and loyalty
8. Enhanced brand authority and credibility

Tools:

1. Content reuse and repurposing software (e.g., ContentForge)
2. Video editing software (e.g., Adobe Premiere)
3. Graphic design software (e.g., Canva)
4. Audio editing software (e.g., Audacity)
5. E-learning platforms (e.g., Teachable)
6. Social media scheduling tools (e.g., Hootsuite)
7. Blogging platforms (e.g., WordPress)
8. Infographic creation tools (e.g., Piktochart)

Best Practices:

1. Identify content gaps and opportunities
2. Analyze content performance and engagement
3. Involve team members in repurposing decisions
4. Consider audience preferences and formats
5. Ensure consistency across content formats
6. Optimize content for SEO and search
7. Use analytics to track repurposed content performance
8. Continuously evaluate and refine repurposing strategy

Common Mistakes:

1. Lack of strategic planning
2. Insufficient content analysis
3. Poor content quality
4. Inconsistent branding
5. Failure to update outdated content
6. Ignoring audience feedback
7. Not considering content format preferences
8. Inadequate promotion and distribution

☐ Measuring content effectiveness

Measuring content effectiveness involves tracking and analyzing metrics to determine the success of your content strategy.

Key Performance Indicators (KPIs):

1. **Engagement metrics:**
   - Likes
   - Comments
   - Shares
   - Views
2. **Traffic metrics:**
   - Page views
   - Unique visitors
   - Bounce rate
   - Time on page
3. **Conversion metrics:**
   - Leads generated
   - Sales
   - Sign-ups
   - Downloads
4. **SEO metrics:**
   - Search engine rankings
   - Organic traffic
   - Keyword density
5. **Social media metrics:**
   - Follower growth
   - Engagement rate
   - Social media referrals

Content Metrics Tools:

1. Google Analytics
2. Google Tag Manager
3. Mixpanel
4. Chartbeat
5. Ahrefs
6. SEMrush
7. Hootsuite Insights
8. Sprout Social
9. Content Management Systems (CMS) analytics
10. Social media platform insights (e.g., Facebook, Twitter)

Content Effectiveness Metrics:

1. Content ROI (Return on Investment)
2. Content Engagement Rate
3. Content Conversion Rate
4. Content Shareability Index
5. Content Relevance Score
6. Time-to-Read (TTR)
7. Scroll Depth
8. Bounce Rate
9. Average Watch Time (AWT)
10. Completion Rate

How to Measure Content Effectiveness:

1. Set clear goals and objectives
2. Choose relevant metrics and KPIs
3. Track and analyze data regularly
4. Use A/B testing to optimize content
5. Conduct content audits
6. Monitor user feedback and surveys
7. Adjust content strategy based on data insights
8. Continuously refine and improve content

Common Mistakes:

1. Lack of clear goals and objectives
2. Insufficient data tracking
3. Focusing on vanity metrics
4. Not adjusting content strategy
5. Ignoring user feedback
6. Not considering content format and channel
7. Inadequate content promotion
8. Not measuring ROI

Part 2: Social Media Marketing

Chapter 5: Facebook Marketing

▢ What is Facebook and how it's work for you?

Facebook is a social networking platform that connects people from around the world. Here's an overview:

What is Facebook?

Facebook is a free online social networking service that allows users to:

1. Create profiles with personal information, interests, and photos
2. Connect with friends, family, and colleagues
3. Share updates, photos, and videos
4. Join groups based on interests
5. Follow pages from businesses, organizations, and public figures
6. Engage with others through comments, likes, and shares

Key Features:

1. **News Feed:** A personalized feed displaying updates from friends and pages
2. **Profiles:** User-created profiles showcasing information and interests
3. **Friends:** Connecting with others and managing relationships
4. **Groups:** Communities centered around shared interests
5. **Pages:** Official profiles for businesses, organizations, and public figures
6. **Messenger:** Private messaging service for individuals and groups
7. **Events:** Creating and joining events
8. **Marketplace:** Buying and selling goods and services

Facebook Statistics:

1. Over 2.7 billion monthly active users
2. 1.8 billion daily active users
3. 70% of online adults use Facebook
4. Average user spends 38 minutes per day on Facebook
5. 80 million businesses use Facebook Pages

Facebook History:

6. Launched in 2004 by Mark Zuckerberg, Dustin Moskovitz, Chris Hughes, and Eduardo Saverin
7. Initially exclusive to Harvard University students
8. Expanded to colleges, universities, and eventually the general public
9. Acquired Instagram (2012) and WhatsApp (2014)
10. Introduced features like Facebook Live, Reactions, and Stories

Facebook's Impact:

1. Revolutionized social networking
2. Changed how people connect, share, and consume information
3. Influenced online advertising and marketing

4. Facilitated global communication and community building
5. Raised concerns about data privacy, security, and social media addiction

☐ Creating engaging Facebook content (posts, stories, reels)

Creating engaging Facebook content involves understanding your audience and crafting posts, stories, and reels that resonate with them.

Types of Facebook Content:

1. Posts: Text, images, videos, links
2. Stories: Ephemeral content (24 hours)
3. Reels: Short-form videos (up to 60 seconds)
4. Live Streams: Real-time video
5. Groups: Community-driven discussions

Facebook Content Strategies:

1. Know your audience: Understand demographics, interests, behaviors
2. Define content goals: Engagement, conversions, brand awareness
3. Content calendar: Plan and schedule content
4. Visual content: Use images, videos, graphics
5. Storytelling: Share customer stories, behind-the-scenes
6. Interactive content: Polls, quizzes, questions
7. User-generated content: Encourage audience participation
8. Consistency: Post regularly
9. Engagement: Respond to comments, messages
10. Analytics: Track performance, adjust strategy

Facebook Post Ideas:

1. Promotions and sales
2. Product showcases
3. Customer testimonials
4. Behind-the-scenes content
5. Industry news and updates
6. Educational content
7. Humor and entertainment
8. Inspirational quotes
9. User-generated content
10. Seasonal and timely content

Facebook Story Ideas:

1. Sneak peeks
2. Exclusive deals
3. Q&A sessions
4. Polls and surveys
5. Behind-the-scenes content
6. Product demos
7. User-generated content
8. Events and announcements
9. Personal stories
10. How-to tutorials

Facebook Reel Ideas:

1. Short product demos
2. Customer testimonials
3. Before-and-after videos
4. Product showcases
5. Dance or music performances
6. Comedy skits
7. Educational content
8. DIY tutorials
9. Time-lapse videos
10. Stop-motion animations

Facebook Content Tools:

1. Facebook Creator Studio

2. Facebook Insights
3. Canva
4. Adobe Creative Cloud
5. Hootsuite
6. Buffer
7. Sprout Social
8. Facebook Live
9. Reels editor
10. Storyteller tool

Best Practices:

1. Optimize content for mobile
2. Use eye-catching visuals
3. Keep content concise
4. Post consistently
5. Engage with audience
6. Monitor analytics
7. Adjust content strategy
8. Utilize Facebook Groups
9. Leverage user-generated content
10. Run contests and giveaways

☐ Facebook advertising (targeting, budgeting, ad creative)

Facebook advertising involves using the platform's advertising capabilities to reach target audiences and drive business outcomes.

Facebook Ad Targeting:

1. Demographic targeting: Age, location, language, interests
2. Behavioral targeting: Purchasing habits, device usage, browsing history
3. Custom audiences: Upload customer data, email lists
4. Lookalike audiences: Target users similar to existing customers
5. Interest-based targeting: Hobbies, interests, job titles

Facebook Ad Budgeting:

1. Daily budget: Set daily spend limits
2. Lifetime budget: Set total campaign spend
3. Cost per click (CPC): Pay for ad clicks
4. Cost per thousand impressions (CPM): Pay for ad views
5. Optimized budget allocation: Facebook's automated budget optimization

Facebook Ad Creative:

1. Image ads: Single images with text overlays
2. Video ads: Video content with sound and captions
3. Carousel ads: Multi-image or video ads
4. Collection ads: Product catalogs with images and prices
5. Story ads: Full-screen, immersive ads
6. Instant Experience ads: Fast-loading, interactive ads

Facebook Ad Formats:

1. Facebook Feed Ads
2. Instagram Feed Ads
3. Facebook Story Ads
4. Instagram Story Ads
5. Facebook Marketplace Ads
6. Facebook Video Ads
7. Instagram Reels Ads

Facebook Ad Optimization:

1. Conversion tracking: Measure actions taken on website
2. Pixel tracking: Monitor website activity
3. A/B testing: Compare ad creative performance
4. Ad rotation: Automatically rotate ad creative
5. Automated bidding: Facebook's automated bidding strategies

Facebook Ad Metrics:

1. Reach: Number of users who viewed ad

2. Impressions: Number of times ad was viewed
3. Click-through rate (CTR): Percentage of users who clicked ad
4. Conversion rate: Percentage of users who took action
5. Return on ad spend (ROAS): Revenue generated per dollar spent

Facebook Ad Tools:

1. Facebook Ads Manager
2. Facebook Ads API
3. Facebook Pixel
4. Facebook Insights
5. Facebook Audience Network

Best Practices:

1. Define clear campaign objectives
2. Set realistic budgets and bids
3. Optimize ad creative for mobile
4. Target specific audiences
5. Monitor and adjust campaigns regularly
6. Use A/B testing and ad rotation
7. Track conversions and revenue
8. Utilize Facebook's automated features

☐ Facebook groups and community building (Join and participate in relevant groups)

Facebook groups and community building involve leveraging groups to connect with your target audience, build relationships, and establish your brand as an authority.

Benefits of Facebook Groups:

1. Targeted audience engagement
2. Increased brand visibility
3. Community building and loyalty
4. Valuable feedback and insights
5. Networking opportunities
6. Content sharing and collaboration
7. Support and customer service

Types of Facebook Groups:

1. Public groups: Open to anyone
2. Closed groups: Invitation-only or moderator approval
3. Secret groups: Hidden from non-members
4. Private groups: Exclusive, invitation-only

Joining and Participating in Relevant Groups:

1. Research relevant groups using keywords
2. Request to join groups aligned with your niche
3. Engage with group members through comments and posts
4. Share valuable content and insights
5. Collaborate with group administrators
6. Follow group rules and guidelines
7. Monitor and respond to comments and messages

Creating and Managing Your Own Facebook Group:

1. Define group purpose and objectives
2. Set clear rules and guidelines
3. Choose group type (public, closed, or secret)
4. Invite initial members and moderators
5. Create engaging content and discussions
6. Moderate and manage group activity
7. Analyze group performance using Facebook Insights

Facebook Group Features:

1. Group posts and comments
2. Live streaming and video chat
3. File sharing and collaboration
4. Polls and quizzes
5. Events and meetups
6. Group insights and analytics
7. Moderator tools and settings

Community Building Strategies:

1. Host Q&A sessions or webinars
2. Share exclusive content or offers
3. Recognize and reward members
4. Encourage user-generated content
5. Collaborate with influencers or experts
6. Run contests or giveaways
7. Provide support and resources

Best Practices:

1. Be authentic and transparent
2. Engage consistently and respond promptly
3. Respect group rules and members
4. Share valuable and relevant content
5. Monitor and adjust your strategy
6. Utilize Facebook Group features
7. Leverage user-generated content

Common Mistakes:

1. Spamming or self-promotion
2. Ignoring group rules and guidelines
3. Lack of engagement and participation
4. Inconsistent content quality
5. Failure to moderate and manage
6. Not utilizing group insights
7. Inadequate community building

▢ Facebook Messenger marketing

Facebook Messenger marketing involves using Messenger to connect with customers, promote products, and provide customer support.

Benefits of Facebook Messenger Marketing:

1. Personalized communication
2. High engagement rates
3. Increased conversions
4. Improved customer support
5. Reduced costs
6. Enhanced customer experience
7. Targeted messaging

Facebook Messenger Marketing Strategies:

1. Broadcast messages: Send updates to subscribers
2. Sequences: Automated message series
3. Chatbots: Automated customer support
4. Sponsored messages: Paid advertising
5. Customer support: Responsive and helpful support
6. Surveys and feedback: Collect customer insights
7. Promotions and offers: Exclusive deals

Facebook Messenger Features:

1. Messaging: Text, images, videos, and files
2. Quick Replies: Pre-defined responses
3. Chatbots: Automated messaging
4. Handover Protocol: Transfer conversations
5. Messaging Tags: Organize conversations
6. Customer Chat Plugin: Website integration
7. Messenger API: Custom integrations

Best Practices for Facebook Messenger Marketing:

1. Obtain explicit consent
2. Personalize messages
3. Keep messages concise
4. Use visual content
5. Respond promptly
6. Segment audiences
7. Monitor performance

Common Facebook Messenger Marketing Mistakes:

1. Spamming or unsolicited messages
2. Lack of personalization
3. Inconsistent messaging
4. Ignoring customer responses
5. Not utilizing chatbots
6. Insufficient segmentation
7. Not tracking performance

Facebook Messenger Marketing Tools:

1. ManyChat
2. Chatfuel
3. MobileMonkey
4. Conversational Flow
5. Messenger API
6. Facebook Business Suite
7. Hootsuite

Facebook Messenger Marketing Metrics:

1. Open rates
2. Click-through rates (CTR)
3. Conversion rates
4. Response rates
5. Customer satisfaction (CSAT)
6. Net Promoter Score (NPS)
7. Return on Investment (ROI)

☐ Facebook analytics and tracking

Facebook analytics and tracking involve monitoring and measuring the performance of your Facebook content, ads, and overall presence.

Facebook Analytics Tools:

1. Facebook Insights: Page and content performance
2. Facebook Ads Manager: Ad performance and ROI
3. Facebook Pixel: Website tracking and conversion optimization
4. Facebook Analytics: Cross-device and cross-platform tracking
5. Google Analytics: Website traffic and conversion tracking

Facebook Metrics to Track:

1. Engagement metrics:
   - Likes
   - Comments
   - Shares
   - Reactions
2. Reach metrics:
   - Impressions
   - Views
   - Unique users
3. Traffic metrics:
   - Click-through rate (CTR)
   - Conversions
   - Website traffic
4. Ad metrics:
   - Cost per click (CPC)
   - Cost per thousand impressions (CPM)
   - Return on ad spend (ROAS)
5. Audience metrics:
   - Demographics
   - Interests
   - Behaviors

Facebook Tracking Parameters:

1. Facebook Pixel: Track website conversions and events
2. Facebook SDK: Track mobile app events
3. UTM parameters: Track URL parameters
4. Conversion tracking: Track specific actions
5. Event tracking: Track custom events

Facebook Analytics Best Practices:

1. Set clear goals and objectives

2. Track relevant metrics
3. Monitor and adjust campaigns
4. Use A/B testing
5. Analyze audience insights
6. Optimize for mobile
7. Use Facebook's automated features

Common Facebook Analytics Mistakes:

1. Lack of clear goals
2. Insufficient tracking
3. Inaccurate metrics
4. Not monitoring campaigns
5. Ignoring audience insights
6. Not optimizing for mobile
7. Inadequate A/B testing

Facebook Analytics Tools Integration:

1. Google Analytics
2. Mixpanel
3. HubSpot
4. Marketo
5. Salesforce
6. Hootsuite Insights
7. Sprout Social

- Facebook advertising approximate cast in India and international

Facebook advertising costs in India and internationally can vary based on several factors, including:
1. Target audience
2. Ad format (image, video, carousel, etc.)
3. Bidding strategy (CPC, CPM, etc.)
4. Ad placement (Facebook, Instagram, Audience Network)
5. Industry/niche
6. Time of year (seasonal fluctuations)
7. Ad creative quality

Approximate Facebook Advertising Costs in India:

1. CPC (Cost Per Click):
   - Average: ₹15-₹30 (USD 0.20-0.40)
   - E-commerce: ₹20-₹50 (USD 0.25-0.65)
   - Finance: ₹30-₹70 (USD 0.40-0.90)
   - Education: ₹15-₹30 (USD 0.20-0.40)
2. CPM (Cost Per Thousand Impressions):
   - Average: ₹50-₹150 (USD 0.65-1.95)
   - E-commerce: ₹80-₹250 (USD 1.05-3.25)
   - Finance: ₹100-₹350 (USD 1.30-4.55)
   - Education: ₹50-₹150 (USD 0.65-1.95)
3. Daily Budget:
   - Average: ₹500-₹2,000 (USD 6.50-26)
   - E-commerce: ₹1,000-₹5,000 (USD 13-65)
   - Finance: ₹2,000-₹10,000 (USD 26-130)
   - Education: ₹500-₹2,000 (USD 6.50-26)

Approximate Facebook Advertising Costs Internationally:

1. CPC (Cost Per Click):
   - USA: USD 0.70-2.50
   - UK: USD 0.50-1.50
   - Australia: USD 0.50-1.50
   - Europe: USD 0.30-1.20
2. CPM (Cost Per Thousand Impressions):
   - USA: USD 5-20
   - UK: USD 3-15
   - Australia: USD 3-15
   - Europe: USD 2-10
3. Daily Budget:
   - USA: USD 50-500
   - UK: USD 30-300
   - Australia: USD 30-300
   - Europe: USD 20-200

Factors Affecting Facebook Advertising Costs:

1. Competition
2. Ad relevance
3. Target audience size

4. Ad creative quality
5. Bidding strategy
6. Industry/niche
7. Seasonal fluctuations

Tips to Optimize Facebook Advertising Costs:

1. Target specific audiences
2. Use relevant ad creative
3. Optimize for conversions
4. Use lookalike audiences
5. Monitor and adjust bids
6. Utilize Facebook's automated bidding
7. Split test ad creative

Chapter 6: Instagram Marketing

☐ What is Instagram and how is it useful to the peoples in the world?

Instagram is a social networking platform focused on visual content, primarily photography and videography.

What is Instagram?

Instagram is a free online platform where users can:

1. Share photos and videos
2. Follow other users and view their content
3. Engage with others through likes, comments, and stories
4. Discover content through hashtags and explore pages
5. Utilize features like IGTV, Reels, and Live Streaming

History of Instagram

1. Launched in 2010 by Kevin Systrom and Mike Krieger
2. Acquired by Facebook in 2012
3. Introduced features like Stories (2016), IGTV (2018), and Reels (2020)

How is Instagram useful to people?

1. Visual storytelling and self-expression
2. Community building and social networking
3. Business and marketing opportunities
4. Inspiration and creativity
5. Education and learning
6. News and current events
7. Personal branding and portfolio building
8. Entertainment and leisure

Instagram Statistics

1. Over 1 billion active users
2. 71% of online adults aged 18-29 use Instagram
3. Average user spends 53 minutes per day on Instagram
4. 95 million posts shared daily
5. 70% of businesses use Instagram

Instagram Features

1. Feed: Curated content from followed accounts
2. Stories: Ephemeral content (24 hours)
3. Reels: Short-form videos (up to 60 seconds)

4. IGTV: Long-form videos (up to 60 minutes)
5. Live Streaming: Real-time video
6. Hashtags: Content discovery and organization
7. Instagram Shopping: E-commerce integration
8. Instagram Insights: Analytics and performance tracking

Benefits of Instagram

1. Visual inspiration and creativity
2. Community engagement and networking
3. Business growth and marketing
4. Personal branding and self-expression
5. Education and learning

6. Entertainment and leisure
7. Real-time information and news
8. Portfolio building and showcase

Instagram's Impact

1. Revolutionized visual content sharing
2. Influenced social media marketing
3. Changed how people consume and interact with content
4. Facilitated community building and social networking
5. Raised concerns about mental health, data privacy, and online safety

☐ Creating visually appealing Instagram content

Creating visually appealing Instagram content involves using a combination of visual elements, captions, and hashtags to capture users' attention.

Visual Elements:

1. High-quality images and videos
2. Consistent color palette and branding
3. Text overlays and graphics
4. Emojis and icons
5. Backgrounds and textures

Content Types:

1. Photos
2. Videos
3. Stories
4. Reels
5. IGTV
6. Live Streaming
7. Carousels (multi-image posts)
8. GIFs

Design Tips:

1. Use a consistent aesthetic
2. Balance text and images
3. Experiment with colors and textures
4. Add depth with layers and dimensions
5. Keep it simple and concise

Caption Strategies:

1. Keep it short and sweet
2. Use humor and storytelling
3. Ask questions and spark conversations
4. Include relevant hashtags
5. Provide context and explanations

Hashtag Strategies:

1. Research relevant hashtags
2. Use a mix of niche and broad hashtags
3. Limit hashtags to 5-10 per post
4. Create branded hashtags
5. Monitor hashtag performance

Instagram-Friendly Formats:

1. Square (1080 x 1080 px)
2. Portrait (1080 x 1350 px)
3. Landscape (1080 x 608 px)
4. Story (1080 x 1920 px)
5. Reel (1080 x 1920 px)

Content Calendar Tools:

1. Planoly
2. Hootsuite
3. Buffer
4. Sprout Social
5. Canva

Visual Content Creation Tools:

1. Adobe Creative Cloud
2. Canva
3. Sketch
4. Figma
5. VSCO

Best Practices:

1. Post consistently
2. Engage with audience
3. Monitor analytics
4. Experiment with content types
5. Stay up-to-date with Instagram trends

Common Mistakes:

1. Poor image quality
2. Inconsistent branding
3. Overuse of hashtags
4. Lack of engagement
5. Ignoring analytics

Instagram hashtags and tagging

Instagram hashtags and tagging are essential tools for increasing discoverability, engagement, and reach.

Hashtags:

1. Keywords or phrases preceded by "#" symbol
2. Categorize and make content discoverable
3. Used in captions, comments, and stories

Types of Hashtags:

1. Niche hashtags (specific industry/community)
2. Broad hashtags (general topics)
3. Branded hashtags (unique to your business)
4. Event hashtags (conferences, festivals, etc.)
5. Seasonal hashtags (holidays, trends, etc.)

Best Practices:

1. Use 5-10 relevant hashtags per post
2. Research and test hashtags
3. Mix niche and broad hashtags
4. Create a unique branded hashtag
5. Monitor hashtag performance

Tagging:

1. Mentioning other users in captions or comments
2. Notifies tagged users and adds post to their profile
3. Increases engagement and collaboration

Types of Tags:

1. User tags (@username)
2. Location tags (geotagging)
3. Product tags (shopping)
4. Hashtag tags (#hashtag)

Tagging Best Practices:

1. Tag relevant users and brands
2. Use tags consistently
3. Limit tags to 5-10 per post
4. Respond to tags and comments
5. Utilize tagging for collaborations

Tools for Hashtag Research:

1. Instagram's built-in hashtag suggestions
2. Hashtagify
3. RiteTag
4. TagCrowd
5. Hootsuite Insights

Tools for Tagging:

1. Instagram's tagging feature
2. Hootsuite's tagging tool
3. Sprout Social's tagging feature
4. Buffer's tagging tool
5. (link unavailable)

Common Mistakes:

1. Overusing hashtags
2. Using irrelevant hashtags
3. Not researching hashtags
4. Not responding to tags
5. Not utilizing tagging for collaborations

☐ Instagram Stories and Reels

Instagram Stories and Reels are essential features for businesses and creators to engage with their audience.

Instagram Stories:

1. Ephemeral content (24 hours)
2. Photos, videos, and text-based content
3. Swipe-up links, polls, quizzes, and more
4. Engagement metrics (views, swipes, taps)

Instagram Reels:

1. Short-form videos (up to 60 seconds)
2. Music, effects, and editing tools
3. Captioning, tagging, and hashtagging
4. Engagement metrics (views, likes, comments)

Benefits of Instagram Stories and Reels:

1. Increased engagement and reach
2. Improved brand awareness and visibility
3. Enhanced customer connection and loyalty
4. Drive website traffic and sales
5. Share behind-the-scenes content

Instagram Stories Features:

1. Swipe-up links
2. Polls and quizzes
3. Question stickers
4. Shopping tags
5. Location tags
6. Hashtag stickers
7. GIFs and emojis

Instagram Reels Features:

1. Music library
2. Effects and filters
3. Editing tools
4. Captioning and tagging
5. Hashtagging
6. Shopping tags
7. Reels tab on profile

Best Practices for Instagram Stories and Reels:

1. Post consistently
2. Use engaging visuals and audio
3. Keep content concise and informative
4. Utilize interactive features
5. Monitor and respond to engagement
6. Use relevant hashtags
7. Collaborate with influencers and users

Common Mistakes:

1. Lack of consistency
2. Poor content quality

3. Insufficient engagement
4. Overuse of hashtags
5. Ignoring analytics
6. Not utilizing interactive features
7. Inadequate branding

Tools for Instagram Stories and Reels:

1. Instagram's built-in editing tools
2. Adobe Creative Cloud
3. Canva
4. InShot
5. VSCO
6. Hootsuite
7. Sprout Social

▢ Instagram Influencer marketing

Instagram Influencer Marketing involves partnering with influencers to promote products, services, or brands to their followers.

Benefits:

1. Increased brand awareness and reach
2. Authentic endorsements and credibility
3. Targeted audience engagement
4. Improved sales and conversions
5. Cost-effective marketing

Types of Influencers:

1. Nano-influencers(1,000-10,000 followers)
2. Micro-influencers(10,000-100,000 followers)
3. Mid-tier influencers (100,000-500,000 followers)
4. Macro-influencers (500,000-1,000,000 followers)
5. Celebrity influencers (1,000,000+ followers)

Influencer Selection Criteria:

1. Relevance to target audience
2. Follower count and engagement
3. Content quality and consistency
4. Authenticity and credibility
5. Past collaborations and reviews

Influencer Collaboration Ideas:

1. Sponsored posts
2. Product reviews
3. Giveaways and contests
4. Exclusive discounts
5. Long-term ambassador programs
6. Instagram Takeovers
7. Live streaming and events

Influencer Marketing Platforms:

1. AspireIQ
2. HYPR
3. Upfluence
4. Influencer Marketing Hub
5. Grin
6. Traackr
7. IZEA

Measuring Influencer Marketing ROI:

1. Engagement metrics (likes, comments, etc.)
2. Reach and impressions
3. Conversion tracking (sales, website traffic, etc.)
4. Brand awareness and sentiment analysis
5. Influencer-specific promo codes

Best Practices:

1. Clearly define campaign objectives
2. Choose influencers aligning with brand values
3. Set realistic expectations and budgets
4. Monitor and measure campaign performance
5. Disclose sponsored content

6. Build long-term relationships with influencers
7. Ensure FTC compliance

Common Mistakes:

1. Partnering with irrelevant influencers
2. Insufficient campaign planning
3. Lack of clear objectives
4. Inadequate tracking and measurement
5. Overemphasis on follower count
6. Ignoring influencer authenticity
7. Not disclosing sponsored content

Instagram Influencer Marketing Tools:

1. Instagram Brand Content Ads
2. Instagram Shopping
3. Instagram Insights
4. Facebook Creator Studio
5. Hootsuite Influencer Marketing
6. Sprout Social Influencer Management
7. AspireIQ Influencer Discovery

Instagram shopping and ecommerce integration

Instagram Shopping and ecommerce integration enable businesses to tag products directly in their Instagram posts and stories, making it easy for customers to purchase from their feed.

Benefits:

1. Seamless shopping experience
2. Increased conversions and sales
3. Enhanced customer engagement
4. Simplified product discovery
5. Detailed analytics and insights

Instagram Shopping Features:

1. Product Tags: Tag products in posts and stories
2. Shopping Cart: Customers can purchase from your feed
3. Product Catalog: Centralized product management
4. Shopping Bag: Customers can view and edit orders
5. Checkout: Secure, in-app payment processing

Ecommerce Integration Options:

1. Instagram Shopping API
2. Facebook Shop
3. BigCommerce
4. Shopify
5. Magento
6. WooCommerce
7. Salesforce Commerce Cloud

Setup Requirements:

1. Instagram Business Account
2. Facebook Shop
3. Product Catalog
4. Ecommerce platform integration
5. Verified website and domain

Best Practices:

1. High-quality product images
2. Accurate product information
3. Clear calls-to-action (CTAs)
4. Consistent branding
5. Regular product updates
6. Engage with customers
7. Monitor analytics

Common Mistakes:

1. Inaccurate product information
2. Poor image quality
3. Insufficient CTAs
4. Lack of product updates
5. Inadequate analytics tracking
6. Non-compliant ecommerce integration
7. Ignoring customer engagement

Instagram Shopping Analytics:

1. Product views

2. Website clicks
3. Purchases
4. Revenue
5. Conversion rate
6. Average order value (AOV)
7. Return on ad spend (ROAS)

Tools for Instagram Shopping:

1. Instagram Shopping API
2. Facebook Commerce Manager
3. Shopify Instagram Shopping
4. BigCommerce Instagram Shopping
5. Hootsuite Instagram Shopping
6. Sprout Social Instagram Shopping
7. SocialPilot Instagram Shopping

Instagram advertising costs internationally and in India

Instagram advertising costs can vary greatly depending on several factors, including ad objectives, placement, audience demographics, seasonality, and competition [1].

Factors Influencing Instagram Ad Costs

- Ad Objectives and Goals: What you want to achieve with your Instagram ads, such as boosting brand awareness or driving website traffic, affects your cost per click (CPC) or cost per impression (CPM).
- Ad Placement and Formats: Different ad placements, like feed or stories, and formats, such as static images or videos, impact costs.
- Target Audience and Demographics: Targeting a specific audience, like doctors in major Indian cities, can increase costs due to competition.
- Seasonality and Timing: Advertising during festive seasons or major events can lead to higher costs.
- Competition in the Industry or Niche: Highly competitive industries or niches result in higher ad costs.

Average Instagram Ad Costs in India

While costs vary, here are some rough estimates of average costs for different ad types in India:

- Average CPC: ₹45-₹70

- Average CPM: ₹150-₹300

Industry-Specific Costs

- E-commerce and tech tend to have higher costs due to competition.
- Education and travel might have lower costs.

Keep in mind that these are general estimates, and actual costs depend on your specific ad campaign and targeting. To optimize your ad spend, consider A/B testing, tracking performance metrics, and adjusting your bidding strategy.

Chapter 7: X (Formally Twitter) Marketing (x.com)

☐ What is X (formally Twitter) and how to use it?

Note: Twitter has been renamed to X and the domain has been changed to x.com

Rebranding
Twitter was rebranded to X in July 2023, shortly after Elon Musk took over as CEO.

Domain change
The domain name was changed from twitter.com to x.com on May 17, 2024. The Twitter.com URL now redirects to x.com.

Login page
The X login page displays a notification that the URL is changing, but privacy and data protection settings remain the same

X (Twitter) is a social networking and microblogging platform that enables users to share short messages (tweets) of up to 280 characters.

What is Twitter?

Twitter is a real-time social networking platform where users can:

1. Share thoughts, opinions, and experiences
2. Follow others and view their tweets
3. Engage with others through replies, likes, and retweets
4. Discover trending topics and hashtags
5. Share multimedia content (images, videos, GIFs)

History of Twitter

1. Launched in 2006 by Jack Dorsey, Evan Williams, Biz Stone, and Noah Glass
2. Initially called "twttr"
3. Acquired by Elon Musk in 2022

How is Twitter useful to people?
1. Real-time news and updates
2. Networking and community building

3. Self-expression and creativity
4. Business and marketing opportunities
5. Education and learning
6. Entertainment and leisure
7. Political discourse and activism
8. Customer service and support

Twitter Statistics

1. Over 440 million monthly active users
2. 192 million daily active users
3. 1.3 billion registered users
4. 500 million tweets sent daily
5. 75% of users are outside the US

Twitter Features

1. Tweets
2. Hashtags (#)
3. @Mentions
4. Direct Messages (DMs)
5. Retweets
6. Likes
7. Twitter Polls
8. Twitter Live
9. Twitter Moments

Benefits of Twitter

1. Real-time information sharing
2. Global connectivity
3. Personal branding and self-expression
4. Business and marketing opportunities
5. Community building and engagement
6. Education and learning
7. Entertainment and leisure
8. Social activism and awareness

Twitter's Impact

1. Revolutionized real-time communication
2. Changed how people consume news
3. Influenced social media marketing
4. Facilitated global connectivity
5. Raised concerns about online safety and harassment

Twitter Tools and Integrations

1. Twitter Analytics
2. Twitter Ads
3. Hootsuite
4. Sprout Social
5. Buffer
6. TweetDeck
7. Twitterific

Best Practices for Twitter

1. Post consistently
2. Engage with others
3. Use relevant hashtags
4. Keep tweets concise
5. Utilize multimedia content
6. Monitor and respond to mentions
7. Use Twitter Analytics

☐ Crafting compelling tweets

Crafting compelling tweets requires a combination of creativity, strategy, and attention to detail.

Key Elements of a Compelling Tweet:

1. Clear and concise language
2. Relevant hashtags
3. Engaging visuals (images, videos, GIFs)
4. Strong call-to-action (CTA)
5. Personal touch and authenticity
6. Timeliness and relevance
7. Emotional connection

Tweet Structure:

1. Introduction (hook)
2. Main message
3. Call-to-action (CTA)
4. Hashtags
5. Visuals (optional)

Tips for Crafting Compelling Tweets:

1. Know your audience
2. Keep it short and sweet (280 characters)
3. Use active voice
4. Ask questions
5. Use humor and emotion
6. Utilize storytelling
7. Include a clear CTA
8. Use relevant hashtags (2-3)
9. Add visuals to enhance engagement
10. Proofread and edit

Types of Tweets:

1. Informational
2. Promotional
3. Engagement-driven
4. Conversational
5. Inspirational
6. Educational
7. Entertaining

Visual Content:

1. Images (1024 x 512 px)
2. Videos (up to 2 minutes)
3. GIFs (up to 5MB)
4. Infographics
5. Quotes and text overlays

Hashtag Strategies:

1. Research relevant hashtags
2. Use niche and broad hashtags
3. Limit hashtags to 2-3
4. Create branded hashtags
5. Monitor hashtag performance

Twitter Analytics:

1. Engagement rate
2. Reach and impressions
3. Click-through rate (CTR)
4. Conversion rate
5. Hashtag performance

Tools for Crafting Compelling Tweets:

1. Twitter Composer
2. Hootsuite
3. Sprout Social
4. Buffer
5. TweetDeck
6. Canva
7. Adobe Creative Cloud

☐ Twitter Chats and hashtag participation

Twitter Chats and hashtag participation are excellent ways to engage with others, build community, and increase visibility.

Twitter Chats:

1. Real-time conversations around a specific topic
2. Moderated by a host or organization
3. Use a designated hashtag
4. Participants share thoughts, experiences, and expertise

Benefits of Twitter Chats:

1. Networking and community building
2. Thought leadership and expertise
3. Real-time engagement and feedback
4. Increased visibility and reach
5. Learning and professional development

Popular Twitter Chats:

1. #TwitterChat (general discussions)

2. #BlogChat (blogging and writing)
3. #SocialMediaChat (social media marketing)
4. #MarketingChat (marketing and advertising)
5. #SmallBizChat (small business and entrepreneurship)

How to Participate in Twitter Chats:

1. Research and find relevant chats
2. Follow the chat's hashtag
3. Introduce yourself and join the conversation
4. Share your thoughts and expertise
5. Engage with others and respond to comments
6. Use the chat's hashtag in your tweets
7. Follow up with new connections

Hashtag Participation:

1. Research relevant hashtags
2. Use hashtags in your tweets
3. Participate in hashtag conversations
4. Monitor hashtag performance
5. Create branded hashtags

Benefits of Hashtag Participation:

1. Increased visibility and reach
2. Improved engagement and conversations
3. Networking and community building
4. Thought leadership and expertise
5. Brand awareness and recognition

Tools for Twitter Chats and Hashtag Participation:

1. TweetDeck
2. Hootsuite
3. Sprout Social
4. Buffer
5. Hashtagify
6. RiteTag
7. Twitter Chat Schedule

Best Practices:

1. Research and understand the chat's topic and tone
2. Be respectful and professional
3. Add value to the conversation
4. Use relevant hashtags
5. Engage with others and respond to comments
6. Follow up with new connections
7. Monitor and adjust your strategy

☐ Twitter Polls and surveys

Twitter Polls and surveys enable users to gather opinions, feedback, and insights from their audience.

Twitter Polls:

1. Create polls with up to 7 options
2. Poll duration: 1-7 days
3. Real-time results
4. Engage audience and spark conversations

Benefits of Twitter Polls:

1. Increase engagement and participation
2. Gather opinions and feedback
3. Conduct market research
4. Enhance brand awareness
5. Drive website traffic

Twitter Survey Tools:

1. Twitter Polls (native feature)
2. SurveyMonkey
3. PollDaddy
4. Typeform
5. Google Forms

Best Practices for Twitter Polls:

1. Keep polls concise and clear
2. Use relevant and engaging questions
3. Limit options to 3-5
4. Set poll duration strategically

5. Promote polls through tweets and hashtags
6. Analyze and share results
7. Encourage discussion and feedback

Twitter Survey Questions:

1. Multiple-choice questions
2. Rating scales (1-5)
3. Open-ended questions
4. Likert scale questions
5. Demographic questions

Tips for Effective Twitter Surveys:

1. Define survey objectives
2. Identify target audience
3. Keep surveys concise
4. Use clear and simple language
5. Test survey questions
6. Analyze and share results
7. Follow up with respondents

Analytics for Twitter Polls and Surveys:

1. Vote count and percentage
2. Response rate
3. Engagement metrics (likes, retweets)
4. Demographic insights
5. Sentiment analysis

Integrating Twitter Polls with Other Tools:

1. Website integration
2. Email marketing integration
3. CRM integration
4. Social media management tools
5. Analytics platforms

Twitter advertising

Twitter advertising enables businesses to reach their target audience and achieve specific marketing goals.

Twitter Ad Types:

1. Promoted Tweets: Boost tweets for increased visibility
2. Promoted Accounts: Increase followers and visibility
3. Promoted Trends: Sponsor trending topics
4. Video Ads: Share video content
5. Carousel Ads: Showcase multiple images or videos
6. Website Cards: Drive website traffic
7. App Cards: Promote mobile apps
8. Shopping Ads: Tag products for easy purchasing

Twitter Ad Targeting:

1. Demographics (age, location, language)
2. Interests (keywords, hashtags)
3. Behaviors (user actions, device usage)
4. Tailored Audiences (custom lists)
5. Lookalike Audiences (similar users)
6. Keyword Targeting (conversation topics)
7. Event Targeting (specific events)

Twitter Ad Pricing:

1. Cost Per Click (CPC)
2. Cost Per Thousand Impressions (CPM)
3. Cost Per View (CPV)
4. Cost Per Engagement (CPE)
5. Auction-based pricing

Twitter Ad Benefits:

1. Increased brand awareness
2. Website traffic and conversions
3. Lead generation
4. App installs
5. Sales and revenue growth
6. Customer engagement
7. Market research and insights

Twitter Ad Analytics:

1. Engagement metrics (likes, retweets)
2. Conversion tracking
3. Click-through rate (CTR)
4. Cost per acquisition (CPA)
5. Return on ad spend (ROAS)
6. Impressions and reach
7. Audience insights

Twitter Ad Tools:

1. Twitter Ads Manager
2. Twitter Analytics
3. Hootsuite Ads
4. Sprout Social Ads
5. AdEspresso
6. TweetDeck
7. Twitter Ad API

Best Practices for Twitter Ads:

1. Define clear objectives
2. Target specific audiences
3. Optimize ad creative
4. Monitor and adjust bidding
5. Track and measure performance
6. Rotate ad creative
7. Use Twitter's ad automation

☐ Twitter analytics and tracking

Twitter analytics and tracking provide valuable insights into your Twitter performance, helping you refine your strategy and optimize results.

Twitter Analytics Tools:

1. Twitter Analytics (native tool)
2. Hootsuite Insights
3. Sprout Social Analytics
4. TweetDeck
5. Google Analytics (for website tracking)
6. (link unavailable) (for link tracking)
7. Twitter Counter

Twitter Metrics to Track:

1. Engagement rate
2. Follower growth
3. Tweet impressions
4. Click-through rate (CTR)
5. Conversion rate
6. Hashtag performance
7. Mention and reply rate
8. Audience demographics
9. Top-performing content
10. Sentiment analysis

Twitter Analytics Categories:

1. Account metrics (followers, engagement)
2. Tweet metrics (impressions, engagement)
3. Audience metrics (demographics, interests)
4. Engagement metrics (likes, retweets, replies)
5. Conversion metrics (website traffic, sales)

Twitter Tracking Methods:

1. Tracking URLs (e.g., (link unavailable))
2. Conversion tracking (e.g., Twitter Pixel)
3. Hashtag tracking (e.g., Hashtagify)
4. Keyword tracking (e.g., Twitter Search)
5. Influencer tracking (e.g., Social Blade)

Benefits of Twitter Analytics:

1. Data-driven decision making
2. Improved content strategy
3. Enhanced engagement and conversions
4. Better audience understanding
5. Competitive analysis
6. ROI measurement

7. Campaign optimization

Common Twitter Analytics Mistakes:

1. Not tracking key metrics
2. Ignoring audience insights
3. Not adjusting strategy based on data
4. Overemphasizing follower count
5. Not using tracking URLs
6. Not monitoring sentiment analysis
7. Not analyzing competitor performance

Best Practices for Twitter Analytics:

1. Set clear objectives
2. Track relevant metrics
3. Monitor audience insights
4. Adjust strategy based on data
5. Use tracking URLs
6. Analyze sentiment analysis
7. Regularly review and optimize performance

☐ Twitter Advertising cost India and International

Twitter advertising costs vary depending on factors like ad format, targeting, and bidding strategy. Here's a breakdown of what you can expect to pay:

Twitter Ads Packages in India

- Package 1: ₹10,125 (approximately $130) for a daily spend limit of ₹250 and a contract period of 30 days
- Package 2: ₹13,860 (approximately $180) for a daily spend limit of ₹350 and a contract period of 30 days
- Package 3: ₹19,500 (approximately $250) for a daily spend limit of ₹500 and a contract period of 30 days
- Package 4: ₹28,800 (approximately $370) for a daily spend limit of ₹750 and a contract period of 30 days
- Package 5: ₹37,500 (approximately $480) for a daily spend limit of ₹1,000 and a contract period of 30 days
- Package 6: ₹54,900 (approximately $700) for a daily spend limit of ₹1,500 and a contract period of 30 days

International Twitter Ads Packages

- Package 1: $157.21 for a daily spend limit of $3.29 and a contract period of 30 days
- Package 2: $215.20 for a daily spend limit of $4.60 and a contract period of 30 days
- Package 3: $302.76 for a daily spend limit of $6.58 and a contract period of 30 days
- Package 4: $447.16 for a daily spend limit of $9.87 and a contract period of 30 days
- Package 5: $582.24 for a daily spend limit of $13.16 and a contract period of 30 days
- Package 6: $852.40 for a daily spend limit of $17.74 and a contract period of 30 days

Keep in mind that these prices are subject to change and may vary based on your specific advertising needs and goals. Additionally, Twitter ads pricing can be influenced by factors like ad format, targeting options, and bidding strategy.

Chapter 8: WhatsApp Business Marketing

What is WhatsApp and WhatsApp business?

WhatsApp is a popular messaging app for personal and group conversations, while WhatsApp Business provides additional features for businesses to manage customer communications.

WhatsApp:

1. Free messaging app for individuals
2. End-to-end encryption for secure conversations
3. Text, voice, and video messaging
4. Group chats and broadcasts
5. File sharing and location sharing
6. Cross-platform compatibility (Android, iOS, Web)

WhatsApp Business:

1. Designed for businesses to manage customer communications
2. Verified business profiles with contact information
3. Business-specific features:
   - Auto-replies
   - Greeting messages
   - Quick replies
   - Labels for organizing conversations
   - Statistics for message delivery and reading
4. API for integrating with CRM systems
5. Support for automated messaging and chatbots
6. WhatsApp Business App (Android, iOS) and WhatsApp Business API

WhatsApp Business Features:

1. Business Profile: Verified profile with business information
2. Auto-replies: Automated responses to frequent queries
3. Greeting Messages: Customizable welcome messages
4. Quick Replies: Pre-defined responses to common questions
5. Labels: Organize conversations by topic or customer
6. Statistics: Track message delivery and reading
7. API: Integrate with CRM systems and automate messaging
8. Chatbots: Automated conversational interfaces
9. Group Messaging: Communicate with multiple customers
10. File Sharing: Share documents, images, and videos

Benefits of WhatsApp Business:

1. Enhanced customer engagement
2. Improved response times
3. Automated messaging and support
4. Increased efficiency
5. Better customer insights
6. Secure and reliable communication
7. Scalable solution for growing businesses

WhatsApp Business Pricing:

1. Free for small businesses
2. Enterprise pricing: Custom plans for large businesses
3. API pricing: Based on message volume and frequency

WhatsApp Business Requirements:

1. Business phone number
2. Verified business profile
3. WhatsApp Business App or API
4. Comply with WhatsApp Business policies

WhatsApp Business Use Cases:

1. Customer support
2. Sales and marketing
3. Order tracking and updates
4. Appointment scheduling
5. Survey and feedback collection
6. Transactional messaging (e.g., receipts, confirmations)

Setting up WhatsApp Business

Setting up WhatsApp Business involves several steps:

Prerequisites:

1. Business phone number (dedicated or existing)
2. Android or iOS device
3. WhatsApp Business App (download from Play Store or App Store)
4. Verified business profile information

Setup Steps:

Option 1: WhatsApp Business App

1. Download and install WhatsApp Business App.
2. Verify business phone number via SMS or call.
3. Create business profile with:
   - Business name
   - Address
   - Category
   - Profile picture
4. Set up auto-replies, greeting messages, and quick replies.
5. Configure business settings (e.g., working hours, email).

Option 2: WhatsApp Business API

1. Apply for WhatsApp Business API access.
2. Provide business information and verification documents.
3. Set up API credentials and integrate with CRM or system.
4. Configure messaging and automation settings.

Verification Process:

1. Phone number verification via SMS or call.
2. Business profile verification through:
   - Facebook Business Manager (if connected)
   - WhatsApp Business API (if applied)
   - Manual verification (document submission)

Post-Setup:

1. Test WhatsApp Business features.
2. Configure additional settings (e.g., labels, statistics).
3. Integrate with CRM or marketing automation tools.
4. Develop messaging strategies and content.

Tips and Best Practices:

1. Use a dedicated business phone number.
2. Ensure accurate business profile information.
3. Set clear auto-replies and greeting messages.
4. Use quick replies for frequent queries.
5. Monitor and respond to customer messages promptly.
6. Comply with WhatsApp Business policies.

Common Issues and Solutions:

1. Verification issues: Check phone number and business profile accuracy.

2. Setup errors: Review setup steps and API documentation.
3. Messaging limitations: Ensure compliance with WhatsApp policies.

WhatsApp Business Support:
1. WhatsApp Business Support Center
2. WhatsApp Business API Documentation
3. WhatsApp Business Community Forum

☐ Creating and sending broadcasts

Creating and sending broadcasts on WhatsApp Business:

Broadcasts:

1. Send messages to multiple contacts or groups
2. Useful for announcements, updates, or promotions
3. Can be text, image, video, or document

Creating Broadcasts:

1. Open WhatsApp Business
2. Tap "Broadcast" (three dots on top-right)
3. Select contacts or groups
4. Type or attach message content
5. Add quick replies or buttons (optional)
6. Review and send

Broadcast List:

1. Create a list of contacts for recurring broadcasts
2. Add/remove contacts as needed
3. Use for regular updates or newsletters

Broadcast Features:

1. Personalization: Use contact names or custom fields
2. Scheduling: Send broadcasts at specific times
3. Tracking: Monitor delivery and reading stats
4. Automation: Use WhatsApp Business API for automated broadcasts

Best Practices:

1. Keep messages concise and relevant
2. Segment broadcast lists for targeted content
3. Use attention-grabbing headings and CTAs
4. Include unsubscribe options
5. Respect contact preferences and frequency

Broadcast Limitations:

1. 256 contacts per broadcast (WhatsApp limit)
2. Message length limits (text, media)
3. File size limits (documents, images)

Broadcast Analytics:

1. Delivery reports
2. Reading stats
3. Engagement metrics (replies, clicks)
4. Use data to refine broadcast strategy

Common Issues:

1. Broadcast not delivered: Check contact lists, message content
2. Error sending broadcast: Review WhatsApp Business API logs

WhatsApp Business Broadcast Tools:

1. WhatsApp Business App
2. WhatsApp Business API
3. Third-party integrations (e.g., Zapier, Mailchimp)

1. **WhatsApp Business API Integration**

The WhatsApp Business API enables businesses to integrate WhatsApp messaging with their systems, automating and scaling customer communications.

Benefits:

1. Automated messaging
2. Customized integrations
3. Scalable messaging solutions
4. Enhanced customer experience
5. Reduced manual effort
6. Improved response times
7. Increased efficiency

Integration Options:

1. CRM integration (e.g., Salesforce, HubSpot)
2. Marketing automation integration (e.g., Mailchimp, Marketo)
3. Customer support platform integration (e.g., Zendesk, Freshdesk)
4. ERP integration (e.g., SAP, Oracle)
5. Custom integrations using WhatsApp Business API

API Features:

1. Message sending and receiving
2. Contact management
3. Group management
4. Message templates
5. Media sharing
6. Location sharing
7. API callbacks for events (e.g., message delivery)

Integration Process:

1. Apply for WhatsApp Business API access
2. Receive API credentials
3. Choose an integration method (e.g., CRM, custom)
4. Develop and test integration
5. Deploy and monitor integration

Popular Integration Tools:

1. Zapier
2. Integromat
3. (link unavailable)
4. WhatsApp Business API SDKs (Java, Python, Node.js)

Best Practices:

1. Ensure API security and authentication
2. Monitor API usage and errors
3. Optimize message content and frequency
4. Use API callbacks for event tracking
5. Test and iterate integration

2. Automating Broadcasts with Chatbots

Chatbots can automate WhatsApp broadcasts, enhancing customer engagement. Benefits include:

Automating Broadcasts with Chatbots:

Benefits:

1. 24/7 availability
2. Personalized responses
3. Reduced manual effort
4. Improved customer engagement
5. Enhanced customer experience
6. Increased efficiency
7. Scalable messaging solutions

Chatbot Features for Broadcast Automation:

1. Keyword-based triggers
2. Natural Language Processing (NLP)
3. Intent identification
4. Message templates
5. Conditional logic
6. Integration with WhatsApp Business API
7. Analytics and reporting

Broadcast Automation Use Cases:

1. Welcome messages
2. Appointment reminders
3. Order updates
4. Promotional offers
5. Event notifications
6. Survey and feedback collection
7. Customer support

Chatbot Platforms for WhatsApp Broadcast Automation:

1. ManyChat
2. Chatfuel
3. MobileMonkey
4. Conversational AI platforms (e.g., Dialogflow, Microsoft Bot Framework)
5. Custom chatbot development

Setup and Integration:

1. Connect WhatsApp Business API to chatbot platform
2. Configure chatbot triggers and responses
3. Design and test broadcast workflows
4. Integrate with CRM or marketing automation tools (optional)
5. Monitor and optimize chatbot performance

3. Automating Broadcasts with Chatbots:
Benefits:

1. 24/7 availability
2. Personalized responses
3. Reduced manual effort
4. Improved customer engagement
5. Enhanced customer experience
6. Increased efficiency
7. Scalable messaging solutions

Chatbot Features for Broadcast Automation:

1. Keyword-based triggers
2. Natural Language Processing (NLP)

Best Practices:

1. Define clear chatbot goals and personas
2. Use conversational language and tone
3. Keep broadcasts concise and relevant
4. Use conditional logic for personalized responses
5. Monitor and analyze chatbot performance
6. Continuously test and improve chatbot workflows
7. Ensure compliance with WhatsApp policies

Common Challenges:

1. Chatbot understanding and accuracy
2. Broadcast content and frequency
3. Integration with existing systems
4. Chatbot maintenance and updates
5. Ensuring compliance with regulations

Success Metrics:

1. Broadcast delivery and open rates
2. Engagement metrics (replies, clicks)
3. Customer satisfaction and feedback
4. Conversion rates (e.g., sales, appointments)
5. Return on Investment (ROI)

3. Intent identification
4. Message templates
5. Conditional logic
6. Integration with WhatsApp Business API
7. Analytics and reporting

Broadcast Automation Use Cases:

1. Welcome messages
2. Appointment reminders
3. Order updates
4. Promotional offers
5. Event notifications
6. Survey and feedback collection
7. Customer support

Chatbot Platforms for WhatsApp Broadcast Automation:

1. ManyChat
2. Chatfuel
3. MobileMonkey
4. Conversational AI platforms (e.g., Dialogflow, Microsoft Bot Framework)
5. Custom chatbot development

Setup and Integration:

1. Connect WhatsApp Business API to chatbot platform
2. Configure chatbot triggers and responses
3. Design and test broadcast workflows
4. Integrate with CRM or marketing automation tools (optional)
5. Monitor and optimize chatbot performance

Best Practices:

1. Define clear chatbot goals and personas
2. Use conversational language and tone
3. Keep broadcasts concise and relevant
4. Use conditional logic for personalized responses
5. Monitor and analyze chatbot performance

6. Continuously test and improve chatbot workflows
7. Ensure compliance with WhatsApp policies

Common Challenges:

1. Chatbot understanding and accuracy
2. Broadcast content and frequency
3. Integration with existing systems
4. Chatbot maintenance and updates
5. Ensuring compliance with regulations

Success Metrics:

1. Broadcast delivery and open rates
2. Engagement metrics (replies, clicks)
3. Customer satisfaction and feedback
4. Conversion rates (e.g., sales, appointments)
5. Return on Investment (ROI)

WhatsApp Business provides broadcast analytics and tracking features. Benefits include:

- Delivery reports
- Reading stats
- Engagement metrics
- Data-driven decision making

4. Best Practices for WhatsApp Business Broadcasts

Best practices for WhatsApp Business broadcasts:

- Keep messages concise
- Segment broadcast lists
- Use attention-grabbing headings
- Include unsubscribe options
- Respect contact preferences

5. Creating Engaging Broadcast Content

Tips for creating engaging broadcast content:

- Use visuals (images, videos)
- Personalize messages
- Use clear CTAs

- Keep messages concise
- Use interactive elements (polls, quizzes)

6. Managing Broadcast Lists and Contacts

Tips for managing broadcast lists and contacts:

- Segment lists for targeted content
- Regularly update contact information
- Remove inactive contacts
- Use clear and descriptive list names
- Respect contact preferences

7. Troubleshooting Broadcast Issues

Common broadcast issues and solutions:

- Broadcast not delivered: Check contact lists, message content
- Error sending broadcast: Review WhatsApp Business API logs
- Message formatting issues: Check media and file sizes
- Contact complaints: Review broadcast content and frequency

☐ Using WhatsApp groups

Using WhatsApp Groups:
Benefits:

1. Real-time communication
2. Group conversations
3. File sharing
4. Location sharing
5. End-to-end encryption
6. Low data usage
7. Cross-platform compatibility
8. Large group capacity (up to 256 people)
9. Easy invitation and joining process
10. Customizable group settings

Features:

1. Group chat
2. File sharing (docs, images, videos)
3. Voice and video calls
4. Location sharing
5. Polls
6. GIFs and stickers
7. Emoji reactions
8. Quote replies
9. Group description
10. Admin controls

WhatsApp Group Types:

1. Public groups (open to everyone)
2. Private groups (invitation-only)
3. Closed groups (admin-approved membership)
4. Secret groups (hidden from search)

WhatsApp Group Management:

1. Create and manage groups
2. Add/remove members
3. Set group description
4. Assign admin roles
5. Manage group settings
6. Mute/ unmute notifications
7. Pin important messages
8. Use group labels

WhatsApp Group Best Practices:

1. Set clear group purpose
2. Establish group rules
3. Use descriptive group names
4. Limit group size
5. Monitor member activity
6. Encourage respectful conversation
7. Use emojis and GIFs wisely
8. Pin important information
9. Regularly clean up conversations
10. Respect member privacy

WhatsApp Group for Business:

1. Customer support groups
2. Sales and marketing groups
3. Employee communication groups
4. Partner and supplier groups
5. Community building groups

WhatsApp Business Features:

1. Business profile
2. Label-based organization
3. Quick replies
4. Automated messages
5. WhatsApp Business API
6. Group messaging
7. File sharing
8. Customer support tools

Common WhatsApp Group Issues:

1. Spam messages
2. Group flooding
3. Member conflicts
4. Information overload
5. Difficulty finding information

Solutions to Common Issues:

1. Set group rules
2. Use admin controls
3. Implement moderation
4. Use labels and filters
5. Limit group size
6. Encourage respectful conversation
7. Regularly clean up conversations
8. Use third-party management tools

☐ Customer support and response

Customer Support and Response:

Importance of Customer Support:

1. Builds trust and loyalty
2. Resolves issues promptly
3. Enhances customer experience
4. Reduces churn and complaints
5. Increases customer retention
6. Provides valuable feedback
7. Improves brand reputation

Customer Support Channels:

1. WhatsApp (text, voice, video)
2. Phone (voice calls)
3. Email
4. Live Chat (website, app)
5. Social Media (Twitter, Facebook, Instagram)
6. Knowledge Base (FAQs, tutorials)
7. Forum/Community Support

WhatsApp Customer Support Benefits:

1. Fast response times

2. Personalized support
3. Convenient (mobile-first)
4. Secure (end-to-end encryption)
5. Cost-effective
6. Easy escalation (voice/video calls)
7. Integrated with CRM/systems

Response Strategies:

1. Timely responses (within hours/mins)
2. Empathetic and personalized responses
3. Clear resolutions/explanations
4. Proactive support (anticipate issues)
5. Multilingual support
6. Automated responses (chatbots)
7. Continuous improvement (feedback analysis)

Customer Support Metrics:

1. Response Time (RT)
2. First Response Time (FRT)
3. Resolution Rate (RR)
4. Customer Satisfaction (CSAT)
5. Net Promoter Score (NPS)
6. Ticket Volume/Throughput
7. Support Team Productivity

Best Practices:

1. Define support processes/procedures
2. Train support staff regularly
3. Use customer feedback for improvement
4. Monitor performance metrics
5. Continuously update knowledge base
6. Ensure seamless channel integration
7. Recognize and reward support staff

Tools for Customer Support:

1. WhatsApp Business API
2. Zendesk
3. Freshdesk
4. HelpScout
5. Intercom
6. Salesforce Service Cloud
7. Conversational AI platforms (e.g., Dialogflow)

Challenges:

1. Handling high volume of requests
2. Ensuring timely responses
3. Resolving complex issues
4. Managing multilingual support
5. Maintaining consistency across channels
6. Measuring support effectiveness
7. Continuously improving support processes

☐ Integrating WhatsApp with other channels

Integrating WhatsApp with Other Channels:

Benefits:

1. Seamless customer experience
2. Unified communication
3. Increased efficiency
4. Better customer insights
5. Enhanced engagement
6. Reduced response times
7. Improved customer satisfaction

Channels to Integrate with WhatsApp:

1. Website (live chat, contact forms)
2. Social Media (Facebook, Twitter, Instagram)
3. Email
4. Phone (voice calls)
5. SMS
6. CRM (customer relationship management)
7. Marketing Automation platforms

Integration Methods:

1. API integration (WhatsApp Business API)
2. Third-party integrations (e.g., Zapier, Integromat)
3. Custom development
4. Plugins (e.g., WordPress, Shopify)
5. SDKs (software development kits)

Popular Integration Tools:

1. Zapier
2. Integromat
3. (link unavailable)
4. WhatsApp Business API SDKs
5. ManyChat
6. Chatfuel
7. Conversational AI platforms (e.g., Dialogflow)

Use Cases:

1. Omnichannel customer support
2. Automated lead generation
3. Personalized marketing campaigns
4. Order tracking and updates
5. Survey and feedback collection
6. Appointment scheduling
7. Customer engagement and retention

Best Practices:

1. Define integration goals and objectives
2. Choose the right integration method
3. Ensure data consistency and synchronization
4. Monitor and analyze integration performance
5. Test and iterate integration workflows
6. Ensure security and compliance
7. Document integration processes

Common Challenges:

1. Technical complexities
2. Data consistency and synchronization
3. Ensuring seamless customer experience
4. Managing multiple channels
5. Integration costs and resources
6. Security and compliance concerns
7. Scalability and reliability

Success Metrics:

1. Customer engagement and satisfaction
2. Response times and resolution rates
3. Conversion rates and sales
4. Customer retention and loyalty
5. Integration ROI (return on investment)
6. Data quality and consistency
7. Support team productivity

☐ WhatsApp Business Polling and Survey Settings:

Polling Settings:

1. Poll type: Multiple choice, Rating scale, Open-ended
2. Question text: Customizable
3. Options: Up to 10 options
4. Allow multiple selections: Yes/No
5. Randomize options: Yes/No
6. Poll duration: Set timer (e.g., 1 day, 1 week)
7. Results visibility: Public/Private

Survey Settings:

1. Survey type: NPS, CSAT, Custom
2. Question text: Customizable
3. Question type: Multiple choice, Rating scale, Open-ended
4. Survey length: Up to 10 questions
5. Logic branching: Yes/No (conditional questions)
6. Survey duration: Set timer (e.g., 1 day, 1 week)
7. Results visibility: Public/Private

Distribution Settings:

1. Broadcast lists: Select specific lists

2. WhatsApp groups: Select specific groups
3. Individual messages: Send to specific contacts
4. QR code: Generate QR code for survey
5. Website integration: Embed survey on website
6. Social media sharing: Share on Facebook, Twitter, etc.
7. Email campaigns: Send survey via email

Notification Settings:

1. Notification type: Email, WhatsApp, Both
2. Notification frequency: Immediate, Daily, Weekly
3. Notification recipients: Select specific contacts
4. Custom notification text: Yes/No

Analytics Settings:

1. Response tracking: Yes/No
2. Response rate tracking: Yes/No
3. Survey completion rate tracking: Yes/No
4. NPS/CSAT scoring: Yes/No
5. Custom analytics: Yes/No

Security Settings:

1. Data encryption: Yes/No
2. Password protection: Yes/No
3. Two-factor authentication: Yes/No
4. GDPR compliance: Yes/No

Integrations:

1. CRM integration (e.g., Salesforce)
2. Marketing automation integration (e.g., Mailchimp)
3. Google Analytics integration
4. Custom integrations via API

WhatsApp Business Polling and Survey Implementation:

Benefits:

1. Gather customer feedback
2. Understand customer preferences
3. Improve customer satisfaction
4. Enhance product/service development
5. Increase engagement and participation
6. Real-time feedback and insights
7. Cost-effective and efficient

Polling and Survey Types:

1. Multiple-choice polls
2. Rating scales (1-5, 1-10)
3. Open-ended questions
4. Net Promoter Score (NPS) surveys
5. Customer Satisfaction (CSAT) surveys
6. Product feedback surveys
7. Event feedback surveys

Implementation Steps:

1. Define survey goals and objectives
2. Choose survey type and questions
3. Design visually appealing templates
4. Set up survey distribution (WhatsApp groups, broadcasts)
5. Track and analyze responses
6. Follow up with respondents (optional)
7. Review and act on feedback

WhatsApp Business Polling Tools:

1. WhatsApp Business API
2. ManyChat
3. Chatfuel
4. MobileMonkey
5. Conversational AI platforms (e.g., Dialogflow)
6. SurveyMonkey integration
7. Google Forms integration

Best Practices:

1. Keep surveys concise and clear
2. Use visually appealing templates
3. Target specific audience segments
4. Monitor response rates and adjust
5. Analyze and act on feedback
6. Follow up with respondents

7. Ensure survey security and compliance

Survey Distribution Methods:

1. WhatsApp groups
2. Broadcast lists
3. Individual messages
4. QR codes
5. Website integration
6. Social media sharing
7. Email campaigns

Analytics and Reporting:

1. Response rates and completion rates
2. Answer distributions and trends
3. Net Promoter Score (NPS) analysis
4. Customer Satisfaction (CSAT) analysis
5. Open-ended question analysis
6. Survey funnel analysis
7. Custom reporting and dashboards

Common Challenges:

1. Ensuring survey relevance and engagement
2. Managing survey distribution and targeting
3. Analyzing and acting on feedback
4. Maintaining survey security and compliance
5. Handling survey fatigue
6. Integrating with existing systems
7. Scaling survey implementation

Success Metrics:

1. Response rates and completion rates
2. Customer satisfaction and Net Promoter Score
3. Feedback quality and actionable insights
4. Survey engagement and participation
5. Return on Investment (ROI)
6. Customer retention and loyalty
7. Product/service improvement

Chapter 9: YouTube Marketing

☐ What is YouTube and YouTube Marketing?

What is YouTube?

YouTube is a video-sharing platform where users can upload, share, and view videos. Founded in 2005, YouTube has become the largest video-sharing platform in the world, with:

1. 2 billion monthly active users
2. 5 billion videos viewed daily
3. 300 hours of content uploaded every minute
4. Available in 80 languages
5. Owned by Google

Types of YouTube Content:

1. Vlogs (personal vlogs)
2. Music videos
3. Educational content (tutorials, how-to)
4. Product reviews
5. Gaming content
6. Live streams
7. Podcasts
8. Movies and TV shows
9. Documentaries
10. Animated content

What is YouTube Marketing?

YouTube marketing is the process of promoting products, services, or brands through video content on YouTube. Goals include:

1. Increasing brand awareness
2. Generating leads
3. Driving website traffic
4. Boosting sales
5. Building customer engagement
6. Improving SEO
7. Enhancing customer retention

YouTube Marketing Strategies:

1. Video optimization (tags, titles, descriptions)
2. Channel optimization (profile, banner, icons)
3. Content creation (high-quality, engaging)
4. Influencer partnerships
5. Paid advertising (YouTube Ads)
6. Sponsorships and product placements
7. Community engagement (comments, social media)
8. Analytics and tracking (YouTube Analytics)
9. Call-to-actions (CTAs)
10. Cross-promotion (social media, websites)

YouTube Marketing Benefits:

1. Increased brand visibility
2. Targeted advertising
3. Measurable ROI
4. Improved customer engagement
5. Enhanced credibility
6. Cost-effective marketing
7. Global reach
8. Diversified content options
9. SEO benefits
10. Competitive advantage

YouTube Marketing Tools:

1. YouTube Analytics
2. Google Ads
3. TubeBuddy
4. VidIQ
5. Hootsuite
6. Sprout Social
7. Adobe Creative Cloud
8. Final Cut Pro
9. Camtasia
10. ScreenFlow

YouTube Marketing Challenges:

1. Competition
2. Content creation
3. Audience engagement
4. Algorithm changes
5. Ad blockers
6. Measuring ROI
7. Brand safety
8. Video quality
9. Audio quality
10. Consistency

☐ Creating engaging YouTube content

Creating Engaging YouTube Content:
Types of Engaging Content:

1. Educational (tutorials, how-to)
2. Entertaining (comedy, music, vlogs)
3. Inspirational (motivational, self-improvement)
4. Informative (news, reviews, analysis)
5. Interactive (live streams, Q&A, challenges)
6. Storytelling (personal stories, documentaries)
7. Product reviews and demos
8. Gaming content
9. Podcasts and interviews
10. Animated explainers

Content Creation Strategies:

1. Know your audience (target demographic)
2. Define your niche (specific topic)
3. Plan content (script, storyboard, schedule)
4. Invest in quality equipment (camera, microphone)
5. Edit and optimize (titles, tags, descriptions)
6. Use attention-grabbing thumbnails
7. Write compelling titles and descriptions
8. Utilize captions and subtitles
9. Promote on social media and websites
10. Engage with audience (comments, responses)

Video Optimization Techniques:

1. Keyword research (tags, titles)
2. Optimize video length (5-15 minutes)
3. Use eye-catching intros and outros
4. Add closed captions and subtitles
5. Utilize annotations and cards
6. Create engaging thumbnails
7. Use end screens and CTAs
8. Analyze and adjust (YouTube Analytics)
9. Collaborate with other creators
10. Consistency is key (regular uploads)

Storytelling Techniques:

1. Start with a hook (grab attention)
2. Build tension and conflict
3. Resolve with a clear message
4. Use emotional connections
5. Make it relatable and authentic
6. Use visuals and graphics
7. Create suspense and anticipation
8. Use humor and wit
9. Make it concise and clear
10. End with a call-to-action

Tools for Content Creation:

1. Adobe Creative Cloud
2. Final Cut Pro
3. Camtasia
4. ScreenFlow
5. OBS Studio
6. Lightworks
7. DaVinci Resolve
8. iMovie
9. WeVideo
10. YouTube Studio

Common Mistakes to Avoid:

1. Poor audio quality
2. Low-quality visuals
3. Lack of consistency
4. Inauthentic content
5. Overuse of ads
6. Ignoring audience engagement
7. Lack of optimization
8. Overly promotional content
9. Not utilizing analytics
10. Not adapting to changes

Best Practices:

1. Be authentic and transparent
2. Engage with audience
3. Optimize for SEO
4. Use high-quality equipment
5. Plan and schedule content
6. Collaborate with others
7. Analyze and adjust
8. Consistency is key
9. Use storytelling techniques
10. Stay up-to-date with trends

☐ YouTube SEO optimization or Channel Optimization

YouTube channel optimization, also known as YouTube SEO, is the process of optimizing your YouTube channel and videos to improve their search engine rankings. The goal is to make your content more visible, which can lead to more traffic, subscribers, and website visits.

- **How it works:** YouTube SEO involves optimizing your channel, playlists, metadata, descriptions, and videos. Some strategies include:
- **Keyword research:** Find popular search terms that people use to find information on a topic
- **Optimizing for keywords:** Include keywords in your titles, meta descriptions, and tags
- **Video accessibility:** Use transcripts, closed captions, and subtitles to improve user experience and SEO
- **Channel name**: Choose a name that accurately reflects your channel and its content
- **Benefits:** SEO can help you attract traffic, grow your following, and increase brand awareness.

YouTube SEO Optimization:

1. Keyword Research:

1. Google Keyword Planner
2. TubeBuddy Keyword Tool
3. VidIQ Keyword Tool
4. Ahrefs Keyword Explorer

5. SEMrush Keyword Magic Tool

Optimization Strategies:

1. Title Optimization: Include target keywords, descriptive, and attention-grabbing.
2. Description Optimization: Include target keywords, detailed, and concise.
3. Tag Optimization: Relevant and specific keywords.
4. Thumbnail Optimization: Eye-catching, relevant, and high-quality.
5. Video Content Optimization: High-quality, engaging, and informative.

Video Optimization Techniques:

1. Closed Captions: Improve watch time and accessibility.
2. Subtitles: Increase engagement and views.
3. Annotations: Add interactive elements.
4. Cards: Provide additional information.
5. End Screens: Encourage engagement and CTAs.

YouTube Algorithm Factors:

1. Watch Time: Video duration and engagement.
2. Engagement: Likes, comments, shares.
3. Relevance: Keyword alignment and content quality.
4. Authority: Channel credibility and trust.
5. User Experience: Video quality, loading speed.

Analytics and Tracking:

1. YouTube Analytics: Monitor views, engagement, earnings.
2. Google Analytics: Track website traffic and conversions.
3. TubeBuddy Analytics: Detailed video performance insights.
4. VidIQ Analytics: Advanced video and channel analytics.

SEO Tools:

1. TubeBuddy
2. VidIQ
3. Ahrefs
4. SEMrush
5. Moz

Best Practices:

1. Consistency: Regular uploads and scheduling.
2. Quality: High-quality video and audio.
3. Relevance: Align content with target audience.
4. Engagement: Interact with audience and respond.
5. Authenticity: Genuine and transparent content.

Common Mistakes:

1. Keyword Stuffing: Overusing keywords.
2. Poor Thumbnails: Low-quality or misleading.
3. Lack of Engagement: Ignoring audience.
4. Duplicate Content: Copying others' work.
5. Inconsistent Uploads: Unpredictable schedule.

Advanced YouTube SEO techniques

Advanced YouTube SEO Techniques:

1. **Video Structuring:**

   - Intro (0-10 seconds): Hook, branding, and context
   - Main Content (10-60 seconds): Key information and value
   - Conclusion (60+ seconds): Summary, CTAs, and engagement

2. **Keyword Clustering:**

   - Group related keywords and phrases
   - Use variations in title, description, and tags

3. Latent Semantic Indexing (LSI) Keywords:

   - Use synonyms and related phrases
   - Enhance video content and relevance

4. **Entity Optimization:**

   - Use specific names, locations, and organizations
   - Enhance video credibility and authority

5. **Timestamps and Chapters:**

   - Improve video navigation and engagement
   - Enhance watch time and retention

6. **Closed Captions and Subtitles:**

   - Increase accessibility and watch time
   - Improve video indexing and crawling

7. **Video Transcripts:**

   - Provide additional content for search engines
   - Enhance video relevance and authority

8. **Internal Linking:**

   - Link to other relevant videos or playlists
   - Enhance video navigation and engagement

9. **YouTube End Screens:**

   - Encourage engagement and CTAs
   - Enhance video retention and conversion

10. **A/B Testing:**

    - Test titles, thumbnails, and descriptions
    - Analyze performance and adjust

Advanced Analytics:

1. YouTube Studio Analytics
2. Google Analytics
3. TubeBuddy Analytics
4. VidIQ Analytics
5. Ahrefs Analytics

SEO Tools:

1. Ahrefs
2. SEMrush
3. Moz
4. TubeBuddy
5. VidIQ

Best Practices:

1. Consistency and quality content
2. Engage with audience and respond
3. Optimize for user experience
4. Use relevant and descriptive metadata
5. Stay up-to-date with algorithm changes

Common Mistakes:

1. Over-optimization
2. Keyword stuffing
3. Poor video quality
4. Lack of engagement
5. Inconsistent uploads

☐ Video optimization strategies

Video Optimization Strategies:
Pre-Upload Optimization

1. Keyword research: Identify relevant keywords.
2. Title optimization: Craft attention-grabbing, descriptive titles.
3. Description optimization: Write detailed, keyword-rich descriptions.
4. Tag optimization: Use relevant, specific tags.
5. Thumbnail optimization: Create eye-catching, descriptive thumbnails.

Video Content Optimization

1. Intro and outro: Branding, hooks, and CTAs.
2. Main content: Valuable, engaging, and informative.
3. Subtitles and closed captions: Improve accessibility and watch time.
4. Annotations and cards: Add interactive elements.
5. End screens: Encourage engagement and CTAs.

Technical Optimization

1. Video format: MP4, 1080p, 60fps.
2. File size: Compress for faster loading.
3. Length: Optimize for audience engagement.
4. Audio quality: Clear, crisp, and synchronized.
5. Frame rate: 24-60fps for smooth playback.

Post-Upload Optimization

1. Video indexing: Ensure proper indexing.
2. Thumbnail testing: Analyze and adjust.
3. Title and description tweaking: Refine for better performance.
4. Tag refinement: Adjust for improved relevance.
5. Engagement optimization: Respond to comments, encourage sharing.

Analytics and Tracking

1. YouTube Analytics: Monitor views, engagement, earnings.
2. Google Analytics: Track website traffic and conversions.
3. TubeBuddy Analytics: Detailed video performance insights.
4. VidIQ Analytics: Advanced video and channel analytics.

Tools and Software

1. Adobe Premiere Pro
2. Final Cut Pro
3. DaVinci Resolve
4. TubeBuddy
5. VidIQ
6. Ahrefs
7. SEMrush
8. Moz

Best Practices

1. Consistency: Regular uploads and scheduling.
2. Quality: High-quality video and audio.
3. Relevance: Align content with target audience.

4. Engagement: Interact with audience and respond.
5. Authenticity: Genuine and transparent content.

Common Mistakes

1. Poor video quality.
2. Inconsistent uploads.
3. Lack of engagement.
4. Over-optimization.
5. Ignoring analytics.

☐ Keyword research tools

Keyword Research Tools:
Free Tools:

1. Google Keyword Planner
2. Google Trends
3. Google Suggest
4. AnswerThePublic
5. Ubersuggest
6. (link unavailable)
7. LSIGraph
8. Soovle
9. SERPs Keyword Research Tool
10. Moz Keyword Explorer (free version)

Paid Tools:

1. Ahrefs Keyword Explorer
2. SEMrush Keyword Magic Tool
3. Moz Keyword Explorer (full version)
4. Long Tail Pro
5. KWFinder
6. SECockpit
7. Keyword Researcher Pro
8. SpyFu Keyword Research Tool
9. WordStream Keyword Tool
10. AdWords Keyword Tool (paid version)

Features to Consider:

1. Keyword suggestions
2. Search volume data
3. Competition analysis
4. Cost-per-click (CPC) data
5. Keyword clustering
6. Long-tail keyword research
7. Question-based research
8. Related keywords
9. Negative keyword research
10. Integration with other SEO tools

Best Practices:

1. Use multiple tools for comprehensive research
2. Focus on relevance and intent
3. Analyze competition and search volume
4. Identify long-tail keywords
5. Refine keywords based on analytics data
6. Use keyword clustering and grouping
7. Monitor keyword trends and seasonality
8. Incorporate keywords in content strategy
9. Track keyword performance and adjust
10. Stay up-to-date with algorithm changes

Common Mistakes:

1. Over-reliance on single tool
2. Ignoring long-tail keywords
3. Not analyzing competition
4. Focusing solely on search volume
5. Not refining keywords based on analytics
6. Not incorporating keywords in content
7. Not tracking keyword performance
8. Not staying up-to-date with algorithm changes
9. Not considering user intent
10. Not using keyword clustering and grouping

YouTube algorithm updates

Recent Updates:

1. 2022: Helpful Content Update - Prioritizes high-quality, helpful content.
2. 2022: Video Length Update - Favors shorter videos.
3. 2021: Algorithm Update - Emphasizes engagement, relevance, and quality.
4. 2020: Video Recommendation Update - Improves video suggestions.
5. 2019: Creator Responsibility Update - Promotes accountability.

Historical Updates:

1. 2018: Adpocalypse Update - Addresses brand safety concerns.
2. 2017: YouTube Redesign Update - Enhances user experience.
3. 2016: Recommendation Algorithm Update - Improves video suggestions.
4. 2015: YouTube Music Update - Introduces music streaming.
5. 2014: Algorithm Update - Favors watch time and engagement.

Algorithm Factors:

1. Watch Time: Video duration and engagement.
2. Engagement: Likes, comments, shares.
3. Relevance: Keyword alignment and content quality.
4. Authority: Channel credibility and trust.
5. User Experience: Video quality, loading speed.
6. Device and Platform: Mobile, desktop, TV.
7. Location and Language: Geotargeting and language.
8. Audience Retention: View duration and drop-off.

Optimization Strategies:

1. High-quality content: Engaging, informative, and relevant.
2. Keyword research: Accurate and descriptive keywords.
3. Thumbnails and titles: Attention-grabbing and descriptive.
4. Tags and descriptions: Relevant and concise.
5. Engage with audience: Respond to comments.
6. Consistency: Regular uploads and scheduling.
7. Analytics: Monitor performance and adjust.
8. Diversify content: Experiment with formats.

Best Practices:

1. Focus on quality content.
2. Understand your audience.
3. Optimize for relevance.
4. Engage with your audience.
5. Stay up-to-date with updates.
6. Diversify your content.
7. Analyze performance.
8. Adjust strategies accordingly.

Common Mistakes:

1. Over-optimization.
2. Ignoring audience engagement.
3. Poor content quality.
4. Inconsistent uploads.
5. Not adapting to updates.
6. Over-reliance on keywords.
7. Neglecting analytics.
8. Not diversifying content.

☐ SEO audit and analysis

Types of SEO Audits:
1. Technical SEO Audit
2. On-Page SEO Audit
3. Off-Page SEO Audit
4. Content SEO Audit
5. Local SEO Audit
6. Mobile SEO Audit
7. E-commerce SEO Audit

SEO Audit Tools:

1. Ahrefs
2. SEMrush
3. Moz
4. Google Search Console
5. Google Analytics
6. Screaming Frog
7. Majestic
8. GTmetrix
9. Pingdom
10. SEO PowerSuite

1. **SEO Analysis Metrics:**

1. Domain Authority (DA)
2. Page Authority (PA)
3. Moz Rank
4. Alexa Rank
5. Google PageSpeed Score
6. Mobile-Friendliness Test
7. Keyword rankings
8. Organic traffic
9. Conversion rate
10. Bounce rate

2. **SEO Audit Benefits:**

1. Improved website visibility
2. Increased organic traffic
3. Better search engine rankings
4. Enhanced user experience
5. Improved conversion rates
6. Increased brand credibility
7. Competitive advantage
8. Data-driven decision making
9. Improved ROI
11. Long-term SEO success

SEO Audit Process:

1. Crawl and indexation analysis
2. Technical SEO analysis (site speed, mobile-friendliness)
3. On-page SEO analysis (titles, descriptions, headers)
4. Content analysis (quality, uniqueness, keyword usage)
5. Link analysis (internal, external, anchor text)
6. Social media analysis (presence, engagement)
7. Local SEO analysis (Google My Business, citations)
8. Analytics and tracking analysis (Google Analytics)
9. Competitor analysis
10. Recommendations and implementation

Common SEO Audit Mistakes:

1. Ignoring technical SEO
2. Over-optimizing content
3. Neglecting local SEO
4. Not analyzing competitors
5. Not tracking analytics
6. Not addressing crawl errors
7. Not optimizing images
8. Not using header tags
9. Not utilizing internal linking
10. Not staying up-to-date with algorithm changes

SEO Audit Best Practices:

1. Regularly perform SEO audits
2. Use multiple audit tools
3. Analyze competitors
4. Focus on user experience
5. Optimize for mobile
6. Use header tags and meta descriptions
7. Internal link and silence broken links
8. Optimize images and videos
9. Use analytics to track performance
10. Stay up-to-date with algorithm change

YouTube marketing case studies

Success Stories:

1. Dollar Shave Club: Increased subscriptions by 25% with YouTube ads.
2. Old Spice: Boosted sales by 27% with humorous YouTube videos.
3. Coca-Cola: Reached 1.5M views with interactive YouTube campaign.
4. Nike: Increased brand awareness by 15% with YouTube influencer partnerships.
5. GoPro: Boosted sales by 20% with user-generated YouTube content.

B2B Case Studies:

1. HubSpot: Increased leads by 50% with YouTube video marketing.
2. Salesforce: Boosted brand awareness by 20% with YouTube thought leadership content.
3. Microsoft: Reached 1M views with YouTube product demo videos.

Non-Profit Case Studies:

1. American Red Cross: Raised $1M with YouTube donation campaign.
2. Charity: Water: Increased donations by 50% with YouTube storytelling.

Small Business Case Studies:

1. Fitness Blender: Grew to 4M subscribers with free workout videos.
2. Marie Forleo: Built a 7-figure business with YouTube coaching videos.

Industry-Specific Case Studies:

1. Gaming: Riot Games increased engagement by 30% with YouTube esports content.
2. Beauty: Sephora boosted sales by 15% with YouTube product tutorials.
3. Travel: Expedia increased bookings by 20% with YouTube destination videos.

Tools and Platforms Used:

1. YouTube Ads
2. YouTube Analytics
3. TubeBuddy
4. VidIQ
5. Hootsuite
6. Sprout Social

Key Takeaways:

1. Define target audience and goals.
2. Create engaging, relevant content.
3. Optimize videos for SEO.
4. Utilize YouTube Ads and sponsorships.
5. Analyze and adjust strategy.

Common Challenges:

1. Measuring ROI.
2. Creating engaging content.
3. Building audience.
4. Managing YouTube algorithm changes.
5. Scaling video production

SEO-friendly title and description writing

Title Writing Best Practices:

1. Keep it concise: 55-60 characters.
2. Use keywords: Primary keyword at beginning.
3. Make it descriptive: Accurately summarize content.
4. Use attention-grabbing words: Questions, numbers, or action verbs.
5. Avoid duplicates: Unique titles for each page.
6. Brand inclusion: Include brand name (if relevant).
7. Emotional appeal: Create curiosity or interest.

Description Writing Best Practices:

1. Keep it concise: 155-160 characters.
2. Use keywords: Primary and secondary keywords.
3. Summarize content: Accurately describe page content.
4. Include CTAs: Encourage click-through.
5. Avoid duplicates: Unique descriptions for each page.
6. Use active voice: Engaging and conversational tone.
7. Emotional appeal: Create interest or urgency.

Meta Description Templates:

1. Product page: "Buy [product name] | [brief description] | [brand name]."
2. Blog post: "[Article title] | Learn [key takeaway] | [brand name]."
3. Service page: "[Service name] | Expert [service description] | [brand name]."
4. Home page: "[Brand name] | [brief description] | [unique value proposition]."

Tools for Writing SEO-Friendly Titles and Descriptions:

1. Google Keyword Planner
2. Ahrefs
3. SEMrush
4. Moz Keyword Explorer
5. Hemingway Editor
6. Title and Description Generator Tools

Common Mistakes to Avoid:

1. Duplicate titles and descriptions.
2. Keyword stuffing.
3. Irrelevant or misleading content.
4. Too long or too short.
5. Lack of emotional appeal.
6. No CTAs.
7. Poor grammar or spelling.

Best Practices for YouTube Titles and Descriptions:

1. Use keywords in title.
2. Include timestamps.
3. Provide detailed description.
4. Use tags.
5. Optimize for watch time.
6. Use attention-grabbing thumbnails.

SEO optimization for live streams

Pre-Stream Optimization

1. Keyword research: Identify relevant keywords.
2. Optimize title: Include keywords, descriptive, and attention-grabbing.
3. Description: Provide detailed, keyword-rich description.

4. Tags: Use relevant keywords and phrases.
5. Thumbnail: Eye-catching, descriptive, and optimized for mobile.

Live Stream Optimization

1. Consistent branding: Use consistent branding across platforms.
2. Engage with audience: Respond to comments, encourage interaction.
3. Quality content: Provide valuable, informative, and engaging content.
4. Timestamps: Use timestamps to highlight key moments.
5. Live chat: Encourage live chat participation.

Post-Stream Optimization

1. Archive stream: Save and archive stream for future viewing.
2. Repurpose content: Convert stream into other formats (blog posts, videos).
3. Optimize video: Edit, trim, and optimize video for YouTube.
4. Distribute content: Share on social media, websites, and blogs.
5. Analyze performance: Track engagement, views, and analytics.

Live Stream Platforms

1. YouTube Live
2. Twitch
3. Facebook Live
4. Instagram Live
5. Periscope
6. Vimeo Live
7. LinkedIn Live

SEO Tools for Live Streams

1. YouTube Analytics
2. Google Analytics
3. TubeBuddy
4. VidIQ
5. Streamlabs
6. OBS Studio
7. XSplit

Best Practices

1. Plan and schedule streams.
2. Promote streams in advance.
3. Engage with audience.
4. Provide quality content.
5. Optimize for mobile.
6. Use consistent branding.
7. Analyze and adjust.

Common Mistakes

1. Poor quality streams.
2. Lack of engagement.
3. Inconsistent scheduling.
4. Insufficient promotion.
5. No archiving or repurposing.
6. Ignoring analytics.
7. Not optimizing for mobile.

YouTube advertising strategies

Types of YouTube Ads:

1. Video Ads (In-Stream, Pre-Roll, Mid-Roll)
2. Display Ads (Overlay, Banner)
3. Sponsored Cards
4. End Screens
5. Shopping Ads
6. TrueView Ads
7. Non-Skippable Ads
8. Bumper Ads

Targeting Options:

1. Demographic Targeting (Age, Location, Language)
2. Interest Targeting (Topics, Keywords)
3. Behavioral Targeting (User Behavior, Interests)
4. Lookalike Targeting (Similar Audiences)
5. Custom Targeting (Upload Your Own List)
6. Contextual Targeting (Video Content)

Ad Optimization Strategies:

1. A/B Testing (Ad Creative, Targeting)
2. Ad Rotation (Rotate Ads for Freshness)
3. Bid Optimization (Cost-Per-View, Cost-Per-Click)
4. Ad Scheduling (Timing, Frequency)
5. Device Targeting (Mobile, Desktop, TV)
6. Location Targeting (Geotargeting)

YouTube Ad Formats:

1. In-Stream Ads (Video Ads)
2. Display Ads (Image Ads)
3. Sponsored Cards (Interactive Ads)
4. End Screens (CTA Ads)
5. Shopping Ads (Product Ads)
6. TrueView Ads (Skippable Ads)
7. Non-Skippable Ads (15-Second Ads)
8. Bumper Ads (6-Second Ads)

YouTube Ad Metrics:

1. View-Through Rate (VTR)
2. Click-Through Rate (CTR)
3. Conversion Rate (CVR)
4. Cost-Per-View (CPV)
5. Cost-Per-Click (CPC)
6. Return on Ad Spend (ROAS)
7. Video Engagement (Likes, Comments)

Best Practices:

1. Define Clear Objectives
2. Know Your Audience
3. Create Engaging Content
4. Optimize for Mobile
5. Use Relevant Targeting
6. Monitor and Adjust
7. Measure ROI

Common Mistakes:

1. Poor Ad Creative
2. Insufficient Targeting
3. Inadequate Budget
4. Lack of Optimization
5. Ignoring Analytics
6. Not Using A/B Testing
7. Not Utilizing YouTube's Features

YouTube Ad Tools:

1. Google AdWords
2. YouTube Studio
3. TubeBuddy
4. VidIQ
5. AdWords Editor
6. YouTube Analytics
7. Google Trends

☐ Influencer marketing on YouTube

Benefits:

1. Increased brand awareness
2. Reach niche audiences
3. Authentic endorsements
4. Improved credibility
5. Drive website traffic and sales
6. Access to influencer's audience
7. Content creation and distribution

Types of Influencers:

1. Nano-influencers (1,000-10,000 subscribers)
2. Micro-influencers (10,000-100,000 subscribers)
3. Mid-tier influencers (100,000-1,000,000 subscribers)
4. Macro-influencers (1,000,000+ subscribers)
5. Celebrity influencers

Influencer Selection Criteria:

1. Relevance to brand niche
2. Audience demographics and engagement
3. Content quality and consistency
4. Past collaborations and success

5. Authenticity and credibility
6. Reach and impressions
7. Cost and budget alignment

Influencer Collaboration Ideas:

1. Sponsored videos
2. Product reviews
3. Unboxing videos
4. Challenges and contests
5. Giveaways and sweepstakes
6. Exclusive discounts and promotions
7. Brand ambassador programs
8. Live streaming and events

Influencer Marketing Platforms:

1. AspireIQ
2. Upfluence
3. HYPR
4. InfluencerDB
5. Grin
6. Traackr
7. IZEA
8. YouTube's BrandConnect

Measuring Influencer Marketing Success:

1. Engagement metrics (likes, comments, views)
2. Reach and impressions
3. Website traffic and sales
4. Conversion rates
5. Return on Investment (ROI)
6. Brand awareness and sentiment
7. Influencer's audience growth

Best Practices:

1. Clearly define objectives and goals
2. Choose influencers wisely
3. Disclose sponsored content
4. Monitor and track performance
5. Build long-term relationships
6. Ensure brand safety and guidelines
7. Comply with FTC regulations

Common Mistakes:

1. Lack of clear objectives
2. Insufficient research and due diligence
3. Overpaying influencers
4. Not disclosing sponsored content
5. Ignoring audience engagement
6. Not tracking performance
7. Not complying with regulations

YouTube Influencer Marketing Trends:

1. Increased focus on niche influencers
2. Rise of video shopping
3. Growing importance of authenticity
4. Integration with e-commerce platforms
5. Use of AI and machine learning
6. Increased emphasis on brand safety
7. Evolution of influencer marketing platforms

☐ YouTube Analytics and tracking

YouTube Analytics Tools:

1. YouTube Studio (beta)
2. YouTube Analytics
3. Google Analytics
4. TubeBuddy
5. VidIQ
6. Social Blade
7. YouTube Tracker

Key Metrics to Track:

1. Views
2. Watch Time
3. Engagement (likes, comments, shares)
4. Subscribers
5. Conversion Rate (e.g., sales, sign-ups)
6. Click-Through Rate (CTR)
7. Average View Duration (AVD)
8. Drop-Off Points
9. Audience Retention
10. Earnings (for monetized channels)

YouTube Analytics Reports:

1. Overview Report
2. Views Report
3. Engagement Report
4. Earnings Report
5. Audience Report
6. Traffic Sources Report
7. Device and Platform Report
8. Geo Report
9. Language Report
10. Content ID Report

Tracking and Measurement Tools:

1. Google Tag Manager
2. Google Analytics tracking code
3. UTM parameters
4. YouTube's built-in tracking pixels
5. Third-party tracking tools (e.g., PixelYourSite)

Common Tracking Mistakes:

1. Not setting up tracking codes
2. Incorrectly configuring tracking codes
3. Not using UTM parameters
4. Not tracking conversions
5. Ignoring audience engagement metrics
6. Not monitoring earnings and revenue
7. Not adjusting strategy based on data

Best Practices:

1. Set clear goals and objectives
2. Track key metrics and KPIs
3. Monitor audience engagement
4. Analyze earnings and revenue
5. Adjust strategy based on data
6. Use A/B testing and experimentation
7. Regularly review and update tracking setup

Advanced YouTube Analytics Topics:

1. Cohort analysis
2. Funnel analysis
3. Retention analysis
4. A/B testing and experimentation
5. Machine learning and AI applications
6. Data visualization and storytelling
7. YouTube API integration

Certifications and Courses:

1. YouTube Analytics Certification
2. Google Analytics Certification
3. HubSpot Academy's YouTube Marketing Course
4. Coursera's Digital Marketing Specialization
5. Udemy's YouTube Analytics Course

☐ YouTube marketing case studies

Success Stories:

1. Dollar Shave Club: Increased subscriptions by 25% with YouTube ads.
2. Old Spice: Boosted sales by 27% with humorous YouTube videos.
3. Coca-Cola: Reached 1.5M views with interactive YouTube campaign.
4. Nike: Increased brand awareness by 15% with YouTube influencer partnerships.

5. GoPro: Boosted sales by 20% with user-generated YouTube content.

B2B Case Studies:

1. HubSpot: Increased leads by 50% with YouTube video marketing.
2. Salesforce: Boosted brand awareness by 20% with YouTube thought leadership content.
3. Microsoft: Reached 1M views with YouTube product demo videos.

Non-Profit Case Studies:

1. American Red Cross: Raised $1M with YouTube donation campaign.
2. Charity: Water: Increased donations by 50% with YouTube storytelling.

Small Business Case Studies:

1. Fitness Blender: Grew to 4M subscribers with free workout videos.
2. Marie Forleo: Built a 7-figure business with YouTube coaching videos.

Industry-Specific Case Studies:

1. Gaming: Riot Games increased engagement by 30% with YouTube esports content.
2. Beauty: Sephora boosted sales by 15% with YouTube product tutorials.
3. Travel: Expedia increased bookings by 20% with YouTube destination videos.

Key Takeaways:

1. Define clear objectives and goals.
2. Create engaging, relevant content.
3. Optimize videos for SEO.
4. Utilize YouTube Ads and sponsorships.
5. Analyze and adjust strategy.
6. Leverage influencer partnerships.
7. Focus on user-generated content.

Common Challenges:

1. Measuring ROI.
2. Creating engaging content.
3. Building audience.
4. Managing YouTube algorithm changes.
5. Scaling video production.

Tools and Platforms Used:

1. YouTube Ads
2. YouTube Analytics
3. TubeBuddy
4. VidIQ
5. Hootsuite
6. Sprout Social

Certifications and Courses:

1. YouTube Marketing Certification
2. HubSpot Academy's YouTube Marketing Course
3. Coursera's Digital Marketing Specialization
4. Udemy's YouTube Marketing Course

☐ YouTube marketing tools and software

Video Creation and Editing

1. Adobe Premiere Pro
2. Final Cut Pro
3. DaVinci Resolve
4. Camtasia
5. ScreenFlow

SEO and Optimization

1. TubeBuddy
2. VidIQ
3. Ahrefs
4. SEMrush
5. Google Keyword Planner

Analytics and Tracking

1. YouTube Analytics
2. Google Analytics
3. Social Blade
4. VidIQ
5. TubeBuddy

Advertising and Promotion

1. Google AdWords
2. YouTube Ads
3. Facebook Ads
4. Instagram Ads
5. Influencer marketing platforms (AspireIQ, Upfluence)

Social Media Management

1. Hootsuite
2. Sprout Social
3. Buffer
4. SocialPilot
5. Sendible

Content Scheduling

1. Hootsuite
2. Buffer
3. Sprout Social
4. SocialPilot
5. VidIQ

Thumbnail and Graphics Creation

1. Canva
2. Adobe Creative Cloud
3. PicMonkey
4. Snappa
5. Thumbnail maker tools (TubeBuddy, VidIQ)

Transcription and Subtitles

1. (link unavailable)
2. GoTranscript
3. TranscribeMe
4. YouTube's auto-caption feature
5. Subtitle editor tools (VidIQ, TubeBuddy)

Community Engagement

1. YouTube Comments
2. Social media management tools (Hootsuite, Sprout Social)
3. Community building platforms (Discord, Patreon)
4. Email marketing tools (Mailchimp, ConvertKit)
5. Live streaming software (OBS Studio, XSplit)

Other Tools

1. YouTube Studio (beta)
2. Google Trends
3. Keyword research tools (Ahrefs, SEMrush)
4. Competitor analysis tools (TubeBuddy, VidIQ)
5. Browser extensions (Video Download Helper, YouTube Enhancer)

Pricing

1. Free tools (TubeBuddy, VidIQ)
2. Paid tools ($10-$50/month)
3. Enterprise tools ($50-$500/month)
4. Custom solutions (contact tool providers)

❏ YouTube marketing best practices

Channel Optimization

1. Clear and concise channel description
2. Relevant profile picture and banner
3. Consistent branding across platforms
4. Organized video categories and playlists

5. High-quality thumbnails

Video Creation

1. Define target audience and goals
2. Plan engaging content (script, storyboard)
3. High-quality video and audio production
4. Optimize video length (5-15 minutes)
5. Use captions, subtitles, and translations

SEO Optimization

1. Keyword research (Google Keyword Planner)
2. Optimize video titles, descriptions, and tags
3. Use relevant and descriptive metadata
4. Thumbnail optimization (text, images)
5. Regularly update content

Engagement and Community

1. Respond to comments and questions
2. Encourage engagement (ask questions, polls)
3. Collaborate with influencers and creators
4. Host live streams and Q&A sessions
5. Offer exclusive content or incentives

Analytics and Tracking

1. Monitor YouTube Analytics (views, engagement)
2. Track website traffic and conversions
3. Use Google Analytics (audience, behavior)
4. A/B testing and experimentation
5. Regularly review and adjust strategy

Advertising and Promotion

1. Define target audience and budget
2. Choose ad formats (video, display, sponsored)
3. Optimize ad targeting and bidding
4. Monitor ad performance and adjust
5. Utilize YouTube's advertising features

Content Strategy

1. Develop a content calendar
2. Create diverse content types (vlogs, tutorials)
3. Utilize user-generated content
4. Repurpose content for other platforms
5. Consistency and frequency

Influencer and Partnership

1. Identify relevant influencers and creators
2. Collaborate on content and promotions
3. Sponsor product placements and reviews
4. Partner with brands and organizations
5. Monitor and measure partnership ROI

Common Mistakes to Avoid

1. Poor video quality
2. Inconsistent branding
3. Lack of engagement
4. Insufficient SEO optimization
5. Not tracking analytics
6. Ignoring audience feedback
7. Not adapting to algorithm changes

YouTube Marketing Tools

1. TubeBuddy
2. VidIQ
3. Hootsuite
4. Sprout Social
5. Adobe Creative Cloud
6. Google Analytics
7. YouTube Analytics

Certifications and Courses

1. YouTube Marketing Certification
2. HubSpot Academy's YouTube Marketing Course
3. Coursera's Digital Marketing Specialization
4. Udemy's YouTube Marketing Course
5. Google Analytics Certification

YouTube marketing trends

YouTube marketing trends are constantly evolving, but here are some key strategies to help you stay ahead of the game.

Optimizing Your YouTube Channel

First and foremost, creating and branding your YouTube channel is crucial. This is where you'll publish videos, create playlists, respond to comments, view analytics, and more. Make sure to customize your profile picture, banner image, channel description, social links, and channel trailer to establish consistency and generate brand awareness [1].

Understanding Your Audience

Defining your target audience is vital. Research your audience's interests, age range, location, languages, and online video consumption habits. Use social media market research, analytics, and social listening to understand your audience's problems, questions, and behaviors.

Content Creation Strategies

- High-Quality Video Content: Consistently create high-quality videos that viewers love watching and engaging with. Research audience pain points, analyze trending keywords, and use brand storytelling techniques to connect with your audience [1].
- YouTube Shorts: Experiment with YouTube Shorts and other features like live streams, premieres, and 360 videos to deliver unique video experiences.
- SEO Optimization: Optimize your video titles, descriptions, tags, and thumbnails with primary and secondary keywords to maximize visibility.

Engagement and Community Building

- Respond to Comments: Interact with your audience by responding to comments and creating interactive video content.
- Collaborate with Influencers: Partner with YouTube influencers in your niche to promote products and services.
- Consistent Publishing Schedule: Stick to a consistent publishing schedule to build relationships with your subscribers and keep them engaged.

Advertising and Promotion

- YouTube Ads: Use YouTube ads to drive targeted traffic, promote products, and deliver personalized messaging.
- Influencer Marketing: Partner with influencers to reach your target audience and create sponsored content.

YouTube SEO certifications, YouTube marketing certifications and courses

Here are some popular YouTube SEO certifications, YouTube marketing certifications, and courses:

YouTube SEO Certifications:

1. Google's YouTube SEO Certification
2. HubSpot's YouTube SEO Certification
3. Moz's YouTube SEO Certification
4. Ahrefs' YouTube SEO Certification
5. SEMrush's YouTube SEO Certification

YouTube Marketing Certifications:

1. Google's YouTube Marketing Certification
2. HubSpot's YouTube Marketing Certification
3. Hootsuite's YouTube Marketing Certification
4. Sprout Social's YouTube Marketing Certification
5. YouTube's Official Creator Certification

YouTube Marketing Courses:

Beginner Courses:

1. YouTube's Official Creator Academy (Free)
2. HubSpot's YouTube Marketing Course (Free)
3. Udemy's YouTube Marketing Course ($10-$20)
4. Coursera's Digital Marketing Specialization ($30-$40)
5. Skillshare's YouTube Marketing Course ($10-$20)

Advanced Courses:

1. Ahrefs' YouTube SEO Course ($100-$200)
2. SEMrush's YouTube Marketing Course ($100-$200)
3. Moz's YouTube Marketing Course ($100-$200)
4. Hootsuite's Advanced YouTube Marketing Course ($200-$300)
5. Sprout Social's Advanced YouTube Marketing Course ($200-$300)

Specialized Courses:

1. Video Production and Editing (Udemy, Coursera)
2. YouTube Analytics and Tracking (Google Analytics Academy)
3. Influencer Marketing on YouTube (Influencer Marketing Hub)
4. YouTube Advertising and Sponsorships (Google Ads Academy)
5. YouTube Community Building and Engagement (Social Media Examiner)

Online Training Platforms:

1. Udemy
2. Coursera
3. Skillshare
4. LinkedIn Learning (formerly (link unavailable))
5. YouTube Creator Academy

Industry-Recognized Certifications:

1. Google Analytics Certification
2. HubSpot Inbound Marketing Certification
3. Hootsuite Social Media Marketing Certification
4. Sprout Social Social Media Marketing Certification
5. SEMrush SEO Certification

Course Pricing:

1. Free courses (YouTube Creator Academy, HubSpot)
2. $10-$50 (Udemy, Skillshare)
3. $50-$200 (Coursera, Ahrefs, SEMrush)

4. $200-$500 (Hootsuite, Sprout Social)

Course Duration:

1. Self-paced (Udemy, Skillshare)
2. 1-3 months (Coursera, Ahrefs, SEMrush)
3. 6-12 months (Hootsuite, Sprout Social)

☐ YouTube Analytics and tracking

YouTube Analytics Tools:

1. YouTube Studio (beta)
2. YouTube Analytics
3. Google Analytics
4. TubeBuddy
5. VidIQ
6. Social Blade
7. YouTube Tracker

4. YouTube's built-in tracking pixels
1. 5.Third-party tracking tools (e.g., PixelYourSite)

Common Tracking Mistakes:

1. Not setting up tracking codes
2. Incorrectly configuring tracking codes
3. Not using UTM parameters
4. Not tracking conversions
5. Ignoring audience engagement metrics
6. Not monitoring earnings and revenue
7. Not adjusting strategy based on data

Key Metrics to Track:

1. Views
2. Watch Time
3. Engagement (likes, comments, shares)
4. Subscribers
5. Conversion Rate (e.g., sales, sign-ups)
6. Click-Through Rate (CTR)
7. Average View Duration (AVD)
8. Drop-Off Points
9. Audience Retention
10. Earnings (for monetized channels)

Best Practices:

1. Set clear goals and objectives
2. Track key metrics and KPIs
3. Monitor audience engagement
4. Analyze earnings and revenue
5. Adjust strategy based on data
6. Use A/B testing and experimentation
7. Regularly review and update tracking setup

YouTube Analytics Reports:

1. Overview Report
2. Views Report
3. Engagement Report
4. Earnings Report
5. Audience Report
6. Traffic Sources Report
7. Device and Platform Report
8. Geo Report
9. Language Report
10. Content ID Report

Advanced YouTube Analytics Topics:

1. Cohort analysis
2. Funnel analysis
3. Retention analysis
4. A/B testing and experimentation
5. Machine learning and AI applications
6. Data visualization and storytelling
7. YouTube API integration

Tracking and Measurement Tools:

1. Google Tag Manager
2. Google Analytics tracking code
3. UTM parameters

Certifications and Courses:

1. YouTube Analytics Certification
2. Google Analytics Certification

3. HubSpot Academy's YouTube Marketing Course
4. Coursera's Digital Marketing Specialization
5. Udemy's YouTube Analytics Course

YouTube Analytics Tools Comparison:

1. TubeBuddy vs. VidIQ
2. YouTube Analytics vs. Google Analytics
3. Social Blade vs. YouTube Tracker
4. YouTube Studio (beta) vs. YouTube Analytics

☐ Collaborations sponsorships and partnerships

Collaborations, Sponsorships, and Partnerships:

Collaborations:

1. Influencer collaborations: Partner with influencers in your niche to reach new audiences.
2. Brand collaborations: Partner with complementary brands to create content, products, or services.
3. Creator collaborations: Collaborate with other creators on YouTube, podcasts, or blogs.
4. Community collaborations: Engage with your audience through live streams, Q&A sessions, or contests.

Sponsorships:

1. Product placements: Integrate sponsored products into your content.
2. Sponsored content: Create content specifically for a sponsor.
3. Event sponsorships: Sponsor events, conferences, or meetups.
4. Brand ambassadors: Partner with brands as a representative.

Partnerships:

1. Affiliate partnerships: Earn commissions promoting products or services.
2. Strategic partnerships: Partner with businesses to achieve mutual goals.
3. Content partnerships: Collaborate on content creation.
4. Distribution partnerships: Partner to distribute content.

Benefits:

1. Increased reach and audience
2. Credibility and authority
3. Revenue generation
4. Networking opportunities
5. Access to new markets
6. Enhanced content quality
7. Improved engagement

Types of Partnerships:

1. Exclusive partnerships
2. Non-exclusive partnerships
3. Revenue-sharing partnerships
4. Co-creation partnerships
5. Licensing partnerships

Finding Partners:

1. Industry events and conferences
2. Social media platforms
3. Networking groups
4. Online marketplaces (e.g., AspireIQ)
5. Personal connections

Negotiating Partnerships:

1. Define objectives and goals
2. Establish clear expectations
3. Discuss terms and conditions
4. Agree on compensation
5. Set performance metrics

Measuring Partnership Success:

1. Track engagement metrics
2. Monitor sales and revenue
3. Analyze audience growth
4. Evaluate content performance
5. Conduct regular check-ins

Common Mistakes:

1. Lack of clear objectives
2. Insufficient research
3. Poor communication
4. Unrealistic expectations
5. Inadequate measurement

Best Practices:

1. Align partnerships with your brand values
2. Choose partners with shared goals
3. Establish clear communication channels
4. Set realistic expectations
5. Monitor and adjust partnerships regularly

Tools and Resources:

1. AspireIQ
2. Upfluence
3. HYPR
4. InfluencerDB
5. Partnerize
6. Affiliatly

Certifications and Courses:

1. Influencer Marketing Certification
2. Partnership Marketing Certification
3. Collaborative Marketing Course
4. Sponsorship Marketing Course
5. Strategic Partnerships Course

◻ Live streaming on YouTube

Benefits:

1. Real-time engagement with audience
2. Increased audience retention
3. Improved visibility and discoverability
4. Enhanced community building
5. Monetization opportunities (Super Chat, Memberships)
6. Exclusive content for loyal viewers
7. Feedback and interaction through live comments

Equipment Requirements:

1. Camera (webcam, DSLR, or 4K-resolution camera)
2. Microphone (USB, wireless, or lavalier)
3. Lighting (natural or artificial)

4. Stable internet connection (minimum 5 Mbps upload speed)
5. Encoding software (e.g., OBS Studio, XSplit)
6. Capture card (for console or external device streaming)

Software and Tools:

1. YouTube Live (native streaming platform)
2. OBS Studio (free, open-source encoding software)
2. XSplit (popular encoding software)
3. Streamlabs (live streaming and chat management)
4. Restream (simultaneous streaming to multiple platforms)
5. Google Chrome extensions (e.g., YouTube Live Streaming)

Pre-Stream Preparation:

1. Choose a compelling title and description
2. Set thumbnail image
3. Schedule stream in advance
4. Promote stream on social media
5. Prepare engaging content and visuals
6. Test equipment and internet connection

During the Stream:

1. Interact with audience through live comments
2. Use polls, Q&A sessions, and giveaways
3. Monitor stream performance (viewers, engagement)
4. Adjust stream quality, audio, or visuals as needed
5. Encourage audience participation

Post-Stream:

1. Archive stream for future viewing
2. Analyze stream performance (views, engagement)
3. Engage with audience through comments and social media
4. Optimize and improve future streams
5. Consider repurposing stream content (e.g., blog posts, videos)

Monetization Options:

1. Super Chat (live streaming revenue)
2. Memberships (channel membership program)
3. Merchandise sales
4. Sponsorships and product placements
5. YouTube Premium revenue

Best Practices:

1. Consistency and scheduling
2. Engage with audience
3. High-quality equipment and internet
4. Promote stream in advance
5. Analyze and adjust stream performance
6. Offer exclusive content
7. Interact with other creators

Common Mistakes:

1. Poor equipment quality
2. Insufficient promotion
3. Inconsistent scheduling
4. Lack of engagement
5. Technical issues (e.g., audio, video delays)

YouTube Live Features:

1. Live Streaming
2. Super Chat
3. Memberships
4. Live Polls
5. Live Q&A
6. Live Chat
7. Stream Key

Certifications and Courses:

1. YouTube Live Certification
2. Live Streaming Course (Udemy)
3. YouTube Live Streaming Course (Skillshare)
4. Live Streaming and Video Production Course (Coursera)
5. YouTube Creator Academy (Live Streaming section)

☐ Live streaming equipment and software

Cameras:

1. Logitech C920 (webcam)
2. Canon EOS 80D (DSLR)
3. Sony A7S III (mirrorless)
4. Blackmagic Design URSA Mini Pro (professional camera)
5. GoPro Hero8 (action camera)

Microphones:

1. Blue Yeti (USB microphone)
2. Rode NT-USB (USB microphone)
3. Sennheiser MMD 935 (wireless microphone)
4. Shure SM7B (dynamic microphone)
5. HyperX QuadCast Gaming Microphone (USB microphone)

Lighting:

1. Softbox lights
2. LED panel lights
3. Ring lights
4. Backlights
5. Natural light

Capture Cards:

1. Elgato HD60 (HDMI capture card)
2. AVerMedia Game Capture HD (HDMI capture card)
3. Magewell USB Capture HDMI (USB capture card)
4. Blackmagic Design Intensity Shuttle (Thunderbolt capture card)
5. AJA Io 4K Plus (Thunderbolt capture card)

Encoding Software:

1. OBS Studio (free, open-source)
2. XSplit (popular, user-friendly)
3. Streamlabs OBS (customizable, integrated with Streamlabs)
4. Wirecast (professional, feature-rich)
5. vMix (professional, feature-rich)

Streaming Software:

1. YouTube Live (native streaming platform)
2. Twitch (live streaming platform)
3. Facebook Live (live streaming platform)
4. Periscope (live streaming app)
5. Streamlabs (live streaming and chat management)

Audio Mixers:

1. Behringer Xenyx Q1202USB (USB audio mixer)
2. Presonus AudioBox iTwo (USB audio mixer)
3. Yamaha MG10 (analog audio mixer)
4. Mackie ProFX10v3 (analog audio mixer)
5. Rode RODECASTER Pro (integrated audio mixer and interface)

Internet Connectivity:

1. Ethernet cable
2. Wi-Fi router
3. Cellular data (4G/5G)
4. Bonded internet connection (e.g., Streamlabs Bond)

Other Equipment:

1. Tripods
2. Gimbal stabilizers
3. External monitors
4. Headphones
5. Pop filters

Budget-Friendly Options:

1. Logitech C270 (webcam)
2. Blue Snowball (USB microphone)
3. Softbox lights
4. OBS Studio (free encoding software)
5. YouTube Live (free streaming platform)

Professional-Grade Options:

1. Blackmagic Design URSA Mini Pro (camera)
2. Sennheiser MMD 935 (wireless microphone)
3. AVerMedia Game Capture HD (capture card)
4. Wirecast (encoding software)
1. 5. AJA Io 4K Plus (capture card)

☐ Podcasting on YouTube

Podcasting on YouTube:

Benefits:

1. Increased visibility and reach
2. Diversified content strategy
3. Monetization opportunities (ads, sponsorships)
4. Engagement with audience through comments and live streaming
5. Repurposing content for multiple platforms

Equipment Requirements:

1. Microphone (USB, dynamic, or condenser)
2. Audio interface (e.g., USB, XLR)
3. Headphones
4. Pop filter
5. Boom arm or stand
6. Webcam (optional)

Software and Tools:

1. Recording software (Audacity, Adobe Audition)
2. Video editing software (Adobe Premiere, Final Cut Pro)
3. Audio editing software (Audacity, GarageBand)
4. YouTube video upload and management tools
5. Podcast hosting platforms (Anchor, Buzzsprout)

Podcasting Formats on YouTube:

1. Video podcasts (vlogs, interviews)
2. Audio-only podcasts (uploaded as video files)
3. Live podcasts (streamed on YouTube Live)
4. Animated podcasts (animated videos)
5. Interview-style podcasts

Optimizing Podcasts for YouTube:

1. Use relevant keywords and tags
2. Create engaging thumbnails
3. Write descriptive titles and descriptions
4. Use closed captions and subtitles
5. Promote podcasts on social media

Monetization Strategies:

1. AdSense (YouTube Partner Program)
2. Sponsorships and product placements
3. Affiliate marketing
4. Merchandise sales
5. Patreon or membership programs

Popular Podcasting Niches on YouTube:

1. True crime
2. Comedy
3. Self-improvement

4. Business and entrepreneurship
5. Gaming

Tips for Success:

1. Consistency and scheduling
2. Engage with audience
3. High-quality audio and video
4. Promote podcasts on multiple platforms
5. Analyze performance and adjust strategy

YouTube Podcasting Communities:

1. YouTube Podcasting Community
2. Podcasters on YouTube
3. YouTube Audio Podcasters
4. Podcasting on YouTube Facebook Group

Courses and Resources:

1. YouTube Podcasting Course (Udemy)
2. Podcasting on YouTube (Skillshare)
3. YouTube Creator Academy (Podcasting section)
4. Podcasting 101 (Coursera)
5. The Podcast Host (blog and resources)

▢ Engaging thumbnail design

Engaging Thumbnail Design:

Best Practices:

1. High-contrast colors
2. Clear, readable text
3. Relevant images or graphics
4. Emotive expressions or faces
5. Branded elements (logos, color schemes)
6. Simple, concise design
7. Text overlay (titles, tags, or descriptions)
8. Visual hierarchy (focus on main element)
9. Consistent design style
10. A/B testing and iteration

Design Elements:

1. Images: Photos, illustrations, or graphics
2. Text: Titles, tags, descriptions, or quotes
3. Shapes: Geometric or abstract shapes
4. Icons: Simple, recognizable icons
5. Gradients: Colorful, subtle gradients
6. Effects: Shadows, glows, or textures
1. 7.Branding: Logos, color schemes, or typography

Thumbnail Size and Format:

1. Minimum 640 x 360 pixels (16:9 aspect ratio)
2. Maximum 1280 x 720 pixels (16:9 aspect ratio)
3. JPEG, PNG, GIF, or BMP formats
4. File size: <2MB

Tools for Thumbnail Design:

1. Adobe Photoshop
2. Canva
3. Sketch
4. GIMP
5. PicMonkey
6. Thumbnail makers (TubeBuddy, VidIQ)

Tips for YouTube Thumbnails:

1. Use attention-grabbing images
2. Include text overlays
3. Highlight key information (title, tags)
4. Use consistent branding
5. Avoid clutter and complexity
6. Test and iterate designs
7. Ensure mobile-friendliness

Common Mistakes:

1. Low-quality images
2. Illegible text
3. Insufficient contrast
4. Overcrowding
5. Lack of relevance
6. Ignoring branding guidelines
7. Not testing designs

Thumbnail Psychology:

1. Emotional appeal
2. Curiosity-driven design
3. Color psychology
4. Visual hierarchy
5. Recognition and familiarity
6. Storytelling through images
7. Attention-grabbing techniques

Certifications and Courses:

1. Graphic Design Certification (Canva)
2. Thumbnail Design Course (Udemy)
3. Visual Design Course (Skillshare)
4. YouTube Thumbnail Design Course (TubeBuddy)
5. Digital Marketing Certification (HubSpot)

☐ Animated explainer videos

Animated Explainer Videos:

Benefits:

1. Simplify complex concepts
2. Engage audience and increase conversions
3. Enhance brand awareness and recognition
4. Improve website SEO
5. Reduce support queries
6. Increase social media shares
7. Cost-effective marketing solution

Types:

1. 2D animation
2. 3D animation
3. Stop-motion animation
4. Motion graphics
5. Whiteboard animation
6. Kinetic typography
7. Animated infographics

Style:

1. Cartoon-style
2. Corporate-style
3. Minimalist-style
4. Abstract-style
5. Storytelling-style
6. Humorous-style
7. Educational-style

Scripting:

1. Keep it concise (60-90 seconds)
2. Focus on key message
3. Use simple language
4. Include call-to-action (CTA)
5. Ensure brand consistency

Visual Elements:

1. Characters
2. Icons
3. Graphics
4. Animations
5. Transitions
6. Color scheme
7. Typography

Audio Elements:

1. Voiceover
2. Music

3. Sound effects
4. Narration

Tools:

1. Adobe After Effects
2. Blender
3. GoAnimate (now Vyond)
4. Powtoon
5. Animaker
6. Renderforest
7. OpenToonz

Best Practices:

1. Keep it simple and concise
2. Use high-quality visuals and audio
3. Ensure branding consistency
4. Optimize for mobile devices
5. Test and iterate
6. Use storytelling techniques
7. Measure performance (analytics)

Common Mistakes:

1. Overly complex animation
2. Poor audio quality
3. Lack of branding consistency
4. Insufficient testing
5. Not optimizing for mobile
6. Ignoring call-to-action (CTA)
7. Not measuring performance

Industry Uses:

1. Marketing and advertising
2. Education and training
3. Healthcare and medical
4. Technology and software
5. Finance and banking
6. E-commerce and retail
7. Non-profit and social impact

Cost:

1. DIY tools (free-$100)
2. Freelance animators ($500-$2,000)
3. Animation studios ($2,000-$10,000)
4. Custom animation ($10,000+)

Certifications and Courses:

1. Animation Certification (Adobe)
2. Explainer Video Course (Udemy)
3. Motion Graphics Course (Skillshare)
4. Animation and Visual Effects Course (Coursera)
5. Digital Marketing Certification (HubSpot)

☐ Content calendar planning

Benefits of Content Calendar Planning:

1. Organized content strategy
2. Consistent content publication
3. Reduced content creation stress
4. Improved team collaboration
5. Enhanced content quality
6. Increased audience engagement
7. Better tracking of content performance

Types of Content Calendars:

1. Editorial calendar (blog posts, articles)
2. Social media calendar (social media posts)
3. Video calendar (video content)
4. Podcast calendar (podcast episodes)
5. Email calendar (email newsletters)
6. Influencer calendar (influencer collaborations)

Steps to Create a Content Calendar:

1. Define content goals and objectives
2. Identify target audience and personas
3. Determine content types and formats
4. Plan content themes and topics
5. Assign content creation tasks and deadlines
6. Schedule content publication dates
7. Review and adjust calendar regularly

Content Calendar Templates:

1. Google Sheets
2. Microsoft Excel
3. Trello
4. Asana
5. CoSchedule
6. Hootsuite
7. Sprout Social

Content Calendar Tools:

1. CoSchedule
2. Hootsuite
3. Sprout Social
4. Buffer
5. Trello
6. Asana
7. Google Calendar

Best Practices:

1. Plan content in advance (3-6 months)
2. Consider holidays and events
3. Mix content types and formats
4. Include evergreen content
5. Leave space for spontaneity
6. Track content performance
7. Adjust calendar regularly

Common Mistakes:

1. Lack of planning
2. Inconsistent publication schedule
3. Insufficient content variety
4. Ignoring audience feedback
5. Not tracking content performance
6. Overlooking SEO optimization
7. Not adapting to changes

Content Calendar Examples:

1. Blog post calendar
2. Social media content calendar
3. Video content calendar
4. Podcast episode calendar
5. Email newsletter calendar

Industry-Specific Content Calendars:

1. Fashion and beauty
2. Food and beverage
3. Travel and tourism
4. Healthcare and wellness
5. Technology and software
6. Education and training
7. Finance and banking

- **Video editing software**

Video Editing Software:

Professional-Level:

1. Adobe Premiere Pro (Windows, macOS)
2. Final Cut Pro X (macOS)
3. Avid Media Composer (Windows, macOS)
4. Blackmagic Design DaVinci Resolve (Windows, macOS, Linux)
5. Autodesk Flame (Windows, macOS)

Mid-Range:

1. Adobe Premiere Elements (Windows, macOS)
2. CyberLink PowerDirector (Windows)

3. Magix Movie Edit Pro (Windows)
4. Vegas Pro (Windows)
5. Hitfilm Express (Windows, macOS)

Free and Open-Source:

1. Shotcut (Windows, macOS, Linux)
2. Lightworks (Windows)
3. VSDC Free Video Editor (Windows)
4. OpenShot (Windows, macOS, Linux)
5. Blender (Windows, macOS, Linux)

Online Video Editors:

1. WeVideo (cloud-based)
2. Clipchamp (cloud-based)
3. Kizoa (cloud-based)
4. Wibbitz (cloud-based)
5. InVideo (cloud-based)

Mobile Video Editors:

1. Adobe Premiere Rush (iOS, Android)
2. iMovie (iOS)
3. InShot (iOS, Android)
4. PowerDirector (iOS, Android)
5. Filmic Pro (iOS)

Key Features to Consider:

1. Video and audio editing
2. Color correction and grading
3. Visual effects and transitions
4. Audio mixing and editing
5. Multi-camera editing
6. 360-degree video editing
7. 4K and HDR support
8. Collaboration tools
9. Export options (format, resolution, frame rate)
10. User interface and ease of use

System Requirements:

1. Processor (CPU)
2. Memory (RAM)
3. Graphics Card (GPU)
4. Storage (HDD or SSD)
5. Operating System (Windows, macOS, Linux)

Tutorials and Resources:

1. YouTube tutorials
2. Udemy courses
3. Skillshare classes
4. Online forums and communities
5. Software documentation and manuals

Chapter 10: LinkedIn Marketing

☐ What is LinkedIn and how does it work for you?

LinkedIn is a social networking platform designed for professionals and businesses to connect, share information, and network. Here's an overview of LinkedIn and how it works:

What is LinkedIn?

LinkedIn is a platform where users can:

1. Create a professional profile showcasing their work experience, skills, and education.
2. Connect with colleagues, industry peers, and potential employers.
3. Share updates, articles, and content related to their industry or expertise.
4. Join groups and participate in discussions.
5. Search for job openings and apply directly.
6. Network with other professionals.

Key Features:

1. Profile: Showcase your professional experience, skills, and education.
2. Connections: Connect with others on LinkedIn.
3. Networking: Reach out to people in your industry or profession.
4. Groups: Participate in discussions and share content.
5. Jobs: Search and apply for job openings.
6. Content Sharing: Share articles, posts, and updates.
7. Recommendations: Request and provide recommendations.
8. Endorsements: Endorse skills and expertise.

How LinkedIn Works for You:
Personal Benefits:

1. Establish professional online presence.
2. Expand network and connections.
3. Stay updated on industry news and trends.
4. Enhance career opportunities.
5. Develop personal brand.

Business Benefits:

1. Establish company presence.
2. Promote products or services.
3. Attract top talent.
4. Build thought leadership.
5. Generate leads.

LinkedIn Algorithms:

1. Profile views: Priority to connections and relevance.
2. Post visibility: Engagement, relevance, and timing.
3. Job matching: Skills, experience, and location.

Optimizing LinkedIn:

1. Complete and update profile.
2. Engage with others' content.
3. Share relevant and valuable content.
4. Participate in groups.

5. Request recommendations.

LinkedIn Premium:

1. Enhanced search filters.
2. InMail messaging.
3. Profile views and analytics.
4. Job insights.
5. Career development resources.

LinkedIn Statistics:

1. 700+ million users.
2. 40% of users access daily.
3. 95% of recruiters use LinkedIn.
4. 45% of LinkedIn users are decision-makers.

Certifications and Courses:

1. LinkedIn Learning (formerly (link unavailable)).
2. LinkedIn Certified Professional.
3. LinkedIn Marketing Certification.
4. LinkedIn Sales Certification.

▢ Creating a professional LinkedIn profile

Creating a Professional LinkedIn Profile:
Step 1: Setup and Basics

1. Create a LinkedIn account ((link unavailable))
2. Choose a professional profile picture (400x400 pixels)
3. Write a clear, concise headline (max 220 characters)
4. Add your current and past work experience
5. Include education and relevant certifications

Step 2: Profile Optimization

1. Write a compelling summary (max 2,000 characters)
2. Use relevant keywords in your headline and summary
3. Add relevant skills (max 50)
4. Request endorsements from connections
5. Showcase achievements and accomplishments

Step 3: Work Experience

1. List current and past work experience
2. Include job title, company, and dates
3. Describe job responsibilities and achievements
4. Quantify accomplishments (e.g., "Increased sales by 25%")
5. Emphasize transferable skills

Step 4: Education and Certifications

1. List relevant education (degrees, institutions)
2. Include relevant certifications and licenses
3. Add relevant courses or training programs
4. Highlight academic achievements (e.g., GPA, awards)

Step 5: Additional Sections

1. **Projects:** Showcase relevant projects
2. **Volunteer Experience:** Highlight community involvement
3. **Languages:** List languages spoken
4. **Awards:** Showcase relevant awards or recognition
5. **Patents:** List relevant patents or inventions

Step 6: Profile Completion

1. Ensure profile is 100% complete
2. Review and edit profile for errors

Best Practices:

1. Use a professional profile picture
2. Keep profile up-to-date
3. Use relevant keywords
4. Showcase achievements
5. Engage with others on LinkedIn

Common Mistakes:

1. Incomplete profile
2. Lack of keywords
3. Poor profile picture
4. Insufficient work experience
5. Typos and grammatical errors

LinkedIn Profile Tips:

3. Use LinkedIn's profile strength meter
4. Request feedback from connections

1. Use action verbs (e.g., "Managed," "Created")
2. Quantify accomplishments
3. Emphasize transferable skills
4. Use relevant certifications
5. Showcase soft skills (e.g., communication, teamwork)

Certifications and Courses:

1. LinkedIn Learning (formerly (link unavailable))
2. LinkedIn Certified Professional
3. LinkedIn Marketing Certification
4. LinkedIn Sales Certification
5. LinkedIn Profile Optimization Course (Udemy)

☐ Participating in LinkedIn groups

Benefits:

1. Networking and connections
2. Industry insights and news
3. Thought leadership and expertise
4. Lead generation and business opportunities
5. Personal branding and visibility
6. Learning and professional development
7. Community engagement and support

Types of LinkedIn Groups:

1. Industry-specific groups
2. Professional association groups
3. Geographic-specific groups
4. Alumni groups
5. Special interest groups
6. Networking groups
7. Mastermind groups

Participation Strategies:

1. Join relevant groups (max 100)
2. Read and comment on discussions
3. Share relevant content and articles
4. Ask questions and seek advice
5. Provide valuable insights and expertise
6. Engage with others' content
7. Participate in group challenges and events

Best Practices:

1. Read group rules and guidelines
2. Be authentic and genuine
3. Add value to discussions
4. Avoid self-promotion
5. Use proper etiquette and language
6. Engage regularly
7. Monitor and adjust participation

Common Mistakes:

1. Spamming or self-promotion

2. Lack of engagement
3. Irrelevant content sharing
4. Not reading group rules
5. Being overly negative or critical
6. Not respecting others' opinions
7. Overparticipating

Group Management:

1. Create and manage your own group
2. Set clear group objectives and rules
3. Moderate discussions and content
4. Encourage engagement and participation
5. Invite relevant members
6. Use group analytics
7. Adjust group settings

LinkedIn Group Features:

1. Discussion boards
2. Newsletters
3. Events
4. Polls
5. File sharing
6. @mentions
7. Group messaging

Group Participation Metrics:

1. Engagement rate
2. Comments and likes
3. Post views
4. Group growth rate
5. Member demographics
6. Participation rate
7. Sentiment analysis

Certifications and Courses:

1. LinkedIn Group Management Certification
2. LinkedIn Marketing Certification
3. LinkedIn Sales Certification
4. LinkedIn Learning (formerly (link unavailable))
5. LinkedIn Group Participation Course (Udemy)

☐ **Building connections and networking**

Why Network on LinkedIn?

1. Expand professional network
2. Enhance career opportunities
3. Access industry insights and news
4. Establish thought leadership
5. Generate business leads
6. Improve personal branding
7. Stay connected with colleagues and peers

Building Connections:

1. Invite people you know (colleagues, friends, alumni)
2. Attend LinkedIn events and conferences
3. Join and participate in LinkedIn groups
4. Engage with others' content (like, comment, share)
5. Use LinkedIn's "People You May Know" feature
6. Import contacts from email or other networks
7. Reach out to industry leaders or influencers

Networking Strategies:

1. Personalize connection requests
2. Craft a compelling invitation message
3. Engage in meaningful conversations
4. Offer value and expertise
5. Ask for advice or feedback
6. Participate in LinkedIn challenges
7. Collaborate on content or projects

Best Practices:

1. Be genuine and authentic
2. Respect others' time and boundaries

3. Add value to conversations
4. Avoid spamming or self-promotion
5. Use proper etiquette and language
6. Follow up and follow through
7. Monitor and adjust approach

Common Mistakes:

1. Sending generic connection requests
2. Not engaging with others' content
3. Self-promotion or spamming
4. Ignoring messages or requests
5. Not personalizing invitations
6. Lack of follow-up or follow-through
7. Not respecting boundaries

LinkedIn Networking Features:

1. Connection requests
2. Messaging
3. InMail
4. Groups
5. Events
6. People You May Know
7. Who's Viewed Your Profile

Networking Metrics:

1. Connection growth rate
2. Engagement rate
3. Message response rate
4. InMail open rate
5. Group participation rate
6. Event attendance
7. Profile views

☐ Sharing content and engaging (Publishing articles and posts)

Benefits of Sharing Content:

1. Establish thought leadership
2. Increase visibility and reach
3. Drive engagement and conversations
4. Generate leads and business opportunities
5. Improve personal branding
6. Enhance career opportunities
7. Stay top of mind with connections

Types of Content to Share:

1. Articles
2. Blog posts
3. Videos
4. Infographics
5. Podcasts
6. News stories
7. Industry insights
8. Personal stories
9. How-to guides
10. Listicles

Best Practices for Sharing Content:

1. Post high-quality, relevant content
2. Use attention-grabbing headlines
3. Optimize for SEO (keywords, tags)
4. Include visuals (images, videos)
5. Keep content concise and scannable
6. Use calls-to-action (CTAs)
7. Engage with commenters and messagers
8. Share consistently
9. Monitor analytics
10. Adjust content strategy

Publishing Articles on LinkedIn:

1. LinkedIn Pulse (long-form content)
2. LinkedIn Articles (short-form content)
3. LinkedIn Newsletters (curated content)
4. LinkedIn Live (real-time video content)

Post Formats:

1. Text-only posts
2. Image posts
3. Video posts
4. Link posts
5. Document posts

6. Poll posts
7. Event posts

1. Engagement Strategies:

1. Ask questions
2. Request feedback
3. Host Q&A sessions
4. Create polls
5. Share user-generated content
6. Host LinkedIn Live sessions
7. Participate in comments

Analytics and Tracking:

1. Post views
2. Engagement rate
3. Comments
4. Likes
5. Shares
6. Click-through rate (CTR)
7. Conversion rate

Content Calendar Tools:

1. Hootsuite
2. Sprout Social
3. Buffer
4. CoSchedule
5. LinkedIn's built-in scheduling tool

◻ Job searching and recruitment

Job Searching:

1. Update LinkedIn profile (100% completeness)
2. Utilize job search filters (location, industry, etc.)
3. Browse LinkedIn Jobs (job postings)
4. Network with connections (referrals)
5. Join job-related groups
6. Follow companies (job postings)
7. Use LinkedIn's Job Search feature

Recruitment:

1. Post job openings on LinkedIn Jobs
2. Utilize LinkedIn Recruiter (recruitment tool)
3. Search for candidates (filters, keywords)
4. Reach out to potential candidates (InMail)
5. Manage applicant tracking (LinkedIn's ATS)
6. Utilize LinkedIn's Recruitment Ads
7. Measure recruitment metrics (applicant source, time-to-hire)

Best Practices:

1. Tailor resume and profile to job openings
2. Network and build relationships
3. Personalize applications (cover letters)
4. Follow up with recruiters/hiring managers
5. Prepare for interviews (research, practice)
6. Utilize LinkedIn's Job Search resources (resume builder, interview prep)
7. Continuously develop skills and knowledge

LinkedIn Job Search Features:

1. Job Alerts (customizable notifications)
2. Job Recommendations (algorithm-driven)
3. Salary Insights (average salary data)

4. Skills Assessments (verify skills)
5. LinkedIn Learning (skill development courses)
6. Resume Builder (template-based resume creation)
7. Interview Prep (practice interviews)

Recruitment Tools:

1. LinkedIn Recruiter
2. LinkedIn Jobs
3. LinkedIn Talent Finder
4. LinkedIn Recruitment Ads
5. Workday Recruitment
6. BambooHR
7. Greenhouse

- **LinkedIn advertising and marketing**

LinkedIn Advertising and Marketing:

Benefits:

1. Targeted advertising (professionals, industries)
2. Increased brand awareness
3. Lead generation and conversion
4. Thought leadership establishment
5. Talent acquisition and recruitment
6. Enhanced credibility and reputation
7. Measurable ROI

Ad Formats:

1. Sponsored Content (posts, articles)
2. Sponsored InMail (direct messaging)
3. Text Ads (banners, side rails)
4. Display Ads (banners, leaderboards)
5. Video Ads (in-stream, display)
6. Carousel Ads (multi-image)
7. Lead Gen Forms (pre-filled forms)

Targeting Options:

1. Job title and function
2. Industry and company size
3. Location and language
4. Skills and expertise
5. Education and experience
6. Interests and behaviors
7. Lookalike audiences

Budgeting and Pricing:

1. Cost-per-click (CPC)
2. Cost-per-thousand impressions (CPM)
3. Cost-per-send (CPS)
4. Daily and total budget
5. Bidding strategies (manual, automated)

Marketing Strategies:

1. Account-based marketing (ABM)
2. Lead nurturing and generation
3. Thought leadership and content marketing
4. Employee advocacy and engagement
5. Event marketing and webinars
6. Retargeting and remarketing
7. Social selling and sales enablement

LinkedIn Marketing Tools:

1. LinkedIn Ads Manager
2. LinkedIn Campaign Manager
3. LinkedIn Insights (analytics)
4. LinkedIn Lead Gen Forms
5. LinkedIn Messaging (chatbots)
6. LinkedIn Video (native video)
7. LinkedIn Analytics (website tracking)

Best Practices:

1. Define clear objectives and targeting
2. Create engaging and relevant content
3. Optimize ad creative and messaging
4. Monitor and adjust budget and bidding
5. Track and measure campaign performance

6. Utilize LinkedIn's marketing resources
7. Integrate with existing marketing strategies

☐ LinkedIn Marketing advertising cost in India and international

LinkedIn Advertising Costs in India:

1. Cost-per-click (CPC): ₹50-₹500 (average)
2. Cost-per-thousand impressions (CPM): ₹500-₹5,000 (average)
3. Sponsored Content: ₹1,500-₹15,000 per month (average)
4. Sponsored InMail: ₹500-₹5,000 per month (average)
5. Display Ads: ₹1,000-₹10,000 per month (average)

International LinkedIn Advertising Costs:

1. CPC (USA): $5-$50 (average)
2. CPM (USA): $50-$500 (average)
3. Sponsored Content (USA): $1,500-$15,000 per month (average)
4. Sponsored InMail (USA): $500-$5,000 per month (average)
5. Display Ads (USA): $1,000-$10,000 per month (average)

Factors Affecting LinkedIn Ad Costs:

1. Targeting options (location, industry, job title)
2. Ad format (sponsored content, display ads)
3. Budget and bidding strategy
4. Ad relevance and quality score
5. Competition and ad auctions
6. Time of day and day of week
7. Device and platform (desktop, mobile)

LinkedIn Advertising Pricing Models:

1. Cost-per-click (CPC)
2. Cost-per-thousand impressions (CPM)
3. Cost-per-send (CPS)
4. Cost-per-conversion (CPC)
5. Fixed budget (daily/total)

LinkedIn Ad Budget Allocation:

1. Small businesses: ₹5,000-₹50,000 per month
2. Medium businesses: ₹50,000-₹500,000 per month
3. Large businesses: ₹500,000-₹5,000,000 per month

☐ LinkedIn premium features

LinkedIn Premium Plans:

1. Career: $29.99/month (job search, resume builder)
2. Business: $59.99/month (sales, marketing, recruitment)
3. Sales Navigator: $64.99/month (sales, lead generation)

4. Recruiter: $119.99/month (recruitment, talent management)
5. Learning: $29.99/month (online courses, skill development)

Premium Features:

1. InMail (direct messaging)
2. Who's Viewed Your Profile
3. Premium Search Filters
4. Salary Insights
5. Skill Assessments
6. LinkedIn Learning (online courses)
7. Resume Builder
8. Career Coach
9. Job Search Analytics
10. Sales Navigator (lead generation)

Business Premium Features:

1. Business Insights (company data)
2. Lead Recommendations
3. Sales Opportunities
4. Account Targeting
5. Content Suggestions
6. Analytics (post performance)
7. Sponsored Content (advertising)
8. Display Ads (advertising)

Sales Navigator Premium Features:

1. Lead Generation
2. Account Targeting
3. Sales Insights
4. Opportunity Alerts

5. Relationship Building
6. Sales Analytics
7. Content Sharing
8. CRM Integration

Recruiter Premium Features:

1. Talent Pipeline
2. Candidate Management
3. Job Posting
4. Resume Search
5. Interview Management
6. Recruitment Analytics
7. Employer Branding
8. Talent Insights

Learning Premium Features:

1. Online Courses (4,000+)
2. Skill Development
3. Certification Programs
4. Personalized Learning
5. Course Recommendations
6. Progress Tracking
7. Badge Earned (skill verification)

Benefits of LinkedIn Premium:

1. Enhanced networking
2. Improved job search
3. Increased sales and lead generation
4. Better recruitment and talent management
5. Advanced learning and skill development
6. Enhanced business insights
7. Increased visibility and credibility

- **Optimizing LinkedIn profile**

Optimizing LinkedIn Profile:

Profile Completion

1. Professional profile picture
2. Clear and concise headline
3. Detailed and up-to-date work experience
4. Relevant skills and endorsements
5. Education and certifications

6. Personalized summary statement

Keyword Optimization

1. Use relevant industry keywords
2. Incorporate keywords in headline, summary, and work experience
3. Utilize LinkedIn's keyword suggestions

Visual Optimization

1. High-quality profile picture
2. Consistent branding (color scheme, fonts)
3. Relevant background image
4. Infographics and visual content

Content Optimization

1. Engaging and informative summary
2. Relevant and timely posts
3. Participate in LinkedIn groups
4. Publish articles and thought leadership pieces

Connection and Engagement

1. Connect with relevant professionals
2. Engage with others' content (likes, comments, shares)
3. Participate in LinkedIn groups
4. Collaborate with others on content

Profile SEO

1. Use relevant keywords in profile
2. Optimize profile for LinkedIn search
3. Utilize LinkedIn's search algorithm

Best Practices

1. Keep profile up-to-date
2. Use action verbs and numbers
3. Showcase achievements and results
4. Utilize LinkedIn's profile analytics
5. Monitor and adjust profile regularly

Tools and Resources

1. LinkedIn Profile Builder
2. LinkedIn Profile Optimization Tool
3. Canva (visual content creation)
4. Grammarly (writing and editing)
5. LinkedIn Learning (profile optimization courses)

- **LinkedIn algorithms**

Feed Algorithm:

1. Engagement-based ranking (likes, comments, shares)
2. Relevance-based ranking (keywords, hashtags)
3. Relationship-based ranking (connections, interactions)
4. Timing-based ranking (recency, frequency)
5. Content type-based ranking (articles, videos, posts)

Search Algorithm:

1. Keyword matching (exact, synonyms, related)
2. Profile completeness and accuracy
3. Connection strength and relevance
4. Engagement and activity level
5. Location and language

Post Ranking Factors:

1. Engagement (likes, comments, shares)
2. Relevance (keywords, hashtags)
3. Timeliness (recency, frequency)

4. Content quality (informative, entertaining)
5. User behavior (clicks, views)

Profile Ranking Factors:

1. Profile completeness and accuracy
2. Connection strength and relevance
3. Engagement and activity level
4. Keywords and hashtags
5. Recommendations and endorsements

Algorithm Updates:

1. 2020: "Related Content" update (contextualized search results)
2. 2019: "Feed Integrity" update (reduced spam and low-quality content)
3. 2018: "Video First" update (prioritized video content)
4. 2017: "Relevance" update (improved search results)

Optimizing for LinkedIn Algorithms:

1. Create high-quality, engaging content
2. Use relevant keywords and hashtags
3. Engage with others' content
4. Maintain a complete and accurate profile
5. Build strong connections and relationships
6. Post consistently and timely
7. Utilize LinkedIn's publishing features (articles, videos)

Tools and Resources:

1. LinkedIn Analytics (post and profile performance)
2. LinkedIn Insights (industry trends and data)
3. LinkedIn Learning (algorithm-focused courses)
4. Hootsuite (social media management)
5. Sprout Social (social media analytics)

☐ Advanced LinkedIn strategies

Content Strategy

1. Long-form content (articles, whitepapers)
2. Video content (native, YouTube)
3. Podcasting and audio content
4. Infographics and visual content
5. Repurposing and updating existing content

Influencer and Thought Leadership

1. Identify and collaborate with influencers
2. Develop thought leadership content
3. Participate in LinkedIn groups
4. Host LinkedIn Live sessions
5. Publish books and eBooks

Lead Generation and Sales

1. LinkedIn Lead Gen Forms
2. Sponsored content and ads
3. Email marketing integration
4. Sales Navigator and CRM integration
5. Account-based marketing (ABM)

Personal Branding

1. Develop a unique value proposition
2. Create a consistent visual brand
3. Engage in personal storytelling
4. Leverage employee advocacy

5. Monitor and manage online reputation

Employee Advocacy

1. Develop an employee advocacy program
2. Encourage employee sharing and engagement
3. Create employee-generated content
4. Recognize and reward employee advocates
5. Integrate with existing marketing efforts

Analytics and Measurement

1. LinkedIn Analytics (post, profile, audience)
2. Google Analytics integration
3. Track engagement and conversion metrics
4. Monitor ROI and campaign effectiveness
5. Adjust strategy based on data insights

Tools and Resources

1. LinkedIn Sales Navigator
2. LinkedIn Marketing Solutions
3. Hootsuite Insights
4. Sprout Social
5. LinkedIn Learning (advanced courses)

Certifications and Courses

1. LinkedIn Certified Marketing Professional
2. LinkedIn Certified Sales Professional
3. Digital Marketing Course (HubSpot)
4. Social Media Marketing Course (Udemy)
5. Advanced LinkedIn Strategy Course (Coursera)

Industry-Specific Strategies

1. Financial services: compliance-focused content
2. Healthcare: thought leadership and industry insights
3. Technology: product-focused content and demos
4. Non-profit: donor engagement and fundraising
5. Education: alumni engagement and recruitment

Best Practices

1. Align LinkedIn strategy with business goals
2. Create high-quality, engaging content
3. Engage with audience and build relationships
4. Monitor and adjust strategy regularly
5. Leverage LinkedIn's features and tools

☐ LinkedIn Networking and connections

LinkedIn Networking and Connections:

Benefits of LinkedIn Networking:

1. Expand professional network
2. Establish thought leadership
3. Generate business opportunities
4. Enhance career prospects
5. Stay updated on industry news
6. Access valuable resources and knowledge
7. Build relationships with influencers
8. Improve personal branding
9. Increase visibility and credibility
10. Access job opportunities

Types of LinkedIn Connections:

1. 1st-degree connections (direct contacts)
2. 2nd-degree connections (friends of friends)
3. 3rd-degree connections (friends of friends of friends)
4. LinkedIn groups
5. LinkedIn communities

LinkedIn Networking Strategies:

1. Optimize profile
2. Engage with others' content
3. Participate in LinkedIn groups
4. Publish valuable content
5. Use LinkedIn messaging
6. Attend LinkedIn events
7. Leverage LinkedIn's "Who's Viewed Your Profile" feature
8. Use LinkedIn's "People You May Know" feature
9. Connect with influencers
10. Monitor and adjust strategy

LinkedIn Connection Best Practices:

1. Personalize connection requests
2. Use relevant and clear messaging
3. Engage with others' content
4. Respond to messages promptly
5. Be authentic and genuine
6. Respect others' time and boundaries
7. Use LinkedIn's built-in messaging features
8. Keep connections organized
9. Regularly review and update connections
10. Follow LinkedIn's community guidelines

LinkedIn Group Best Practices:

1. Choose relevant groups
2. Participate actively
3. Provide valuable insights
4. Engage with others' content
5. Follow group rules
6. Use group messaging wisely
7. Share relevant content
8. Collaborate with group members
9. Monitor group activity
10. Report spam or inappropriate content

Common LinkedIn Networking Mistakes:

1. Sending spam messages
2. Not personalizing connection requests
3. Ignoring others' messages
4. Overposting or self-promoting
5. Not engaging with others' content
6. Using automated messaging tools
7. Not respecting others' boundaries
8. Lack of profile optimization
9. Not monitoring group activity
10. Not reporting spam or inappropriate content

LinkedIn Networking Tools:

1. LinkedIn Sales Navigator
2. LinkedIn Recruiter
3. LinkedIn Learning
4. LinkedIn Pulse
5. LinkedIn Groups
6. LinkedIn Messaging
7. LinkedIn Connect
8. LinkedIn Who's Viewed Your Profile
9. LinkedIn People You May Know
10. LinkedIn Analytics

- LinkedIn certifications and courses

LinkedIn offers various certifications and courses to enhance your skills and advance your career. Here are some of the free courses and certifications available:

1. **Free Certificate Learning Paths**
    - Career Essentials in Generative AI by Microsoft and LinkedIn
    - Build Your Generative AI Productivity Skills with Microsoft and LinkedIn
    - AI for Organizational Leaders by Microsoft and LinkedIn
    - Microsoft Copilot for Productivity by Microsoft and LinkedIn
    - Finding a Job during Challenging Economic Times
    - Professional Soft Skills Learning Pathway

2. **Free Certificate Courses**
    - Communication Foundations
    - Microsoft Foundational Career Certificate in Data Analytics
    - Project Management Foundations
    - What Is Business Analysis?
    - Developing Your Emotional Intelligence
    - Entrepreneurship Foundations
    - Administrative Professional Foundations

To access these free courses and certifications, sign up for LinkedIn Learning and ignore the payment details screen after signing up. Then, select the course link and start learning

Additionally, LinkedIn Learning offers over 12,000 courses and 600 learning paths, including free certificates of completion. Some popular courses include:

- Artificial Intelligence: 12,373 courses

- Marketing: 7,811 courses

- Cybersecurity: 16,090 courses

- AP Microeconomics from Massachusetts Institute of Technology

- Comprendere la filosofia from University of Naples Federico II

- Extreme Geological Events from Cardiff University

Part 3: Content Creation and Funnel Building

Chapter 11: Content Creation Strategy

▢ Blogging

Benefits of Blogging:

1. Establish thought leadership
2. Increase online visibility
3. Drive traffic and engagement
4. Generate leads and sales
5. Improve SEO and search rankings
6. Build brand awareness and credibility
7. Develop writing and communication skills

Types of Blogs:

1. Personal blogs
2. Business blogs
3. Niche blogs (industry-specific)
4. Affiliate blogs
5. Educational blogs
6. News blogs
7. Review blogs

Blogging Platforms:

1. WordPress
2. Blogger
3. Medium
4. LinkedIn Pulse
5. Ghost
6. Wix
7. Squarespace

Content Creation:

1. Define target audience and niche
2. Conduct keyword research
3. Plan and schedule content
4. Write engaging and informative posts
5. Optimize for SEO (meta tags, images)
6. Use visual content (images, videos)
7. Repurpose and update existing content

Promotion and Marketing:

1. Social media sharing
2. Email newsletters
3. Collaborate with influencers
4. Participate in blogging communities
5. Guest blogging
6. Content aggregators (Alltop, Blogarama)
7. Paid advertising (Google AdWords, Facebook Ads)

Monetization Strategies:

1. Advertising (display ads, sponsored content)
2. Affiliate marketing
3. Sponsored posts and product reviews
4. Selling digital products (eBooks, courses)
5. Membership and subscription-based models
6. Consulting and coaching services
7. Donations and crowdfunding

Analytics and Tracking:

1. Google Analytics
2. WordPress analytics plugins (Jetpack, MonsterInsights)
3. Social media analytics tools (Hootsuite, Sprout Social)

4. Email marketing analytics (Mailchimp, ConvertKit)
5. SEO tools (Ahrefs, SEMrush)

Certifications and Courses:

1. Blogging Certification (HubSpot)
2. Content Marketing Certification (American Marketing Association)
3. Digital Marketing Course (Udemy)
4. Blogging and Content Creation Course (Coursera)
5. WordPress Development Course ((link unavailable))

Best Practices:

1. Consistency and regular posting
2. High-quality and engaging content
3. SEO optimization
4. Social media integration
5. Engagement with readers and comments
6. Continuous learning and improvement
7. Authenticity and transparency

How to create a Blog
1. **Starting a Blog**

   1. To start a blog, follow these steps:

   1. Choose a niche (topic)
   2. Select a blogging platform (WordPress, Blogger)
   3. Register a domain name
   4. Set up hosting (Bluehost, SiteGround)
   5. Install a theme (template)
   6. Customize and design your blog
   7. Plan and create content

2. **Content Creation and Writing**

   3. For effective content creation:

   1. Define your target audience
   2. Conduct keyword research
   3. Plan and schedule content
   4. Write engaging and informative posts
   5. Optimize for SEO (meta tags, images)
   6. Use visual content (images, videos)
   7. Repurpose and update existing content

4. **Promotion and Marketing Strategies**

   5. Promote your blog with:

   1. Social media sharing
   2. Email newsletters
   3. Collaborate with influencers
   4. Participate in blogging communities
   5. Guest blogging
   6. Content aggregators (Alltop, Blogarama)
   7. Paid advertising (Google AdWords, Facebook Ads)

3. **Monetization and Revenue Streams**

   6. Monetize your blog with:

   1. Advertising (display ads, sponsored content)
   2. Affiliate marketing
   3. Sponsored posts and product reviews
   4. Selling digital products (eBooks, courses)
   5. Membership and subscription-based models
   6. Consulting and coaching services
   7. Donations and crowdfunding

4. **Analytics and Tracking Tools**

   7. Use analytics tools to track:

   1. Website traffic (Google Analytics)
   2. Social media engagement (Hootsuite, Sprout Social)

3. Email marketing metrics (Mailchimp, ConvertKit)
4. SEO performance (Ahrefs, SEMrush)
5. Content performance (WordPress analytics plugins)
6. Audience demographics and interests
7. Conversion rates and goal completion

- **Video creation**

Video Creation:

Types of Videos:

1. Explainer videos
2. Tutorial videos
3. Product demos
4. Testimonial videos
5. Brand stories
6. Event coverage
7. Vlogs (personal videos)
8. Animated videos
9. Live streaming
10. 360-degree videos

Video Creation Tools:

1. Adobe Premiere Pro
2. Final Cut Pro
3. DaVinci Resolve
4. iMovie
5. Camtasia
6. ScreenFlow
7. Loom
8. Vimeo
9. YouTube Video Editor
10. Mobile apps (InShot, PowerDirector)

Pre-Production:

1. Scriptwriting
2. Storyboarding
3. Location scouting
4. Talent casting
5. Scheduling
6. Budgeting
7. Equipment planning

Production:

1. Camera selection
2. Lighting setup
3. Sound recording
4. Filming
5. Direction
6. Capturing B-roll footage

Post-Production:

1. Editing
2. Visual effects
3. Color correction
4. Sound design
5. Music composition
6. Voiceover recording
7. Final cut

Video Marketing Strategies:

1. Social media distribution
2. YouTube optimization
3. Email marketing integration
4. Embedded videos on websites
5. Influencer partnerships
6. Paid advertising (YouTube, Facebook)
7. Video SEO

Video Analytics:

1. View count
2. Engagement metrics (likes, comments)
3. Watch time
4. Drop-off points
5. Conversion tracking
6. Click-through rates
7. Return on investment (ROI)

Certifications and Courses:

1. Video Production Certification (Adobe)
2. Video Marketing Certification (HubSpot)
3. Video Editing Course (Udemy)
4. Video Production Course (Coursera)
5. YouTube Creator Academy

Best Practices:

1. Keep videos concise
2. Use high-quality visuals and audio
3. Optimize for mobile devices
4. Use captions and subtitles
5. Consistency in branding
6. Engage with audience
7. Measure and analyze performance

Here's more information on the selected topics:

1. Video Scriptwriting

Video scriptwriting involves:

1. Defining the purpose and target audience
2. Developing a concept and storyline
3. Writing engaging dialogue and narration
4. Creating a storyboard and shot list
5. Revising and refining the script

Tips:

1. Keep it concise and focused
2. Use visual language
3. Show, don't tell
4. Use humor and emotion
5. Collaborate with others

2. Storyboarding

Storyboarding involves:

1. Visualizing the sequence of events
2. Sketching each scene and shot
3. Defining camera angles and movements
4. Planning transitions and pacing
5. Revising and refining the storyboard

Tools:

1. Paper and pencil
2. Digital drawing tools (Adobe Illustrator)
3. Storyboarding software (Storyboard Pro)
4. Online templates and resources

3. Video Marketing Strategies

Effective video marketing strategies:

1. Define target audience and goals
2. Create engaging and relevant content
3. Distribute on multiple platforms
4. Optimize for SEO and social media
5. Measure and analyze performance

Tactics:

1. Social media contests
2. Influencer partnerships
3. Email marketing integration
4. Paid advertising
5. User-generated content campaigns

4. YouTube Optimization

YouTube optimization techniques:

1. Keyword research and tagging
2. Eye-catching thumbnails
3. Engaging titles and descriptions
4. High-quality video content
5. Consistent uploading schedule

Analytics:

1. View count and engagement metrics
2. Watch time and drop-off points
3. Conversion tracking and ROI

5. Video Analytics Tools

Popular video analytics tools:

1. YouTube Analytics
2. Google Analytics
3. Vimeo Analytics
4. Wistia

5. Vidyard

Metrics:

1. View count and engagement
2. Watch time and drop-off points
3. Conversion tracking
4. Click-through rates
5. Return on investment (ROI)

Video Scriptwriting (Additional Information)

Additional scriptwriting tips:

1. Show, don't tell
2. Use visual language
3. Create compelling characters
4. Use conflict and resolution
5. Edit and revise extensively

Resources:

1. Scriptwriting books and courses
2. Online scriptwriting communities
3. Scriptwriting software and tools

▢ Infographics

Infographics:

Definition: Visual representations of information that combine images, charts, and text to communicate data, statistics, or knowledge.

Types:

1. Statistical infographics
2. Informational infographics
3. Process infographics
4. Comparative infographics
5. Interactive infographics
6. Animated infographics
7. Social media infographics

Benefits:

1. Visual communication
2. Increased engagement
3. Improved comprehension
4. Enhanced sharing
5. Brand awareness
6. SEO benefits
7. Storytelling

Design Tools:

1. Adobe Illustrator
2. Canva
3. Piktochart
4. (link unavailable)
5. Visme
6. Infogram
7. PowerPoint

Design Principles:

1. Keep it simple
2. Use colors effectively
3. Choose fonts wisely
4. Organize information
5. Use images and icons
6. Make it interactive
7. Optimize for mobile

Content Creation:

1. Research and gather data
2. Define the message
3. Sketch and wireframe
4. Design and visualize
5. Refine and edit
6. Publish and share

Distribution Channels:

1. Social media
2. Blogs and websites
3. Email newsletters
4. Presentations
5. Print materials
6. Embedded in articles
7. Shared on visual platforms (Pinterest, Instagram)

Metrics and Analysis:

1. Views and engagement
2. Shares and likes
3. Click-through rates
4. Time spent viewing
5. Conversion rates
6. ROI analysis
7. A/B testing

Certifications and Courses:

1. Infographic Design Certification (Canva)
2. Data Visualization Course (Coursera)
3. Visual Design Course (Udemy)
4. Infographic Marketing Course (HubSpot)
5. Graphic Design Certification (Adobe)

Best Practices:

1. Keep it concise
2. Use high-quality images
3. Make it interactive
4. Optimize for mobile
5. Use clear typography
6. Test and refine
7. Measure and analyze performance

Here's more information on the selected topics:

1. Infographic Design Principles

Infographic design principles:

1. Simplicity
2. Clarity
3. Visual hierarchy
4. Color harmony
5. Typography
6. Balance and alignment
7. Consistency

Best practices:

1. Use high-quality images
2. Limit text
3. Choose fonts wisely
4. Use icons and graphics
5. Ensure accessibility

2. Data Visualization Techniques

Data visualization techniques:

1. Bar charts
2. Pie charts
3. Line graphs
4. Scatter plots
5. Heat maps
6. Interactive visualizations
7. Storytelling with data

Tools:

1. Tableau
2. Power BI
3. D3.js
4. Matplotlib
5. Seaborn

3. Infographic Marketing Strategies

Infographic marketing strategies:

1. Social media sharing
2. Embedding on websites
3. Email marketing
4. Content marketing
5. SEO optimization
6. Influencer partnerships
7. Paid advertising

Benefits:

1. Increased engagement
2. Improved brand awareness
3. Lead generation
4. Website traffic
5. Social shares

4. Distribution Channels

Distribution channels:

1. Social media (Facebook, Twitter, LinkedIn)
2. Blogs and websites
3. Email newsletters
4. Presentations
5. Print materials
6. Embedded in articles
7. Visual platforms (Pinterest, Instagram)

Tips:

1. Optimize for mobile
2. Use eye-catching thumbnails
3. Share consistently
4. Engage with audience
5. Monitor analytics

5. Metrics and Analysis

Metrics and analysis:

1. Views and engagement
2. Shares and likes
3. Click-through rates
4. Time spent viewing
5. Conversion rates
6. ROI analysis
7. A/B testing

Tools:

1. Google Analytics
2. Social media insights
3. Email marketing analytics
4. Infographic tracking tools

6. Best Practices for Infographic Creation

Best practices:

1. Keep it concise
2. Use high-quality images
3. Make it interactive
4. Optimize for mobile
5. Use clear typography
6. Test and refine
7. Measure and analyze performance

7. Tools for Creating Interactive Infographics

Tools:

1. Adobe Illustrator
2. Canva
3. Piktochart
4. Visme
5. Infogram
6. Easelly
7. Coggle

8. Using Infographics in Presentations

Using infographics in presentations:

1. Visualize data
2. Illustrate concepts
3. Break up text
4. Add visual interest
5. Enhance storytelling
6. Support key messages
7. Encourage engagement

9. Measuring ROI on Infographic Campaigns

Measuring ROI:
1. Track website traffic
2. Monitor social shares
3. Measure engagement
4. Analyze conversion rates
5. Calculate ROI
6. Compare to benchmarks
7. Refine and adjust strategy

Podcasting

Podcasting:

Benefits

1. Increased brand awareness
2. Establish thought leadership
3. Build audience engagement
4. Generate leads and sales
5. Improve SEO
6. Diversify content offerings
7. Cost-effective marketing

Types of Podcasts

1. Interview-style
2. Solo shows
3. Panel discussions
4. Storytelling
5. Educational
6. Comedy
7. News and current events

Equipment and Software

1. Microphones (USB, dynamic)
2. Audio interfaces
3. Recording software (Audacity, Adobe Audition)
4. Editing software (GarageBand, Logic Pro)
5. Hosting platforms (Anchor, Buzzsprout)
6. Portable recorders
7. Pop filters and accessories

Production Process

1. Planning and research
2. Scriptwriting and outlining
3. Recording and editing
4. Mixing and mastering
5. Publishing and distribution
6. Promotion and marketing
7. Analytics and feedback

Distribution Channels

1. Apple Podcasts
2. Spotify
3. Google Podcasts
4. Stitcher
5. TuneIn
6. YouTube
7. Podcast directories (Overcast, Pocket Casts)

Monetization Strategies

1. Sponsorships and ads
2. Affiliate marketing
3. Selling products or services
4. Premium content or memberships
5. Crowdfunding
6. Donations
7. Dynamic ad insertion

Analytics and Tracking

1. Listenership metrics
2. Engagement metrics (comments, shares)
3. Download numbers
4. Ratings and reviews
5. Conversion tracking
6. ROI analysis
7. Audience demographics

Certifications and Courses

1. Podcasting Certification (Apple)
2. Podcast Production Course (Udemy)

3. Podcast Marketing Course (HubSpot)
4. Audio Production Course (Coursera)
5. Podcasting for Business Course (LinkedIn Learning)

Best Practices

1. Consistency and scheduling
2. High-quality audio and production
3. Engaging and informative content
4. Strong branding and identity
5. Active community building
6. Continuous improvement
7. Authenticity and transparency

Here's some more information:
1. Starting a Podcast

Steps to start a podcast:

1. Define your niche and target audience
2. Choose a format (interview-style, solo, panel)
3. Pick a name and tagline
4. Register a domain and hosting
5. Design artwork and branding
6. Plan content and scheduling
7. Invest in necessary equipment
8. Record and edit episodes
9. Publish and distribute
10. Promote and market
11. Podcast Equipment and Software

2. Essential equipment:

1. Microphone (USB, dynamic)
2. Audio interface
3. Headphones
4. Pop filter
5. Boom arm

Software:

1. Audacity (free)
2. Adobe Audition (paid)
3. GarageBand (for Mac)
4. Logic Pro (paid)
5. Anchor (free hosting)

3. Production and Editing Techniques

Recording techniques:

1. Scriptwriting and outlining
2. Setting recording levels
3. Using noise reduction tools
4. Editing and mixing
5. Mastering and finalizing

Editing software:

1. Audacity
2. Adobe Audition
3. GarageBand
4. Logic Pro

4. Distribution and Promotion Strategies

Distribution channels:

1. Apple Podcasts
2. Spotify
3. Google Podcasts
4. Stitcher
5. TuneIn

Promotion strategies:

1. Social media sharing
2. Email marketing
3. Collaborations and guest appearances
4. Paid advertising
5. SEO optimization

5. Monetization and Revenue Streams

Monetization strategies:

1. Sponsorships and ads
2. Affiliate marketing
3. Selling products or services
4. Premium content or memberships
5. Crowdfunding

Revenue streams:

1. Ad revenue
2. Sponsorships
3. Affiliate marketing

4. Product sales
5. Membership fees

6. Analytics and Tracking Tools

Analytics tools:

1. Apple Podcasts Analytics
2. Spotify Podcast Analytics
3. Google Podcasts Analytics
4. Anchor Analytics
5. Chartable

Tracking metrics:

1. Listenership
2. Engagement
3. Downloads
4. Ratings and reviews
5. Conversion tracking
6. Advanced Podcasting Strategies

7. Growth strategies:

1. Repurposing content
2. Creating video podcasts
3. Hosting live events
4. Building a community
5. Collaborating with influencers

Optimization techniques:

1. SEO optimization
2. Audio optimization
3. Editing for clarity
4. Using call-to-actions
5. Tracking and analyzing performance

8. Podcast SEO Optimization

SEO strategies:

1. Keyword research
2. Optimizing titles and descriptions
3. Using relevant tags
4. Creating transcripts
5. Internal linking

Tools:

1. Google Keyword Planner
2. Ahrefs
3. SEMrush
4. Moz
5. Yoast SEO

9. Measuring Podcast ROI

Measuring ROI:

1. Tracking listenership and engagement
2. Monitoring conversion rates
3. Analyzing revenue streams
4. Calculating ROI
5. Adjusting strategy

Tools:

1. Google Analytics
2. Apple Podcasts Analytics
3. Spotify Podcast Analytics
4. Chartable
5. Ad revenue tracking software

Chapter 12: Building Sales Funnels

☐ **What is funnel and how it is work for me in my business**

A funnel is a marketing and sales process that guides potential customers through a series of steps, converting them into paying customers.

How a Funnel Works:

1. Awareness: Potential customers become aware of your business.
2. Interest: They show interest in your product/service.
3. Desire: They develop a desire for your product/service.
4. Action: They take action and make a purchase.
5. Retention: They become repeat customers.
6. Advocacy: They become brand advocates.

Funnel Stages:

1. Lead Magnet (Awareness): Offer a free resource (eBook, webinar) to capture email addresses.
2. Tripwire Offer (Interest): Provide a low-cost, high-value offer (template, course).
3. Core Offer (Desire): Present your main product/service.
4. Upsell/Cross-sell (Action): Offer complementary products/services.
5. Follow-up (Retention): Nurture customers through email, surveys, and support.

Benefits of a Funnel:

1. Increased conversions
2. Improved customer experience
3. Enhanced customer retention
4. Increased revenue
5. Better marketing ROI

Types of Funnels:

1. Sales Funnel: Converts leads into customers.
2. Lead Generation Funnel: Captures email addresses.
3. Webinar Funnel: Promotes webinars.
4. Membership Funnel: Offers exclusive content.
5. E-commerce Funnel: Sells physical products.

Creating a Funnel for Your Business:

1. Identify your target audience.
2. Develop a lead magnet.
3. Create a tripwire offer.
4. Design a core offer.
5. Set up email marketing automation.
6. Track and optimize funnel performance.

Tools for Building a Funnel:

1. Website builders (WordPress, Wix).
2. Email marketing software (Mailchimp, ConvertKit).
3. Marketing automation tools (HubSpot, Infusionsoft).
4. CRM systems (Salesforce, Zoho).
5. Funnel builders (ClickFunnels, Unbounce).

Example Funnel:

1. Lead Magnet: Free eBook on "10 Tips for Starting a Business".
2. Tripwire Offer: $29 Business Plan Template.
3. Core Offer: Business Coaching Services ($500/month).
4. Upsell/Cross-sell: Additional coaching sessions or business software.
5. Follow-up: Monthly email newsletters and support.

By understanding and implementing a funnel, you can:

1. Increase conversions
2. Enhance customer experience
3. Drive revenue growth
4. Improve marketing efficiency
5. Scale your business

☐ Understanding sales funnel stages (awareness, interest, desire, and action)

The sales funnel, also known as the AIDA model, is a framework used to understand the customer's journey from initial awareness to final purchase. Here's a breakdown of each stage:

A - Awareness

1. **Definition:**
   Prospective customers become aware of your product or service.

2. **Goals:**
   - Create awareness and visibility.
   - Generate interest.
   - Drive traffic.

3. **Strategies:**
   - Advertising (social media, Google Ads).
   - Content marketing (blog posts, videos).
   - Social media presence.
   - Email marketing.
   - Referrals.

I - Interest

1. **Definition:**
   Prospects show interest in your product or service.

2. **Goals:**
   - Educate and inform.
   - Build credibility.
   - Generate leads.

3. **Strategies:**

- Content marketing (eBooks, whitepapers).
- Webinars.
- Free trials or demos.
- Email nurturing.
- Lead magnets.

D - Desire

1. **Definition:**
   Prospects develop a desire for your product or service.

2. **Goals:**
   - Build trust.
   - Showcase benefits.
   - Create urgency.

3. **Strategies:**
   - Testimonials and case studies.
   - Product comparisons.
   - Special offers and discounts.
   - Scarcity tactics.
   - Social proof.

A - Action

1. **Definition:**
   Prospects take action and make a purchase.

2. **Goals:**
   - Convert leads into customers.
   - Close sales.
   - Ensure customer satisfaction.

3. **Strategies:**
   - Sales calls and demos.
   - Free trials or pilots.
   - Limited-time offers.
   - Upselling and cross-selling.
   - Customer support.

Additional stages:

Retention

1. **Definition:**
   Customers become repeat customers.

2. **Goals:**
   - Build loyalty.
   - Encourage retention.

- Increase customer lifetime value.

3. Strategies:
- Customer support.
- Loyalty programs.
- Exclusive offers.
- Feedback and surveys.

Advocacy

1. Definition:
   Customers become brand advocates.

2. Goals:
- Encourage word-of-mouth.
- Build brand awareness.
- Drive referrals.

3. Strategies:
- Referral programs.
- User-generated content.
- Social media engagement.
- Brand ambassadors.

Understanding these stages helps businesses:

1. Identify bottlenecks in the sales process.
2. Develop targeted marketing strategies.
3. Improve customer experience.
4. Increase conversion rates.
5. Enhance customer retention and advocacy.

▢ Creating landing pages

Creating Landing Pages:

Definition: A landing page is a dedicated webpage designed to convert visitors into customers, subscribers, or leads.

Purpose:

1. Capture email addresses
2. Generate leads
3. Drive sales
4. Promote products/services
5. Increase conversions

Key Elements:

1. Headline: Clear, concise, and attention-grabbing
2. Subheadline: Supports the headline and provides context
3. Image/Video: Visuals that enhance the message

4. Benefits-oriented copy: Focus on customer benefits
5. Call-to-Action (CTA): Clear and prominent
6. Form/Signup: Simple and minimal fields
7. Trust indicators: Testimonials, security badges, etc.
8. Mobile-friendliness: Ensure responsive design

Types of Landing Pages:

1. **Sales page**: Promotes a product/service
2. **Squeeze page:** Captures email addresses
3. Thank-you page: Post-conversion page
4. **Webinar page:** Promotes webinars
5. Lead generation page: Captures lead information
6. **Micro-sites**: Multi-page landing experiences

Best Practices:

1. Focus on one goal
2. Keep it simple and concise
3. Use social proof
4. Optimize for mobile
5. Test and iterate
6. Use clear and compelling CTAs
7. Use relevant images
8. Ensure fast loading speed

Tools for Creating Landing Pages:

1. Website builders (WordPress, Wix)
2. Landing page builders (Unbounce, Instapage)
3. Marketing automation tools (HubSpot, Marketo)
4. Conversion optimization tools (Optimizely, VWO)
5. Design tools (Adobe XD, Sketch)

Landing Page Optimization:

1. A/B testing
2. Multivariate testing
3. Heatmap analysis
4. User feedback
5. Analytics tracking
6. Continuous iteration

Common Mistakes:

1. Distractions (nav menus, footers)
2. Poor mobile experience
3. Unclear CTAs
4. Too much content
5. Lack of social proof
6. Slow loading speed
7. Insufficient testing

Example Landing Page:

2. Headline: Get Started with Our Free Trial
3. Subheadline: Experience the power of our marketing automation tool
4. Image: Screenshot of the tool
5. CTA: Sign up for Free Trial
6. Form: Simple email and password fields
7. Trust indicators: Security badge, customer testimonials

Here's more information on topics:

1. Creating Effective Headlines:

Key characteristics:

- Clear
- Concise
- Attention-grabbing
- Relevant

- Unique

Techniques:

- Use action verbs
- Ask questions
- Make promises
- Use numbers
- Create curiosity

2. **Writing Compelling Copy:**

Principles:

- Know your audience
- Focus on benefits
- Use storytelling
- Be concise
- Use social proof

Techniques:

- Use persuasive language
- Emphasize key points
- Use rhetorical devices
- Create urgency
- Use humor

3. **Designing Landing Pages:**

Best practices:

- Keep it simple
- Use contrasting colors
- Use whitespace effectively
- Make CTAs prominent
- Optimize for mobile

Design elements:

- Images
- Videos
- Icons
- Typography
- Layout

4. **Optimizing Landing Page Performance:**

Metrics:

- Conversion rate
- Click-through rate
- Bounce rate
- Time on page
- Exit rate

Techniques:

- A/B testing
- Multivariate testing
- Heatmap analysis
- User feedback
- Analytics tracking

1. **A/B Testing Landing Pages:**

Benefits:

- Improved conversions
- Increased revenue
- Enhanced user experience
- Data-driven decisions
- Reduced bounce rates

Tools:

- Optimizely
- VWO
- Unbounce
- Instapage
- Google Optimize

5. **Landing Page Analytics:**

Metrics:

- Page views
- Unique visitors
- Conversion rate
- Bounce rate
- Exit rate

Tools:

- Google Analytics
- Mixpanel
- Kissmetrics
- Chartbeat
- Crazy Egg

6. Mobile-Friendly Landing Pages:

Benefits:

- Improved user experience
- Increased conversions
- Enhanced accessibility
- Better search engine rankings
- Competitive advantage

Design considerations:

- Responsive design
- Clear CTAs
- Simple navigation
- Fast loading speed
- Large tap targets

7. Landing Page Best Practices:

Guidelines:

- Focus on one goal
- Keep it simple
- Use social proof
- Optimize for mobile
- Test and iterate

Checklist:

- Clear headline
- Prominent CTA
- Simple form
- Relevant image
- Fast loading speed

8. Common Landing Page Mistakes:

Mistakes:

- Distractions (nav menus, footers)
- Poor mobile experience
- Unclear CTAs
- Too much content
- Lack of social proof

Consequences:

- Reduced conversions
- Increased bounce rates
- Decreased user engagement
- Negative impact on brand reputation
- Wasted resources

8. Landing Page Tools and Software:

Categories:

- Website builders
- Landing page builders
- Marketing automation tools
- Conversion optimization tools
- Design tools

Examples:

- WordPress
- Unbounce
- HubSpot
- Optimizely
- Adobe XD

☐ Lead magnets and opt-in forms

Lead Magnets and Opt-in Forms:

Lead Magnets:

A lead magnet is a valuable resource offered in exchange for contact information.

Types of Lead Magnets:

1. eBooks
2. Webinars
3. Templates
4. Checklists
5. Free trials
6. Consultations
7. Quizzes
8. Video series
9. Podcasts
10. Whitepapers

Characteristics of Effective Lead Magnets:

1. Relevant to target audience
2. Valuable and informative
3. Easy to consume
4. Unique and exclusive
5. Aligns with business goals

Opt-in Forms:

An opt-in form is a web form that captures contact information.

Best Practices for Opt-in Forms:

1. Clear and concise language
2. Minimal fields (name, email)
3. Prominent call-to-action (CTA)
4. Visible and accessible
5. Mobile-friendly
6. Secure (HTTPS, GDPR compliant)
7. Integrated with email marketing software

Types of Opt-in Forms:

1. Embedded forms
2. Pop-up forms
3. Slide-in forms
4. Hover forms
5. Squeeze pages
6. Overlay forms
7. Welcome gates

Opt-in Form Optimization:

1. A/B testing
2. Color and design experimentation
3. Field reduction
4. CTA optimization
5. Form placement testing
6. Mobile-specific optimization
7. Analytics tracking

Lead Magnet Delivery:

1. Instant download
2. Email delivery
3. Membership site access
4. Webinar registration
5. Consultation scheduling

Tools for Creating Lead Magnets and Opt-in Forms:

1. Email marketing software (Mailchimp, ConvertKit)
2. Landing page builders (Unbounce, Instapage)
3. Website builders (WordPress, Wix)
4. Form builders (Gravity Forms, Formstack)
5. Design tools (Adobe Creative Cloud, Canva)

Benefits of Lead Magnets and Opt-in Forms:

1. Increased email list growth
2. Improved lead quality
3. Enhanced customer engagement
4. Better segmentation and targeting
5. Increased conversions and sales

Common Mistakes:

1. Unclear or misleading language
2. Too many form fields
3. Poor form placement
4. Lack of mobile optimization
5. Ineffective lead magnet

Example Lead Magnet and Opt-in Form:

Lead Magnet: "10 Tips to Improve Your Marketing Strategy" eBook

Opt-in Form:

Headline: Get Your Free eBook!
Fields: Name, Email
CTA: Download Now
Design: Simple, contrasting colors

☐ Integrating Lead Magnets with Email Marketing

Benefits:

1. Increased email list growth
2. Improved lead quality
3. Enhanced customer engagement
4. Better segmentation and targeting
5. Increased conversions and sales

Email Marketing Platforms:

1. Mailchimp
2. ConvertKit
3. HubSpot
4. MailerLite
5. ActiveCampaign

Integration Steps:

1. Create a lead magnet
2. Set up an opt-in form
3. Connect form to email marketing platform
4. Configure automated email sequence
5. Segment and personalize emails

Automated Email Sequence:

1. Welcome email with lead magnet delivery
2. Follow-up email with additional resources
3. Nurture email with educational content
4. Promotional email with targeted offer
5. Abandoned lead email with re-engagement strategy

Segmentation and Personalization:

1. Segment based on lead magnet download
2. Personalize emails with name and interests
3. Use behavior-based triggers (e.g., email opens)
4. Create custom fields for targeted content
5. Use A/B testing for subject lines and CTAs

Best Practices:

1. Clear and concise email copy
2. Relevant and valuable content
3. Consistent branding and design
4. Mobile-friendly emails
5. Regular list cleaning and maintenance

Common Mistakes:

1. Not delivering lead magnet instantly
2. Not segmenting email list
3. Sending too many promotional emails
4. Not personalizing emails
5. Not tracking email metrics

Tools and Resources:

1. Email marketing platforms (listed above)
2. Lead magnet creation tools (e.g., Canva, Adobe)
3. Form builders (e.g., Gravity Forms, Formstack)
4. Automation tools (e.g., Zapier, IFTTT)
5. Analytics tools (e.g., Google Analytics, Email Metrics)

☐ Email nurturing sequences

Definition: A series of automated emails sent to subscribers to build relationships, educate, and nurture them through the sales funnel.

Benefits:

1. Increased conversions
2. Improved customer engagement
3. Enhanced brand awareness
4. Better lead qualification
5. Reduced sales cycle time

Types of Email Nurturing Sequences:

1. Welcome sequence
2. Educational sequence
3. Promotional sequence
4. Abandoned lead sequence
5. Re-engagement sequence
6. Onboarding sequence
7. Upsell/Cross-sell sequence

Email Nurturing Sequence Structure:

1. Introduction/Welcome email
2. Value-added content emails (3-5)
3. Soft promotion/offer email
4. Hard promotion/offer email
5. Follow-up/reminder email
6. Final follow-up/feedback email

Best Practices:

1. Personalize emails
2. Segment email list
3. Use relevant and valuable content
4. Optimize subject lines and CTAs
5. Use social proof and testimonials
6. Mobile-friendly emails
7. Track and analyze metrics

Email Nurturing Sequence Examples:

1. Welcome sequence:
   - Email 1: Introduction and thank-you
   - Email 2: Free resource/download
   - Email 3: Product/service overview

2. Educational sequence:
   - Email 1: Industry insights
   - Email 2: Tips and best practices
   - Email 3: Case study/webinar invite

3. Promotional sequence:
   - Email 1: Exclusive offer
   - Email 2: Limited-time discount
   - Email 3: Final reminder

Tools for Creating Email Nurturing Sequences:

1. Email marketing platforms (Mailchimp, HubSpot)
2. Marketing automation tools (Marketo, Pardot)
3. CRM systems (Salesforce, Zoho)
4. Email builders (Mailjet, Sendinblue)
5. Analytics tools (Google Analytics, Email Metrics)

Metrics to Track:

1. Open rates
2. Click-through rates
3. Conversion rates
4. Unsubscribe rates
5. Email ROI

Common Mistakes:

1. Not segmenting email list
2. Sending too many emails
3. Not personalizing emails
4. Lack of relevant content
5. Not tracking metrics

☐ Conversion rate optimization

Conversion Rate Optimization (CRO):

Definition: The process of increasing the percentage of website visitors who complete a desired action (conversion).

Benefits:

1. Increased revenue
2. Improved user experience
3. Enhanced brand credibility
4. Better ROI on marketing spend
5. Data-driven decision making

CRO Process:

1. Research and analysis
2. Hypothesis formation
3. Testing and experimentation
4. Data analysis and interpretation
5. Implementation and iteration

CRO Techniques:

1. A/B testing (split testing)
2. Multivariate testing (MVT)
3. Heatmap analysis
4. User feedback and surveys
5. Usability testing
6. Analytics and tracking
7. Landing page optimization
8. Email optimization
9. Mobile optimization
10. Social proof and trust indicators

Tools for CRO:

1. Google Optimize
2. Optimizely
3. VWO (Visual Website Optimizer)
4. Unbounce
5. Crazy Egg
6. Hotjar
7. Adobe Target
8. Sentient Ascend
9. Convert
10. AB Tasty

CRO Metrics:

1. Conversion rate
2. Click-through rate (CTR)
3. Bounce rate
4. Time on page
5. Exit rate
6. Average order value (AOV)
7. Return on investment (ROI)
8. Customer lifetime value (CLV)

Common CRO Mistakes:

1. Lack of clear goals
2. Insufficient data
3. Poor testing methodology
4. Inadequate segmentation
5. Ignoring user feedback
6. Not iterating and refining
7. Overemphasis on minor changes
8. Underestimating technical constraints

Best Practices:

1. Start with low-hanging fruit
2. Test iteratively and incrementally
3. Use data to inform decisions
4. Prioritize user experience
5. Segment and target specific audiences
6. Continuously monitor and analyze
7. Collaborate with stakeholders
8. Stay up-to-date with industry trends

CRO Strategy:

1. Identify conversion goals
2. Analyze user behavior
3. Develop testing hypotheses
4. Design and execute tests
5. Analyze and interpret results
6. Implement winning variations
7. Refine and iterate

Industry Benchmarks:

1. Average conversion rate: 2-5%
2. Average CTR: 1-3%
3. Average bounce rate: 40-60%

Free and paid tools for creating funnels with Email nurturing sequences and WhatsApp auto-messages

Free Tools:

1. HubSpot (Free Plan) - Includes funnel builder, email marketing, and WhatsApp integration.
2. Mailchimp (Free Plan) - Offers email marketing automation and WhatsApp integration through Zapier.
3. Tars (Free Plan) - Provides conversational funnel builder with WhatsApp integration.
4. Sendinblue (Free Plan) - Includes email marketing automation and WhatsApp integration.
5. Google Forms + Zapier (Free) - Create simple funnels with email and WhatsApp automation.

Paid Tools:

Indian Pricing (INR)

1. HubSpot (Starter) - ₹2,300/month (billed annually)
2. Mailchimp (Essentials) - ₹1,300/month (billed annually)
3. Tars (Pro) - ₹4,500/month (billed annually)
4. Sendinblue (Lite) - ₹1,500/month (billed annually)
5. ClickFunnels (Basic) - ₹5,500/month (billed annually)
6. Unbounce (Essential) - ₹4,200/month (billed annually)
7. GetResponse (Basic) - ₹1,800/month (billed annually)
8. ConvertKit (Basic) - ₹2,500/month (billed annually)
9. ActiveCampaign (Lite) - ₹3,500/month (billed annually)
10. Pabbly (Pro) - ₹2,000/month (billed annually)

International Pricing (USD)

1. HubSpot (Starter) - $40/month (billed annually)
2. Mailchimp (Essentials) - $9.99/month (billed annually)
3. Tars (Pro) - $99/month (billed annually)
4. Sendinblue (Lite) - $25/month (billed annually)
5. ClickFunnels (Basic) - $97/month (billed annually)
6. Unbounce (Essential) - $79/month (billed annually)
7. GetResponse (Basic) - $15/month (billed annually)
8. ConvertKit (Basic) - $29/month (billed annually)
9. ActiveCampaign (Lite) - $9/month (billed annually)
10. Pabbly (Pro) - $29/month (billed annually)

WhatsApp Auto-Message Tools:

1. Twilio (WhatsApp Business API) - Pricing varies based on usage
2. Nexmo (WhatsApp Business API) - Pricing varies based on usage
3. MessageBird (WhatsApp Business API) - Pricing varies based on usage
4. Wati (WhatsApp Automation) - ₹1,500/month (billed annually)

5. WhatsApp Business API (Direct) - Pricing varies based on usage

Comprehensive guide to creating funnels with mail sequences and WhatsApp auto-messages:

Funnel Creation Tools

1. HubSpot
2. Mailchimp
3. Tars
4. Sendinblue
5. ClickFunnels
6. Unbounce
7. GetResponse
8. ConvertKit
9. ActiveCampaign
10. Pabbly

WhatsApp Auto-Message Tools

1. Twilio (WhatsApp Business API)
2. Nexmo (WhatsApp Business API)
3. MessageBird (WhatsApp Business API)
4. Wati (WhatsApp Automation)
5. WhatsApp Business API (Direct)

Email Marketing Automation Tools

1. Mailchimp
2. HubSpot
3. Sendinblue
4. GetResponse
5. ConvertKit
6. ActiveCampaign
7. Pabbly

Funnel Analytics and Tracking Tools

1. Google Analytics
2. HubSpot Analytics
3. Mixpanel
4. Kissmetrics
5. Chartbeat

Funnel Optimization Strategies

1. A/B testing
2. Multivariate testing
3. Heatmap analysis
4. User feedback and surveys
5. Usability testing

WhatsApp Automation Strategies

1. Welcome messages
2. Abandoned cart reminders
3. Order confirmations
4. Product recommendations
5. Customer support

Funnel Creation Best Practices

1. Define clear goals
2. Identify target audience
3. Create relevant content
4. Optimize landing pages
5. Test and iterate

Email Marketing Best Practices

1. Personalize emails
2. Segment email list
3. Use relevant subject lines
4. Optimize email design
5. Track email metrics

WhatsApp Marketing Best Practices

1. Use clear and concise messages
2. Use relevant and personalized content
3. Avoid spamming
4. Use WhatsApp Business API
5. Track WhatsApp metrics

Pricing (INR)

1. HubSpot - ₹2,300/month
2. Mailchimp - ₹1,300/month
3. Tars - ₹4,500/month
4. Sendinblue - ₹1,500/month
5. ClickFunnels - ₹5,500/month
6. Unbounce - ₹4,200/month
7. GetResponse - ₹1,800/month

8. ConvertKit - ₹2,500/month
9. ActiveCampaign - ₹3,500/month
10. Pabbly - ₹2,000/month

Pricing (USD)

1. HubSpot - $40/month
2. Mailchimp - $9.99/month
3. Tars - $99/month
4. Sendinblue - $25/month
5. ClickFunnels - $97/month
6. Unbounce - $79/month
7. GetResponse - $15/month
8. ConvertKit - $29/month
9. ActiveCampaign - $9/month
10. Pabbly - $29/month

Note: Prices may vary based on usage, features, and plans. It's essential to review each tool's pricing page for the most up-to-date information.

Here's a comprehensive guide on some important topics (based on situation Information may be repeated more time :

1. Creating a Funnel Strategy

- Define business goals and objectives
- Identify target audience and customer segments
- Determine funnel stages (awareness, interest, desire, action)
- Develop a unique value proposition (UVP)
- Establish key performance indicators (KPIs)

2. Building a Sales Funnel

- Choose a funnel builder (e.g., ClickFunnels, Unbounce)
- Design and create landing pages
- Set up email marketing automation
- Integrate payment gateways
- Configure analytics and tracking

3. Optimizing Funnel Performance

- Conduct A/B testing and experimentation
- Analyze funnel metrics (conversion rates, drop-off points)
- Refine and iterate funnel design and copy
- Improve email open and click-through rates
- Enhance user experience

4. Integrating Funnels with CRM

- Choose a CRM (e.g., HubSpot, Salesforce)
- Connect funnel tools to CRM
- Sync contact and lead data
- Automate sales follow-ups
- Track customer interactions

5. Funnel Analytics and Reporting

- Track key metrics (conversion rates, revenue)
- Use analytics tools (Google Analytics, Mixpanel)
- Monitor funnel performance
- Identify bottlenecks and areas for improvement
- Create data-driven reports

6. Personalizing Funnel Experiences

- Use segmentation and targeting
- Create personalized content and offers
- Leverage user behavior and preferences
- Implement dynamic content and recommendations
- Enhance user engagement

7. Funnel Best Practices

- Clear and concise messaging

- Relevant and valuable content
- Simple and intuitive design
- Mobile-friendly and responsive
- Secure and trustworthy

8. Common Funnel Mistakes

- Poorly defined target audience
- Ineffective messaging
- Insufficient testing
- Lack of segmentation
- Inadequate analytics

9. Funnel Automation Tools

- Marketing automation platforms (Marketo, Pardot)
- Email marketing automation tools (Mailchimp, HubSpot)
- CRM automation tools (Salesforce, Zoho)
- Funnel optimization tools (Optimizely, Unbounce)

Additional Tools:

- Funnel builders: ClickFunnels, Unbounce, Instapage
- Email marketing automation: Mailchimp, HubSpot, ConvertKit
- CRM: HubSpot, Salesforce, Zoho
- Analytics: Google Analytics, Mixpanel, Kissmetrics

Pricing:

- Funnel builders: $97-$297/month
- Email marketing automation: $9.99-$50/month
- CRM: $40-$100/month
- Analytics: $29-$500/month

Chapter 13: Email Marketing

☐ **What is Email Marketing and how it works?**

Email Marketing

Email marketing is a form of digital marketing that uses electronic mail to send commercial messages to customers and potential customers. It involves sending targeted and personalized messages to subscribers via email to build relationships, promote products/services, and drive sales.

How Email Marketing Works

1. List Building: Create an email list by collecting subscribers' email addresses through opt-in forms on your website, social media, or offline events.
2. Email List Segmentation: Divide your list into segments based on demographics, interests, or behaviors to send targeted emails.
3. Email Campaign Creation: Design and write compelling email campaigns using email marketing software.
4. Email Sending: Send emails to subscribers via email service providers (ESPs).
5. Tracking and Analytics: Monitor email metrics (open rates, click-through rates, conversion rates) to measure campaign success.
6. Follow-up and Automation: Set up automated email sequences to nurture leads and encourage conversions.

Email Marketing Types

1. Newsletters: Regular updates about your company, products, or services.
2. Promotional Emails: Special offers, discounts, or announcements.
3. Transactional Emails: Automated emails triggered by user actions (e.g., password reset).
4. Abandoned Cart Emails: Reminders to complete purchases.
5. Welcome Emails: Introduction to your brand and services.

Email Marketing Benefits

1. Cost-Effective: Low cost compared to traditional marketing.
2. Targeted: Reach specific audiences.
3. Measurable: Track campaign performance.
4. Increased Conversions: Drive sales and revenue.
5. Improved Customer Engagement: Build relationships.

Email Marketing Software

1. Mailchimp
2. HubSpot
3. Constant Contact
4. Sendinblue
5. ConvertKit
6. ActiveCampaign
7. GetResponse
8. AWeber

Best Practices

1. Segment Your List: Personalize emails.
2. Optimize Subject Lines: Increase open rates.

3. Use Clear CTAs: Encourage actions.
4. Mobile-Friendly: Ensure compatibility.
5. Comply with Regulations: Follow anti-spam laws.

Common Email Marketing Mistakes

1. Spamming: Sending unsolicited emails.
2. Poor Subject Lines: Low open rates.
3. Lack of Personalization: Irrelevant content.
4. Inadequate Tracking: Missing metrics.
5. Non-Compliance: Violating regulations.

Building an email list

Building an Email List:

Why Build an Email List?

1. Direct communication with customers
2. Increased conversions and sales
3. Improved customer engagement
4. Targeted marketing
5. Measurable results

How to Build an Email List:

1. Opt-in Forms: Add to website, blog, or social media
2. Load Magnets: Offer free resources (eBooks, webinars)
3. Sign-up Incentives: Discounts, free trials, or exclusive content
4. Content Upgrades: Enhance existing content with email opt-in
5. Paid Advertising: Facebook, Google, or LinkedIn ads
6. Offline Events: Collect email addresses at conferences, trade shows
7. Referrals: Encourage subscribers to refer friends
8. Partnerships: Collaborate with other businesses

Email List Building Strategies:

1. Pop-up Forms: Timed or scroll-triggered pop-ups
2. Slide-in Forms: Less intrusive, scroll-triggered forms
3. Embedded Forms: Integrate with website content
4. Welcome Gates: Full-screen opt-in forms
5. Content Locking: Require email address to access content
6. Gamification: Reward subscribers for referrals
7. Segmentation: Offer targeted content and incentives

Email List Building Tools:

1. Mailchimp
2. HubSpot
3. Sumo
4. OptinMonster
5. Unbounce

6. ConvertKit
7. GetResponse
8. AWeber

Best Practices:

1. Clear opt-in language
2. Visible and accessible forms
3. Relevant incentives
4. Mobile-friendly forms
5. Compliance with anti-spam laws
6. Regular list cleaning
7. Segmentation and targeting

Common Mistakes:

1. Buying email lists
2. Using fake or misleading opt-in language
3. Not providing clear incentives
4. Ignoring list segmentation
5. Not complying with regulations

Email List Building Metrics:

1. Conversion rate
2. Opt-in rate
3. List growth rate
4. Email open rate
5. Click-through rate

Email List Building Cost:

1. Email marketing software (Mailchimp, HubSpot): $9.99-$50/month
2. Lead magnet creation: $100-$500
3. Paid advertising: $500-$5,000/month
4. Opt-in form design: $100-$500

▯ Crafting effective email campaigns

**Crafting Effective Email Campaigns:
Key Components:**

1. Clear objective
2. Targeted audience
3. Compelling subject line
4. Engaging content
5. Strong call-to-action (CTA)
6. Effective design
7. Mobile-friendliness
8. Personalization
9. Timing and frequency
10. Tracking and analysis

Email Campaign Types:

1. Newsletters
2. Promotional emails
3. Abandoned cart emails
4. Welcome emails
5. Transactional emails
6. Educational emails
7. Survey emails
8. Event invitations
9. Follow-up emails
10. Re-engagement emails

Best Practices:

1. Segment your list
2. Use attention-grabbing subject lines
3. Keep content concise and scannable
4. Use clear and prominent CTAs
5. Optimize for mobile devices
6. Personalize content and sender name
7. Use social proof and testimonials
8. Test and iterate
9. Use automation
10. Comply with anti-spam laws

Email Campaign Metrics:

1. Open rate
2. Click-through rate (CTR)
3. Conversion rate
4. Bounce rate
5. Unsubscribe rate
6. Spam complaints
7. Email sharing/forwarding
8. Revenue generated

Tools for Crafting Email Campaigns:

1. Mailchimp
2. HubSpot
3. Constant Contact
4. Sendinblue
5. ConvertKit
6. ActiveCampaign
7. GetResponse
8. AWeber
9. Campaign Monitor
10. Klaviyo

Common Mistakes:

1. Poor subject lines
2. Lack of personalization
3. Too many links
4. Insufficient testing
5. Inadequate tracking
6. Non-compliance with regulations
7. Over-sending
8. Lack of relevance
9. Poor design
10. Ineffective CTAs

Email Campaign Cost:

1. Email marketing software: $9.99-$50/month
2. Content creation: $100-$500
3. Design services: $100-$500
4. Testing and optimization: $100-$500

Email Campaign ROI:

5. 1. Average ROI: 4400%
6. 2. Revenue generated per email: $0.11-$5.50
7. Conversion rate: 1%-5%

☐ Email automation and sequencing

Email Automation and Sequencing:
Email Automation:

1. Define triggers (e.g., sign-up, purchase)
2. Set up automated workflows
3. Use if-then logic for personalization
4. Integrate with CRM and marketing tools
5. Monitor and optimize performance

Email Sequencing:

1. Welcome sequence (onboarding)
2. Abandoned cart sequence
3. Nurture sequence (education)
4. Promotional sequence (offers)
5. Re-engagement sequence (inactivity)
6. Win-back sequence (inactive subscribers)
7. Survey sequence (feedback)

Types of Automated Emails:

1. Transactional emails (order confirmations)
2. Triggered emails (birthday wishes)
3. Behavioral emails (abandoned cart)
4. Educational emails (tutorial series)
5. Promotional emails (limited-time offers)

Email Automation Tools:

1. Mailchimp
2. HubSpot
3. Marketo
4. Pardot
5. ActiveCampaign
6. ConvertKit
7. GetResponse
8. AWeber

9. Klaviyo
10. Automizy

Benefits of Email Automation:

1. Increased efficiency
2. Improved consistency
3. Enhanced personalization
4. Better engagement
5. Increased conversions
6. Reduced manual labor

Best Practices:

1. Segment your list
2. Use clear and concise language
3. Optimize subject lines and CTAs
4. Use relevant and timely content
5. Monitor and adjust frequency
6. Test and optimize performance

Common Mistakes:

1. Over-automating
2. Lack of personalization
3. Insufficient testing
4. Inadequate segmentation
5. Poor timing

Email Automation Metrics:

1. Open rate
2. Click-through rate (CTR)
3. Conversion rate
4. Unsubscribe rate
5. Spam complaints

Email Automation Cost:

1. Email marketing software: $9.99-$50/month
2. Automation tools: $20-$100/month
3. Content creation: $100-$500

1. Email Automation ROI:

1. Average ROI: 4400%
2. Revenue generated per email: $0.11-$5.50
3. Conversion rate: 1%-5%

Email Automation Cost in India:

2. Email Marketing Software:

1. Mailchimp: ₹1,300 - ₹6,500/month (billed annually)
2. HubSpot: ₹2,300 - ₹45,000/month (billed annually)
3. Zoho Campaigns: ₹1,200 - ₹12,000/month (billed annually)
4. Sendinblue: ₹1,500 - ₹15,000/month (billed annually)
5. ConvertKit: ₹2,500 - ₹25,000/month (billed annually)

Automation Tools:

1. ActiveCampaign: ₹2,000 - ₹20,000/month (billed annually)
2. Marketo: ₹15,000 - ₹150,000/month (billed annually)
3. Pardot: ₹20,000 - ₹200,000/month (billed annually)
4. Automizy: ₹1,500 - ₹15,000/month (billed annually)
5. Klaviyo: ₹2,500 - ₹25,000/month (billed annually)

Indian Email Automation Providers:

1. Zoho Campaigns: ₹1,200 - ₹12,000/month
2. Sendinblue: ₹1,500 - ₹15,000/month
3. Mailchimp (India): ₹1,300 - ₹6,500/month
4. HubSpot (India): ₹2,300 - ₹45,000/month
5. Karix: ₹1,000 - ₹10,000/month

Cost Breakdown:

1. Setup and integration: ₹5,000 - ₹50,000
2. Monthly subscription: ₹1,000 - ₹50,000
3. Content creation: ₹5,000 - ₹50,000
4. Automation workflow design: ₹5,000 - ₹50,000

Total Cost:

1. Basic automation: ₹15,000 - ₹100,000/year
2. Advanced automation: ₹50,000 - ₹500,000/year
3. Enterprise automation: ₹100,000 - ₹1,000,000/year

ROI on Email Automation:

1. Average ROI: 400% - 1000%
2. Revenue generated per email: ₹0.50 - ₹50
3. 3. Conversion rate: 1% - 10

Personalization and segmentation

Personalization and Segmentation:
Personalization:

1. Define personalization goals
2. Collect and integrate customer data
3. Use segmentation and targeting
4. Create personalized content
5. Use dynamic content and recommendations
6. Leverage AI and machine learning
7. Test and optimize personalization

Segmentation:

1. Demographic segmentation (age, location, etc.)
2. Behavioral segmentation (purchase history, etc.)
3. Psychographic segmentation (interests, values, etc.)
4. Firmographic segmentation (company size, industry, etc.)
5. Transactional segmentation (purchase frequency, etc.)
6. Engagement segmentation (email opens, clicks, etc.)

Benefits of Personalization:

1. Increased engagement
2. Improved conversion rates
3. Enhanced customer experience
4. Increased loyalty
5. Better ROI

Benefits of Segmentation:

1. Targeted marketing
2. Improved conversion rates
3. Enhanced customer insights
4. Better resource allocation
5. Increased efficiency

Tools for Personalization and Segmentation:

1. Email marketing automation platforms (Mailchimp, HubSpot)
2. CRM systems (Salesforce, Zoho)
3. Marketing automation platforms (Marketo, Pardot)
4. Data analytics tools (Google Analytics, Mixpanel)
5. AI-powered personalization tools (Adobe Target, Evergage)

Best Practices:

1. Start with simple segmentation
2. Use clear and concise language
3. Use relevant and timely content
4. Test and optimize regularly
5. Respect customer preferences
6. Ensure data quality and accuracy
7. Continuously refine and improve

Common Mistakes:

1. Over-segmentation

2. Lack of data quality
3. Insufficient testing
4. Inadequate content creation
5. Non-compliance with regulations

Metrics for Personalization and Segmentation:

1. Open rate
2. Click-through rate (CTR)
3. Conversion rate
4. Unsubscribe rate
5. Spam complaints
6. Customer satisfaction
7. Net Promoter Score (NPS)

Cost of Personalization and Segmentation:

1. Email marketing automation platforms: ₹1,300 - ₹45,000/month
2. CRM systems: ₹1,200 - ₹12,000/month
3. Marketing automation platforms: ₹15,000 - ₹150,000/month
4. Data analytics tools: ₹5,000 - ₹50,000/month
5. AI-powered personalization tools: ₹20,000 - ₹200,000/month

☐ Tracking and analytics

Tracking and Analytics:
Types of Tracking:

1. Email tracking (opens, clicks, bounces)
2. Website tracking (page views, sessions, conversions)
3. Social media tracking (engagement, reach, clicks)
4. Campaign tracking (ROI, conversion rate, revenue)
5. Customer tracking (behavior, preferences, demographics)

Analytics Tools:

1. Google Analytics
2. Mixpanel
3. Kissmetrics
4. HubSpot Analytics
5. Mailchimp Analytics
6. Salesforce Analytics
7. Adobe Analytics
8. Chartbeat
9. Clicky
10. Piwik

Key Metrics:

1. Open rate
2. Click-through rate (CTR)
3. Conversion rate
4. Bounce rate
5. Unsubscribe rate
6. Spam complaints
7. Revenue generated
8. Return on Investment (ROI)
9. Customer Lifetime Value (CLV)
10. Net Promoter Score (NPS)

Benefits of Tracking and Analytics:

1. Data-driven decision making
2. Improved campaign performance
3. Enhanced customer insights
4. Increased efficiency
5. Better ROI
6. Improved customer experience
7. Competitive advantage
8. Reduced costs
9. Increased revenue
10. Improved scalability

Best Practices:

1. Set clear goals and objectives
2. Choose the right analytics tools
3. Track relevant metrics

4. Analyze and interpret data
5. Test and optimize regularly
6. Use data to inform decisions
7. Monitor customer behavior
8. Segment and target effectively
9. Use A/B testing
10. Continuously refine and improve

Common Mistakes:

1. Lack of clear goals
2. Insufficient data
3. Poor data quality
4. Inadequate tracking
5. Failure to analyze and interpret data
6. Not testing and optimizing
7. Ignoring customer feedback
8. Not segmenting and targeting
9. Not using A/B testing
10. Not continuously refining and improving

Cost of Tracking and Analytics:

1. Google Analytics: Free - ₹15,000/month
2. Mixpanel: ₹5,000 - ₹50,000/month
4. Kissmetrics: ₹10,000 - ₹100,000/month
5. HubSpot Analytics: ₹2,300 - ₹45,000/month
6. Mailchimp Analytics: ₹1,300 - ₹6,500/month

ROI on Tracking and Analytics:

1. Average ROI: 200% - 500%
2. Revenue generated per dollar spent: ₹2 - ₹10
3. Conversion rate increase: 10% - 50%
4. Customer lifetime value increase: 10% - 50%
5. Net Promoter Score increase: 10% - 50%

Chapter 14: Webinar and Zoom Meeting Strategy

☐ What is a Webinar and Zoom Meeting?

Webinar and Zoom Meeting are online meeting and presentation tools:

Webinar:

A webinar is a live or pre-recorded online presentation, workshop, or conference that connects speakers with attendees remotely. Webinars typically include:

1. Audio and video conferencing
2. Screen sharing and presentations
3. Interactive elements (polls, Q&A, chats)
4. Virtual whiteboards
5. Recordings and playback

Zoom Meeting:

Zoom Meeting is a video conferencing platform that enables virtual meetings, collaborations, and communication. Key features include:

1. High-definition video and audio
2. Screen sharing and collaboration
3. Virtual whiteboards
4. Recording and playback
5. Chat and messaging
6. Virtual events and webinars

Key Differences:

1. **Purpose:**
   Webinars focus on presentations and education, while Zoom Meetings emphasize collaboration and communication.
2. **Audience size:**
   Webinars often accommodate larger audiences, while Zoom Meetings are better suited for smaller groups.
3. **Interactivity:**
   Webinars typically include more interactive elements, such as polls and Q&A sessions.

Benefits:

1. Convenience
2. Cost-effectiveness
3. Increased reach and accessibility
4. Enhanced collaboration and engagement
5. Scalability
6. Flexibility
7. Measurable ROI

Common Use Cases:

1. Education and training
2. Sales and marketing

3. Customer support
4. Product demos
5. Team meetings
6. Conferences and events
7. Coaching and consulting

Popular Platforms:

1. Zoom
2. GoToWebinar
3. Webex
4. Google Meet
5. Skype
6. Microsoft Teams
7. Demio

Features and Pricing:

Varies depending on the platform, but typically includes:

1. Basic plans (free-$20/month)
2. Pro plans ($20-$50/month)
3. Business plans ($50-$100/month)
4. Enterprise plans (custom pricing)

What is a Webinar and Zoom Meeting Strategy and how can I use it?

Webinar Strategy:

1. Define objectives (lead generation, sales, education)
2. Choose a platform (Zoom, GoToWebinar, Webex)
3. Select a topic and format (live, pre-recorded, Q&A)
4. Promote through email, social media, and paid ads
5. Create engaging content and visuals
6. Encourage interaction (polls, chats, Q&A)
7. Follow up with attendees (recordings, additional resources)

Zoom Meeting Strategy:

1. Define meeting objectives (sales, demo, training)
2. Choose a format (one-on-one, group, screen sharing)
3. Schedule and invite participants
4. Prepare visual aids and materials
5. Encourage interaction and discussion
6. Record and share meetings (optional)
7. Follow up with attendees (next steps, additional info)

Tips and Best Practices:

1. Plan and rehearse
2. Use high-quality audio and video
3. Encourage interaction
4. Use visual aids and materials
5. Record and share meetings
6. Follow up with attendees
7. Continuously improve

Industry Applications:

1. Education and training
2. Sales and marketing
3. Customer support
4. Product demos
5. Team meetings
6. Conferences and events
7. Coaching and consulting

☐ Choosing Topics for Webinars and Zoom Meetings

Webinar Topics:

1. Industry trends and updates
2. Product demos and tutorials
3. Thought leadership and expert insights
4. Training and education
5. Case studies and success stories
6. Panel discussions and debates
7. How-to and best practices
8. Research and analysis
9. Product launches and announcements
10. Q&A sessions

Zoom Meeting Topics:

1. Team meetings and updates
2. Client meetings and consultations
3. Sales and product demos
4. Training and onboarding
5. Brainstorming and ideation
6. Project planning and management
7. Customer support and feedback
8. Partner and stakeholder meetings
9. Virtual events and conferences
10. Coaching and mentoring

Topic Selection Criteria:

1. Relevance to target audience
2. Timeliness and urgency
3. Interest and engagement potential
4. Alignment with business goals
5. Competition and market demand
6. Speaker expertise and availability
7. Content quality and depth
8. Format and delivery options
9. Technical requirements and feasibility
10. Budget and resource constraints

Tools for Topic Research:

1. Google Trends
2. Keyword research tools (Ahrefs, SEMrush)
3. Social media listening (Hootsuite, Sprout Social)
4. Online forums and communities
5. Customer feedback and surveys
6. Industry reports and research studies
7. Competitor analysis
8. Content analytics tools (Google Analytics)
9. Topic suggestion tools (AnswerThePublic)
10. Brainstorming and mind mapping tools (MindMeister)

Best Practices:

1. Validate topics with target audience
2. Ensure speaker expertise and passion
3. Keep topics focused and concise
4. Use attention-grabbing titles and descriptions
5. Promote topics through multiple channels
6. Continuously evaluate and refine topics
7. Consider evergreen and timeless topics
8. Use storytelling and visual aids
9. Encourage interaction and Q&A
10. Follow up with additional resources

☐ Hosting Webinars and Zoom Meetings

Hosting Webinars and Zoom Meetings:

Pre-Event Checklist:

1. Define event objectives and goals
2. Choose a platform (Zoom, GoToWebinar, Webex)
3. Select a date and time

4. Invite speakers and panelists
5. Create promotional materials (emails, social media posts)
6. Set up registration and landing pages
7. Configure audio and video settings
8. Test equipment and internet connection
9. Plan for technical support
10. Confirm event details with speakers and attendees

During the Event:

1. Welcome and introduce speakers
2. Share presentation materials and handouts
3. Encourage audience participation (Q&A, polls)
4. Monitor audio and video quality
5. Troubleshoot technical issues
6. Record the event (optional)
7. Take notes and gather feedback
8. Facilitate discussion and engagement
9. Provide clear instructions and guidance
10. Thank attendees and provide next steps

Post-Event:

1. Evaluate event success (attendance, engagement)
2. Send follow-up emails and surveys
3. Share event recordings and materials
4. Provide additional resources and next steps
5. Review event feedback and improve
6. Update event calendar and scheduling
7. Notify speakers and panelists of event outcome
8. Review event expenses and budget
9. Plan for future events and improvements
10. Archive event materials and recordings

Zoom Meeting Best Practices:

1. Use high-quality audio and video
2. Use a stable internet connection
3. Minimize background noise and distractions
4. Use a headset or earbuds
5. Encourage camera use
6. Use screen sharing and collaboration tools
7. Record meetings (optional)
8. Use chat and messaging features
9. Set clear meeting objectives and agendas
10. Follow up with meeting notes and action items

Webinar Best Practices:

1. Use engaging and interactive content
2. Use high-quality audio and video
3. Use polls, Q&A, and chat features
4. Encourage audience participation
5. Use visual aids and presentation materials
6. Record webinars (optional)
7. Provide clear instructions and guidance
8. Use a stable internet connection
9. Test equipment and software beforehand
10. Follow up with attendees and provide next steps

Tools and Platforms:

1. Zoom
2. GoToWebinar
3. Webex
4. Google Meet
5. Skype
6. Microsoft Teams
7. Demio
8. BigMarker
9. Livestorm
10. ClickMeeting

Costs and Pricing:

1. Zoom: $14.99-$49.99/month
2. GoToWebinar: $49-$99/month
3. Webex: $24-$49/month
4. Google Meet: Free-$10/month
5. Skype: Free-$9.99/month

ROI and Metrics:

1. Attendance and engagement rates
2. Lead generation and conversion rates
3. Customer satisfaction and feedback
4. Revenue generated and ROI
5. Event evaluation and survey responses

Promoting webinars and Zoom Meetings

Webinars and Zoom Meetings:

Pre-Promotion

1. Define target audience and objectives
2. Choose promotional channels (email, social media, paid ads)
3. Create compelling event titles and descriptions
4. Design eye-catching visuals (images, videos)
5. Plan promotional calendar and timeline

Email Promotion

1. Create dedicated email invitations
2. Send reminders and follow-ups
3. Use email marketing automation tools (Mailchimp, Constant Contact)
4. Segment email lists for targeted promotion
5. Track email open rates and click-through rates

Social Media Promotion

1. Share event details on LinkedIn, Twitter, Facebook, Instagram
2. Use relevant hashtags and keywords
3. Create social media events and groups
4. Share engaging visuals and videos
5. Collaborate with influencers and industry leaders

Paid Advertising

1. Google Ads (Google AdWords)
2. Facebook Ads
3. LinkedIn Ads
4. Twitter Ads
5. Native advertising (Taboola, Outbrain)

Content Promotion

1. Blog posts and articles
2. Video content (YouTube, Vimeo)
3. Podcasts and audio content
4. Infographics and visual content
5. Guest blogging and guest speaking

Partner and Affiliate Promotion

1. Partner with industry organizations
2. Collaborate with influencers and thought leaders
3. Offer affiliate programs and incentives
4. Leverage user-generated content
5. Host joint webinars and events

Tracking and Analytics

1. Google Analytics
2. Email marketing analytics (Mailchimp, Constant Contact)
3. Social media analytics (Hootsuite, Sprout Social)
4. Paid advertising analytics (Google Ads, Facebook Ads)
5. Event tracking and analytics tools (Zoom, GoToWebinar)

Budget Allocation

1. Email promotion (30-40%)
2. Social media promotion (20-30%)
3. Paid advertising (20-30%)
4. Content promotion (10-20%)
5. Partner and affiliate promotion (5-10%)

Timeline

1. 4-6 weeks before event: Start promotional campaign

2. 2-4 weeks before event: Intensify promotion
3. 1-2 weeks before event: Send reminders and follow-ups
4. Day of event: Send final reminders and encouragement

Tools and Resources

1. Email marketing automation tools (Mailchimp, Constant Contact)
2. Social media scheduling tools (Hootsuite, Sprout Social)
3. Paid advertising platforms (Google Ads, Facebook Ads)
4. Content creation tools (Canva, Adobe Creative Cloud)
5. Event tracking and analytics tools (Zoom, GoToWebinar)

- **Engaging attendees**

Engaging Attendees:

Before the Event

1. Send interactive invitations
2. Create a dedicated event page
3. Host a pre-event survey or poll
4. Offer exclusive content or resources
5. Encourage attendees to invite others

During the Event

1. Use interactive tools (polls, Q&A, chat)
2. Encourage audience participation
3. Use visual aids and multimedia
4. Host live discussions and debates
5. Offer real-time feedback and Q&A

After the Event

1. Send a post-event survey
2. Provide additional resources or content
3. Encourage attendees to share feedback
4. Host a follow-up webinar or meeting
5. Offer exclusive discounts or promotions

Interactive Tools

1. Polling and survey tools (PollEverywhere, SurveyMonkey)
2. Q&A and chat tools (Slido, Chatroll)
3. Virtual whiteboards (Mural, Google Jamboard)
4. Gamification tools (Gamify, Influitive)
5. Social media integration (Twitter, LinkedIn)

Engagement Strategies

1. Recognize and reward attendees
2. Use humor and storytelling
3. Encourage networking and collaboration
4. Use real-life examples and case studies
5. Provide actionable takeaways

Attendee Feedback

1. Collect feedback through surveys
2. Conduct post-event interviews
3. Analyze event metrics (attendance, engagement)
4. Use feedback to improve future events
5. Share feedback with speakers and sponsors

Event Metrics

1. Attendance and engagement rates
2. Survey and feedback responses
3. Social media engagement (tweets, posts)
4. Lead generation and conversion rates
5. Revenue generated and ROI

Best Practices

1. Test interactive tools beforehand

2. Train speakers and moderators
3. Encourage attendee participation
4. Use clear and concise language
5. Follow up with attendees after the event

Tools and Resources

1. Event management software (Eventbrite, Bizzabo)
2. Virtual event platforms (Zoom, GoToWebinar)
3. Interactive tools (PollEverywhere, Slido)
4. Social media management tools (Hootsuite, Sprout Social)
5. Feedback and survey tools (SurveyMonkey, Google Forms)

☐ Follow-up and conversion

Follow-up and Conversion:

Follow-up Strategies

1. Send a thank-you email within 24 hours
2. Provide additional resources or content
3. Offer exclusive discounts or promotions
4. Schedule a follow-up call or meeting
5. Encourage attendees to share feedback

Conversion Strategies

1. Clear and prominent calls-to-action (CTAs)
2. Personalized and targeted follow-up
3. Relevant and valuable content offerings
4. Limited-time offers or incentives
5. Multi-channel follow-up (email, phone, social media)

Email Follow-up

1. Automated email sequences
2. Personalized email content
3. Relevant and timely email sending
4. Clear and prominent CTAs
5. Tracking and analytics (open rates, click-through rates)

Phone Follow-up

1. Scheduled follow-up calls
2. Personalized and targeted conversations
3. Relevant and valuable discussions
4. Clear and prominent CTAs
5. Tracking and analytics (conversion rates)

Social Media Follow-up

1. Targeted social media ads
2. Personalized and relevant content
4. Engaging and interactive content
5. Clear and prominent CTAs
6. Tracking and analytics (engagement rates)

Conversion Metrics

1. Conversion rates (leads, sales, sign-ups)
2. Return on Investment (ROI)
3. Customer Lifetime Value (CLV)
4. Customer Acquisition Cost (CAC)
5. Sales Qualified Leads (SQLs)

Tools and Resources

1. Marketing automation software (Marketo, HubSpot)
2. Email marketing software (Mailchimp, Constant Contact)
3. CRM software (Salesforce, Zoho)
4. Social media management tools (Hootsuite, Sprout Social)
5. Analytics and tracking tools (Google Analytics)

Best Practices

1. Timing is everything (follow up within 24 hours)
2. Personalization is key
3. Relevance and value are crucial
4. Clear and prominent CTAs
5. Track and analyze results

Common Mistakes

1. Lack of follow-up
2. Poor timing
3. Irrelevant or low-value content
4. Unclear or hidden CTAs
5. Insufficient tracking and analytics

☐ Recording and repurposing

Recording and Repurposing:

Recording:

1. Audio and video recording
2. Screen recording and capture
3. Webinar and meeting recording
4. Interview and presentation recording
5. Lecture and training recording

Repurposing:

1. Blog posts and articles
2. Social media content (videos, posts)
3. Email newsletters and campaigns
4. Podcasts and audio content
5. Video courses and tutorials
6. Infographics and visual content
7. eBooks and whitepapers
8. Case studies and success stories
9. Testimonials and reviews
10. Online courses and training

Benefits:

1. Increased content reach and engagement
2. Improved SEO and search rankings
3. Enhanced credibility and authority
4. Reduced content creation time and effort
5. Increased lead generation and conversion
6. Better content utilization and ROI
7. Improved customer education and support
8. Enhanced brand awareness and reputation
9. Increased sales and revenue
10. Better data analysis and insights

Tools and Resources:

1. Recording software (Zoom, GoToWebinar)
2. Video editing software (Adobe Premiere, Final Cut Pro)
3. Audio editing software (Audacity, Adobe Audition)
4. Transcription software ((link unavailable), Trint)
5. Content management systems (WordPress, HubSpot)
6. Social media scheduling tools (Hootsuite, Sprout Social)
7. Email marketing software (Mailchimp, Constant Contact)
8. Podcast hosting platforms (Anchor, Buzzsprout)
9. Online course platforms (Teachable, Udemy)
10. Analytics and tracking tools (Google Analytics)

Best Practices:

1. Plan and script content
2. Invest in quality recording equipment
3. Edit and refine recorded content
4. Optimize content for SEO
5. Repurpose content across multiple channels
6. Track and analyze content performance
7. Continuously improve and refine content
8. Use captions and subtitles for accessibility
9. Use interactive elements and CTAs

10. Monitor and adjust content strategy

Common Mistakes:

1. Poor recording quality
2. Lack of editing and refinement
3. Insufficient optimization for SEO
4. Limited content repurposing
5. Inadequate tracking and analysis
6. Failure to update and refine content
7. Ignoring accessibility features
8. Not using interactive elements
9. Not monitoring content performance
10. Not adjusting content strategy

☐ Webinar and Zoom Meeting cost in India and International

Zoom offers various plans for webinars and events, catering to different needs and budgets.

Zoom Webinar Plans
- Basic: Free, ideal for personal meetings and small webinars
- Pro: $14.99/month/host, supports 100 participants, ideal for small businesses and teams
- Business: $19.99/month/host, supports 300 participants, ideal for larger businesses and organizations
- Enterprise: Custom pricing for large enterprises, supports up to 500 participants

Zoom Events Plans
- Essentials: $39/month/host, supports 100 participants, ideal for small events and webinars
- Professional: $79/month/host, supports 500 participants, ideal for larger events and conferences
- Business: $99/month/host, supports 1,000 participants, ideal for complex events and trade shows
- Enterprise: Custom pricing for large-scale events and conferences

For international pricing, I recommend checking the Zoom website, as prices may vary depending on your location. For India-specific pricing, you can expect to pay around ₹1,300-1,500 per month for the Pro plan, ₹2,300-2,600 per month for the Business plan, and custom pricing for the Enterprise plan.

Keep in mind that prices may change, and it's always best to verify with Zoom's official website or contact their sales team for the most up-to-date pricing information

Part 4: Advertising and Lead Generation

Chapter 15: Google Ads

☐ **What is Google Ads and how to configure and monetize it?**

Google Ads (formerly Google AdWords) is a popular online advertising platform that enables businesses to create and display ads on Google's search engine and other websites across the internet.

Google Ads Types:

1. Search Ads (text-based ads on Google search results)
2. Display Ads (image-based ads on websites and blogs)
3. Shopping Ads (product-based ads for e-commerce)
4. Video Ads (video-based ads on YouTube and other websites)
5. Mobile Ads (ads optimized for mobile devices)

Configuring Google Ads:

1. Create a Google Ads account
2. Set up billing and payment information
3. Choose ad type and campaign settings
4. Define target audience (location, language, interests)
5. Set ad budget and bidding strategy
6. Create ad groups and ads
7. Set up conversion tracking and analytics

Monetizing Google Ads:

1. Cost-Per-Click (CPC) model: pay for each ad click
2. Cost-Per-Thousand Impressions (CPM) model: pay for every 1,000 ad views
3. Conversion-based pricing: pay for specific actions (e.g., sales, sign-ups)
4. Revenue sharing: partner with Google to share ad revenue

Google Ads Optimization:

1. Keyword research and optimization
2. Ad copywriting and testing
3. Landing page optimization
4. Bidding strategy optimization
5. Ad scheduling and targeting
6. Ad extension optimization (e.g., sitelinks, callouts)
7. Continuous monitoring and improvement

Google Ads Metrics:

1. Click-Through Rate (CTR)
2. Conversion Rate (CR)
3. Cost Per Conversion (CPC)
4. Return on Ad Spend (ROAS)
5. Cost Per Click (CPC)
6. Impressions
7. Clicks

Google Ads Tools:

1. Google Ads Editor
2. Google Ads Keyword Planner
3. Google Ads Conversion Tracking
4. Google Analytics
5. Google Tag Manager

Google Ads Best Practices:

1. Clearly define target audience
2. Use relevant and concise ad copy
3. Optimize landing pages
4. Monitor and adjust bidding strategy
5. Use ad extensions
6. Test and iterate ad creative
7. Track and measure campaign performance

Common Google Ads Mistakes:

1. Poor keyword research
2. Ineffective ad copy
3. Insufficient budget
4. Lack of conversion tracking
5. Inadequate targeting
6. Not optimizing for mobile
7. Not monitoring campaign performance

▢ Google Ads account setup and configuration

Google Ads Account Setup and Configuration:

Step 1: Create a Google Ads Account

1. Go to (link unavailable)
2. Click "Start now"
3. Enter business information (name, email, password)
4. Verify email address

Step 2: Set up Billing

1. Add payment method (credit card, bank account)
2. Set currency and time zone
3. Review and accept terms and conditions

Step 3: Configure Account Settings

1. Account type (individual or business)
2. Business location and category
3. Contact information
4. Set up user roles and permissions

Step 4: Create a Campaign

1. Choose campaign type (Search, Display, Shopping)
2. Set campaign name and budget
3. Define target audience (location, language, interests)
4. Set bidding strategy and ad schedule

Step 5: Set up Ad Groups and Ads

1. Create ad groups (related ads and keywords)
2. Add keywords and ad copy
3. Set ad extensions (sitelinks, callouts)
4. Upload image and video ads

Step 6: Set up Conversion Tracking

1. Create conversion actions (e.g., form submissions)
2. Install conversion tracking code
3. Set up conversion tracking in Google Ads

Step 7: Link Google Analytics

1. Create a Google Analytics account
2. Link to Google Ads account
3. Enable auto-tagging

Step 8: Verify Website

1. Verify website ownership
2. Add verification code to website

Google Ads Account Structure:

1. Account
2. Campaigns
3. Ad groups
4. Ads
5. Keywords

Google Ads Account Settings:

1. Account name and contact information
2. Currency and time zone
3. Billing and payment settings
4. User roles and permissions
5. Campaign settings (budget, targeting, bidding)

Common Google Ads Account Setup Mistakes:

1. Incorrect billing information
2. Insufficient campaign targeting
3. Inadequate keyword research
4. Poor ad copy and landing page optimization
5. Lack of conversion tracking

Google Ads Account Setup Tools:

1. Google Ads Editor
2. Google Ads Keyword Planner
3. Google Analytics
4. Google Tag Manager

☐ Google Ads campaign optimization

Google Ads Campaign Optimization: Campaign-Level Optimization

1. Budget optimization: adjust budget allocation
2. Targeting optimization: refine location, language, and audience targets
3. Bidding strategy optimization: adjust CPC, CPM, or CPA bids
4. Ad scheduling optimization: adjust ad serving times
5. Campaign prioritization: adjust campaign hierarchy

Ad Group-Level Optimization

1. Ad group structuring: organize ad groups by theme
2. Keyword optimization: refine keyword lists and match types
3. Ad copy optimization: improve ad relevance and CTR
4. Landing page optimization: enhance user experience and conversion rates
5. Ad extension optimization: add sitelinks, callouts, and call extensions

Ad-Level Optimization

1. Ad creative optimization: test images, videos, and ad formats
2. Ad headline and description optimization: improve ad relevance and CTR
3. Ad URL optimization: ensure accurate and relevant landing pages
4. Ad extension optimization: add sitelinks, callouts, and call extensions
5. Ad rotation optimization: rotate ads for optimal performance

Keyword-Level Optimization

1. Keyword research: identify relevant and high-performing keywords
2. Keyword matching: adjust match types (broad, phrase, exact)
3. Keyword bidding: adjust bids for optimal ROI
4. Negative keyword optimization: prevent irrelevant traffic
5. Keyword grouping: organize keywords into ad groups

Bidding Strategy Optimization

1. Cost-per-click (CPC) bidding
2. Cost-per-thousand impressions (CPM) bidding
3. Cost-per-acquisition (CPA) bidding
4. Enhanced cost-per-click (ECPC) bidding
5. Automated bidding strategies (Target CPA, Target ROAS)

Conversion Rate Optimization

1. Conversion tracking setup
2. Conversion action optimization (e.g., form submissions)
3. Landing page optimization
4. Ad copy optimization
5. Bidding strategy optimization

Google Ads Optimization Tools

1. Google Ads Editor
2. Google Ads Keyword Planner
3. Google Analytics
4. Google Tag Manager
5. Google Optimize

Common Optimization Mistakes

1. Insufficient keyword research
2. Poor ad copy and landing page relevance
3. Inadequate bidding strategy
4. Lack of conversion tracking
5. Infrequent campaign monitoring

Best Practices

1. Regularly monitor campaign performance
2. Test and iterate ad creative and targeting
3. Optimize for user experience and conversion rates
4. Use automated bidding strategies
5. Continuously refine and adjust campaigns

☐ Google Ads bidding strategies

Google Ads Bidding Strategies:

Manual Bidding Strategies

1. Cost-Per-Click (CPC) Bidding: pay for each ad click
2. Cost-Per-Thousand Impressions (CPM) Bidding: pay for every 1,000 ad views
3. Cost-Per-Acquisition (CPA) Bidding: pay for specific actions (e.g., sales, sign-ups)

Automated Bidding Strategies

1. Target Cost-Per-Acquisition (Target CPA) Bidding: automatically adjusts bids for optimal CPA
2. Target Return on Ad Spend (Target ROAS) Bidding: automatically adjusts bids for optimal ROAS
3. Enhanced Cost-Per-Click (ECPC) Bidding: automatically adjusts bids for optimal CPC
4. Cost-Per-View (CPV) Bidding: pay for video ad views
5. View-Through Rate (VTR) Bidding: optimize for video ad views

Smart Bidding Strategies

1. Smart CPC: automatically adjusts bids for optimal CPC

2. Smart CPM: automatically adjusts bids for optimal CPM
3. Smart CPA: automatically adjusts bids for optimal CPA
4. Smart ROAS: automatically adjusts bids for optimal ROAS

Bidding Strategy Settings

1. Bid Type (CPC, CPM, CPA)
2. Bid Amount
3. Daily Budget
4. Target Location
5. Target Audience
6. Ad Schedule
7. Device Targeting

Bidding Strategy Optimization

1. Monitor performance metrics (CPC, CTR, Conversion Rate)
2. Adjust bidding strategy settings
3. Test and iterate bidding strategies
4. Use bidding strategy simulations
5. Monitor and adjust budget allocation

Google Ads Bidding Tools

1. Google Ads Editor
2. Google Ads Keyword Planner
3. Google Analytics
4. Google Tag Manager
5. Google Optimize

Common Bidding Strategy Mistakes

1. Insufficient budget allocation
2. Poor targeting and ad relevance
3. Inadequate bidding strategy
4. Lack of conversion tracking
5. Infrequent campaign monitoring

Best Practices

1. Set clear bidding goals and objectives
2. Monitor and adjust bidding strategy regularly
3. Test and iterate bidding strategies
4. Use automated bidding strategies
5. Continuously refine and adjust campaigns

☐ Ad copywriting and creative

Ad Copywriting and Creative:
Ad Copywriting Principles

1. Clear and concise headline
2. Compelling and relevant description
3. Strong call-to-action (CTA)
4. Focus on benefits, not features
5. Use attention-grabbing keywords
6. Emphasize unique selling proposition (USP)
7. Use social proof (testimonials, reviews)
8. Create sense of urgency

Ad Creative Best Practices

1. Visually appealing images or videos
2. Relevant and high-quality graphics
3. Clear and readable font
4. Consistent branding
5. Use color psychology
6. Optimize for mobile devices
7. Use interactive elements (e.g., animations)
8. Test and iterate creative

Ad Formats

1. Text Ads
2. Image Ads
3. Video Ads
4. Carousel Ads
5. Shopping Ads
6. Native Ads
7. Interactive Ads
8. Dynamic Ads

Ad Copywriting Tools

1. Google Ads Editor

2. AdWords Keyword Planner
3. Hemingway Editor
4. Grammarly
5. Unsplash (image library)
6. Canva (graphic design tool)
7. Adobe Creative Cloud

Ad Creative Tools

1. Adobe Photoshop
2. Adobe Illustrator
3. Sketch
4. Figma
5. Canva
6. Unsplash
7. Pexels
8. Pixabay

Common Ad Copywriting Mistakes

1. Poor headline and description
2. Lack of clear CTA
3. Insufficient keyword usage
4. Weak or irrelevant imagery
5. Inconsistent branding
6. Failure to test and iterate
7. Ignoring mobile optimization
8. Lack of social proof

Best Practices

1. Know your target audience
2. Focus on benefits, not features
3. Use attention-grabbing headlines
4. Optimize for mobile devices
5. Test and iterate creative
6. Use social proof and urgency
7. Continuously refine and improve
8. Monitor ad performance metrics

☐ Landing page optimization

Landing Page Optimization:
Key Elements:

1. Clear and concise headline
2. Relevant and focused content
3. Prominent call-to-action (CTA)
4. Simple and intuitive design
5. Fast loading speed
6. Mobile-friendliness
7. Secure (HTTPS)
8. Social proof (testimonials, reviews)

Optimization Techniques:

1. A/B testing (split testing)
2. Multivariate testing
3. Heatmap analysis
4. User feedback and surveys
5. Analytics and tracking
6. Conversion rate optimization (CRO)
7. Landing page design best practices
8. Content optimization

Landing Page Types:

1. Lead generation landing pages
2. Sales landing pages
3. Click-through landing pages
4. Micro-sites
5. Squeeze pages
6. Thank-you pages
7. Error pages (404)

Landing Page Metrics:

1. Conversion rate
2. Bounce rate
3. Time on page
4. Exit rate
5. Click-through rate (CTR)
6. Average session duration
7. Pages per session

Tools for Landing Page Optimization:

1. Google Optimize
2. Unbounce
3. Instapage
4. ClickFunnels

5. Wix
6. WordPress
7. Crazy Egg
8. Hotjar

Common Landing Page Mistakes:

1. Poor mobile usability
2. Slow loading speed
3. Unclear or confusing content
4. Lack of social proof
5. Insufficient CTA prominence
6. Too many form fields
7. Lack of analytics tracking
8. Inconsistent branding

Best Practices:

1. Keep it simple and focused
2. Use clear and concise language
3. Optimize for mobile devices
4. Use social proof and urgency
5. Test and iterate regularly
6. Use relevant and high-quality images
7. Ensure fast loading speed
8. Continuously refine and improve

Ad extensions and formats

Ad Extensions and Formats:
Ad Extensions:

1. Sitelinks: link to specific website pages
2. Callouts: highlight business benefits
3. Call Extensions: add phone numbers
4. Message Extensions: enable text messaging
5. Location Extensions: show business location
6. Affiliate Location Extensions: partner locations
7. Price Extensions: display prices
8. App Extensions: promote mobile apps
9. Review Extensions: showcase customer reviews
10. Structured Snippets: highlight product/service features

Ad Formats:

1. Text Ads: simple text-based ads
2. Image Ads: visual ads with images
3. Video Ads: video-based ads
4. Shopping Ads: product-based ads
5. Carousel Ads: multi-image ads
6. Native Ads: ads matching website content
7. Interactive Ads: engaging, interactive ads
8. Dynamic Ads: automatically generated ads
9. HTML5 Ads: interactive, animated ads
10. AMP Ads: accelerated mobile pages ads

Benefits of Ad Extensions:

1. Increased ad visibility
2. Improved click-through rates (CTR)
3. Enhanced ad relevance
4. Better user experience
5. Increased conversions
6. Improved ad ranking
7. Increased brand credibility
8. Better ROI

Best Practices for Ad Extensions:

1. Use relevant and concise language
2. Optimize for mobile devices
3. Use attention-grabbing headlines
4. Test and iterate extensions
5. Monitor performance metrics
6. Use extensions consistently
7. Align extensions with ad copy
8. Use social proof and urgency

Common Ad Extension Mistakes:

1. Poorly written extension copy
2. Irrelevant or redundant extensions
3. Insufficient testing

4. Lack of mobile optimization
5. Inconsistent branding
6. Failure to monitor performance
7. Overuse of extensions
8. Lack of relevance to ad copy

▢ Keyword research and targeting

Keyword Research and Targeting:
Keyword Research Tools:

1. Google Keyword Planner (free)
2. Ahrefs Keyword Explorer (paid)
3. SEMrush Keyword Magic Tool (paid)
4. Moz Keyword Explorer (paid)
5. Long Tail Pro (paid)
6. Ubersuggest (free)
7. AnswerThePublic (free)
8. Keyword Tool (free)

Keyword Targeting Strategies:

1. Long-tail keywords
2. Short-tail keywords
3. Branded keywords
4. Non-branded keywords
5. Keyword clustering
6. Keyword mapping
7. Intent-based targeting (informational, navigational, transactional)
8. Location-based targeting (geo-targeting)

Keyword Research Steps:

1. Identify target audience
2. Brainstorm seed keywords
3. Use keyword research tools
4. Analyze competition and search volume
5. Refine and prioritize keywords
6. Create keyword clusters and groups
7. Develop content and meta tags
8. Track and adjust keyword strategy

Keyword Targeting Best Practices:

1. Use relevant and specific keywords
2. Optimize for user intent
3. Use keyword variations and synonyms
4. Avoid keyword stuffing
5. Use header tags and meta descriptions
6. Optimize content and page structure
7. Monitor keyword performance and adjust
8. Use AI-powered keyword research tools

Common Keyword Research Mistakes:

1. Targeting overly broad keywords
2. Ignoring long-tail keywords
3. Not analyzing competition
4. Not tracking keyword performance
5. Using outdated keyword research tools
6. Not considering user intent
7. Not optimizing for voice search
8. Not using keyword clustering

Advanced Keyword Research Techniques:

1. Entity-based keyword research
2. Topic modeling and clustering
3. Keyword gap analysis
4. Competitor keyword analysis
5. Keyword segmentation and filtering
6. AI-powered keyword research
7. Machine learning-based keyword optimization
8. Natural language processing (NLP) for keyword research

Keyword Research Metrics:

1. Search volume
2. Competition level
3. Cost-per-click (CPC)
4. Conversion rate
5. Click-through rate (CTR)
6. Keyword ranking
7. Keyword density
8. Content relevance score

Chapter 16: Facebook and Instagram Ads

☐ Creating ad campaigns

Creating Ad Campaigns for Facebook and Instagram Ads:

Facebook Ads

1. Choose ad objective (Awareness, Consideration, Conversion)
2. Select target audience (location, age, interests, behaviors)
3. Set budget and schedule
4. Create ad creative (image, video, carousel, collection)
5. Optimize for mobile devices
6. Use Facebook Pixel for tracking and retargeting

Instagram Ads

1. Choose ad objective (Awareness, Consideration, Conversion)
2. Select target audience (location, age, interests, hashtags)
3. Set budget and schedule
4. Create ad creative (image, video, stories, reels)
5. Optimize for mobile devices
6. Use Instagram Shopping for product tags
7. Retargeting (target users who visited website)

Ad Formats

1. Image Ads
2. Video Ads
3. Carousel Ads
4. Collection Ads
5. Story Ads
6. Reels Ads
7. Instant Experience Ads
8. Lead Ads

Targeting Options

1. Location targeting
2. Demographic targeting (age, gender, interests)
3. Behavioral targeting (purchase history, device usage)
4. Interest-based targeting (hobbies, activities)
5. Lookalike targeting (similar to existing customers)
6. Custom audiences (upload customer data)

Budgeting and Bidding

1. Daily budget
2. Lifetime budget
3. Cost per click (CPC)
4. Cost per thousand impressions (CPM)
5. Cost per conversion (CPC)
6. Automatic bidding
7. Manual bidding

Tracking and Optimization

1. Facebook Pixel
2. Instagram Insights
3. Conversion tracking
4. Retargeting
5. A/B testing
6. Ad rotation
7. Budget allocation optimization

Common Mistakes

1. Poor targeting
2. Ineffective ad creative
3. Insufficient budget
4. Lack of tracking and optimization
5. Inconsistent branding
6. Failure to test and iterate
7. Ignoring mobile optimization

Best Practices

1. Clearly define ad objectives
2. Choose relevant targeting options
3. Optimize ad creative for mobile
4. Monitor and adjust campaigns regularly
5. Test and iterate ad creative
6. Use tracking and optimization tools
7. Continuously refine and improve

☐ Facebook Ads and Instagram Ads setup and structure

Here's an in-depth look at Facebook Ads and Instagram Ads setup and structure:

Facebook Ads Setup and Structure:
1. Campaign: Define campaign objective (Awareness, Consideration, Conversion)
2. Ad Set: Define budget, schedule, targeting, and placement
3. Ad: Create ad creative (image, video, carousel, collection)

Facebook Ads Objectives:
1. Awareness: Brand Awareness, Reach
2. Consideration: Traffic, Engagement, App Installs
3. Conversion: Conversions, Sales, Lead Generation

Facebook Ads Targeting:
1. Location: Country, Region, City, Zip
2. Demographics: Age, Gender, Interests, Behaviors
3. Interests: Hobbies, Activities, Job Title
4. Behaviors: Purchase History, Device Usage
5. Custom Audiences: Upload customer data
6. Lookalike Audiences: Target similar users

Facebook Ads Placement:
1. Facebook Feed
2. Instagram Feed
3. Audience Network
4. Messenger
5. Instagram Stories
6. Facebook Marketplace

Instagram Ads Setup and Structure:
1. Campaign: Define campaign objective (Awareness, Consideration, Conversion)
2. Ad Set: Define budget, schedule, targeting, and placement
3. Ad: Create ad creative (image, video, stories, reels)

Instagram Ads Objectives:
1. Awareness: Brand Awareness, Reach
2. Consideration: Traffic, Engagement, App Installs
3. Conversion: Conversions, Sales, Lead Generation

Instagram Ads Targeting:
1. Location: Country, Region, City, Zip
2. Demographics: Age, Gender, Interests, Hashtags
3. Interests: Hobbies, Activities, Job Title
4. Behaviors: Purchase History, Device Usage
5. Custom Audiences: Upload customer data
6. Lookalike Audiences: Target similar users

Instagram Ads Placement:
1. Instagram Feed
2. Instagram Stories
3. Instagram Reels
4. Instagram Shopping

Common Facebook and Instagram Ads Mistakes:

1. Poor targeting
2. Ineffective ad creative
3. Insufficient budget
4. Lack of tracking and optimization
5. Inconsistent branding
6. Failure to test and iterate

Best Practices:

1. Clearly define campaign objectives
2. Choose relevant targeting options
3. Optimize ad creative for mobile
4. Monitor and adjust campaigns regularly
5. Test and iterate ad creative
6. Use tracking and optimization tools
7. Continuously refine and improve

▢ Facebook Ads and Instagram Ads automation

Facebook Ads and Instagram Ads Automation:
Benefits of Automation:

1. Increased efficiency
2. Improved scalability
3. Enhanced accuracy
4. Better ROI
5. Reduced manual labor

Facebook Ads Automation Features:

1. Automated Bidding: optimize bids for best results
2. Automated Ad Rotation: rotate ads for optimal performance
3. Automated Targeting: target audiences based on behavior
4. Dynamic Ads: automatically generate ads based on product feed
5. Facebook Pixel: track website conversions and optimize ads

Instagram Ads Automation Features:

1. Automated Bidding: optimize bids for best results
2. Automated Ad Rotation: rotate ads for optimal performance
3. Automated Targeting: target audiences based on behavior
4. Instagram Shopping: tag products in ads and stories
5. Instagram Insights: track ad performance and optimize

Automation Tools:

1. Facebook Ads Manager
2. Facebook Ads API
3. Instagram Ads API
4. Third-party automation tools (e.g., AdEspresso, Hootsuite)
5. Facebook's Automated Ads

Automated Ad Strategies:

1. Cost Cap Bidding
2. Target Cost Per Acquisition (TCPA)
3. Target Return on Ad Spend (ROAS)
4. Automated Ad Rotation
5. Dynamic Ad Targeting

Common Automation Mistakes:

1. Over-reliance on automation
2. Insufficient monitoring
3. Poor targeting settings
4. Inadequate budget allocation
5. Lack of A/B testing

Best Practices:

1. Set clear automation goals
2. Monitor and adjust automation regularly

3. Test and iterate ad creative
4. Use automated bidding strategies
5. Continuously refine and improve

Advanced Automation Techniques:

1. Using Facebook's Automated Ads
2. Creating custom automation scripts
3. Integrating with CRM data
4. Using AI-powered ad optimization
5. Implementing automated ad scheduling

☐ Facebook Ads and Instagram Ads for e-commerce

Facebook Ads and Instagram Ads for E-commerce:
Benefits:

1. Increased online sales
2. Improved brand awareness
3. Enhanced customer engagement
4. Targeted advertising
5. Measurable ROI

E-commerce Ad Objectives:

1. Conversions (sales, sign-ups)
2. Traffic (website visits)
3. Product sales
4. Lead generation
5. Brand awareness

Facebook Ads for E-commerce:

1. Dynamic Product Ads (DPA)
2. Product Carousel Ads
3. Collection Ads
4. Shopping Ads
5. Retargeting Ads

Instagram Ads for E-commerce:

1. Shopping Ads
2. Product Tags
3. Instagram Stories Ads
4. Reels Ads
5. Influencer Partnerships

Targeting Options:

1. Demographic targeting
2. Interest-based targeting
3. Behavioral targeting
4. Custom audiences (customer lists)
5. Lookalike audiences (similar to customers)

E-commerce Ad Strategies:

1. Abandoned cart campaigns
2. Product recommendation ads
3. Upsell and cross-sell campaigns
4. Seasonal and promotional campaigns
5. Social proof ads (customer testimonials)

Tracking and Optimization:

1. Facebook Pixel
2. Instagram Insights
3. Conversion tracking
4. Return on Ad Spend (ROAS) tracking
5. A/B testing and ad rotation

Common Mistakes:

1. Poor targeting
2. Ineffective ad creative
3. Insufficient budget
4. Lack of tracking and optimization
5. Inconsistent branding

Best Practices:

1. Clearly define ad objectives
2. Choose relevant targeting options
3. Optimize ad creative for mobile
4. Monitor and adjust campaigns regularly
5. Test and iterate ad creative

Advanced E-commerce Strategies:

1. Using Facebook's Automated Ads
2. Creating custom product feeds
3. Implementing dynamic ad targeting
4. Using AI-powered ad optimization
5. Integrating with e-commerce platforms (e.g., Shopify, Magento)

E-commerce Platforms Integration:

1. Shopify
2. Magento
3. WooCommerce
4. BigCommerce
5. Salesforce Commerce Cloud

☐ Target audience selection

Target Audience Selection:
Target Audience Types:

1. Demographic targeting (age, gender, location)
2. Interest-based targeting (hobbies, activities)
3. Behavioral targeting (purchase history, device usage)
4. Custom audiences (customer lists, email subscribers)
5. Lookalike audiences (similar to customers)

Facebook Target Audience Options:

1. Location targeting (country, region, city)
2. Age targeting (18-65+)
3. Gender targeting (male, female, custom)
4. Interest targeting (hobbies, activities)
5. Behavioral targeting (purchase history, device usage)
6. Connection targeting (friends, followers)
7. Custom audiences (customer lists, email subscribers)
8. Lookalike audiences (similar to customers)

Instagram Target Audience Options:

1. Location targeting (country, region, city)
2. Age targeting (18-65+)
3. Gender targeting (male, female, custom)
4. Interest targeting (hobbies, activities)
5. Hashtag targeting (relevant hashtags)
6. User targeting (followers, engagements)
7. Custom audiences (customer lists, email subscribers)
8. Lookalike audiences (similar to customers)

Target Audience Selection Strategies:

1. Identify customer personas
2. Analyze customer data (purchase history, demographics)
3. Research industry trends and insights
4. Use social media listening tools
5. Conduct market research and surveys

Common Target Audience Selection Mistakes:

1. Targeting too broad or too narrow
2. Insufficient data analysis
3. Lack of customer insight
4. Failure to update targeting regularly
5. Inconsistent targeting across channels

Best Practices:

1. Clearly define target audience
2. Use data-driven targeting decisions
3. Continuously monitor and adjust targeting
4. Test and iterate targeting strategies
5. Integrate targeting across channels

Advanced Target Audience Selection Techniques:

1. Using Facebook's Advanced Matching
2. Creating custom audiences from website traffic
3. Using Instagram's "Also Targeted" feature
4. Implementing AI-powered targeting tools
5. Integrating CRM data with targeting options

☐ Ad creative and copy

Ad Creative and Copy:
Ad Creative:

1. Image Ads: static images with text overlay
2. Video Ads: motion graphics, animations, or live-action
3. Carousel Ads: multiple images or cards
4. Collection Ads: product catalogs with images
5. Story Ads: full-screen, immersive ads

Ad Copy:

1. Headline: attention-grabbing title
2. Description: brief, descriptive text
3. Call-to-Action (CTA): actionable phrase (e.g., "Sign Up")
4. Tagline: memorable slogan or phrase

Best Practices:

1. Keep it simple, clear, and concise
2. Use high-quality, visually appealing images
3. Focus on benefits, not features
4. Use social proof (testimonials, reviews)
5. Include a clear CTA
6. Test and iterate ad creative
7. Use branding consistency
8. Optimize for mobile devices

Ad Creative Strategies:

1. Emotional storytelling
2. Humor and entertainment
3. Educational and informative
4. Promotional and offer-based
5. User-generated content (UGC)
6. Influencer partnerships
7. Dynamic ad creative
8. Interactive ad experiences

Ad Copywriting Tips:

1. Use attention-grabbing headlines
2. Focus on customer pain points
3. Use clear, concise language
4. Emphasize benefits and value
5. Include social proof
6. Use actionable CTAs
7. Test and iterate ad copy
8. Use storytelling techniques

Common Ad Creative Mistakes:

1. Poor image quality
2. Inconsistent branding
3. Unclear messaging
4. Lack of CTA
5. Insufficient testing
6. Ignoring mobile optimization
7. Overuse of graphics
8. Lack of social proof

Tools for Ad Creative:

1. Adobe Creative Cloud
2. Canva
3. Sketch
4. Figma
5. Google Web Designer
6. Facebook Ads Creative Hub
7. Instagram Creative Tools

☐ Budgeting and bidding

Budgeting and Bidding:
Budgeting:

1. Daily budget: set daily spend limit
2. Lifetime budget: set total campaign spend
3. Budget allocation: distribute budget across ad sets
4. Budget optimization: automatically adjust budget for best ROI

Bidding:

1. Cost Per Click (CPC): pay per ad click
2. Cost Per Thousand Impressions (CPM): pay per 1,000 ad views
3. Cost Per Action (CPA): pay per conversion
4. Cost Per View (CPV): pay per video view

Bidding Strategies:

1. Automatic bidding: Facebook optimizes bids for best ROI
2. Manual bidding: set bid amounts manually
3. Target Cost Per Acquisition (TCPA): bid to achieve target CPA
4. Target Return on Ad Spend (ROAS): bid to achieve target ROAS

Budgeting and Bidding Best Practices:

1. Set clear budget and bidding goals
2. Monitor and adjust budget regularly
3. Optimize budget allocation
4. Test bidding strategies
5. Use automated bidding
6. Set bid caps
7. Consider ad scheduling
8. Continuously refine and improve

Common Budgeting and Bidding Mistakes:

1. Insufficient budget
2. Poor budget allocation
3. Ineffective bidding strategy
4. Lack of monitoring and adjustment
5. Inconsistent bidding
6. Failure to optimize for ROI
7. Ignoring ad scheduling
8. Overbidding

Budgeting and Bidding Tools:

1. Facebook Ads Manager
2. Google Ads
3. AdEspresso
4. Hootsuite Ads
5. Facebook Ads API
6. Google Ads API
7. Third-party bidding platforms

Advanced Budgeting and Bidding Techniques:

1. Dynamic budget allocation
2. Automated bidding scripts
3. Multi-campaign budget optimization
4. Advanced bid strategies (e.g., value-based bidding)
5. Integrating CRM data with budgeting and bidding
6. Using AI-powered budgeting and bidding tools

7. Real-time budgeting and bidding optimization
8. Cross-campaign budget optimization

☐ Optimizing ad performance and Tracking

Optimizing Ad Performance and Tracking:
Ad Performance Optimization:

1. Monitor ad metrics (CTR, CPC, CPM, Conversion Rate)
2. Identify underperforming ads and ad sets
3. Adjust targeting, bidding, and ad creative
4. Test new ad creative and targeting options
5. Use A/B testing and experimentation
6. Optimize for mobile devices
7. Use ad scheduling and rotation
8. Continuously refine and improve

Tracking and Measurement:

1. **Facebook Pixel:** track website conversions and events
2. **Instagram Insights:** track ad performance and audience engagement
3. **Google Analytics:** track website traffic and conversion data
4. **Conversion Tracking:** track specific actions (e.g., purchases, sign-ups)
5. **Event Tracking:** track specific events (e.g., add-to-cart, checkout)
6. **Retargeting:** target users who visited website or engaged with ads
7. **Custom Conversions:** track custom events and actions
8. **Data-Driven Attribution:** measure ad performance across channels

Key Performance Indicators (KPIs):

1. Return on Ad Spend (ROAS)
2. Conversion Rate
3. Cost Per Acquisition (CPA)
4. Cost Per Click (CPC)
5. Click-Through Rate (CTR)
6. Impressions
7. Reach
8. Engagement Rate

Common Optimization Mistakes:

1. Insufficient tracking and measurement
2. Lack of ad testing and experimentation
3. Ineffective targeting and bidding
4. Poor ad creative and messaging
5. Failure to optimize for mobile devices
6. Inconsistent ad scheduling and rotation
7. Ignoring ad fatigue and burnout
8. Lack of data-driven decision-making

Best Practices:

1. Set clear ad performance goals and KPIs
2. Monitor ad performance regularly
3. Test and iterate ad creative and targeting
4. Optimize for mobile devices
5. Use ad scheduling and rotation
6. Continuously refine and improve
7. Use data-driven attribution and tracking
8. Integrate CRM data with ad performance data

Advanced Optimization Techniques:

1. Using AI-powered ad optimization tools
2. Implementing dynamic ad targeting and bidding
3. Using custom algorithms and models
4. Integrating CRM data with ad performance data
5. Using multi-touch attribution modeling
6. Implementing real-time ad optimization
7. Using predictive analytics and modeling
8. Integrating ad performance data with business intelligence tools

Chapter 17: Lead Generation

☐ What is Lead Generation?

Lead Generation:

Definition: Lead generation is the process of attracting and converting strangers into potential customers, also known as leads, who have shown interest in a product or service.

Goal: The ultimate goal of lead generation is to drive sales, revenue, and business growth by capturing and nurturing leads through the sales funnel.

Types of Leads:

1. **Qualified Lead:** A lead that has shown significant interest and has the potential to become a customer.
2. **Unqualified Lead:** A lead that does not meet the qualification criteria.
3. **Sales-Ready Lead:** A lead that is ready to make a purchase.

Lead Generation Channels:

1. Digital Marketing (Social Media, Email, Search Engine Optimization)
2. Content Marketing (Blog Posts, eBooks, Webinars)
3. Paid Advertising (Google Ads, Facebook Ads)
4. Event Marketing (Conferences, Trade Shows)
5. Referral Marketing (Word-of-Mouth)
6. Sales Outreach (Cold Calling, Email Outreach)

Lead Generation Strategies:

1. Create valuable content
2. Optimize landing pages
3. Use social media advertising
4. Leverage email marketing
5. Utilize lead magnets
6. Host webinars and events
7. Offer free trials or demos
8. Partner with influencers

Lead Generation Metrics:

1. Lead Volume
2. Conversion Rate
3. Cost Per Lead (CPL)
4. Lead Quality
5. Sales Qualified Lead (SQL) Rate
6. Return on Investment (ROI)

Lead Generation Tools:

1. Marketing Automation Software (Marketo, HubSpot)
2. CRM Software (Salesforce, Zoho)
3. Email Marketing Tools (Mailchimp, Constant Contact)
4. Landing Page Builders (Unbounce, Instapage)
5. Social Media Management Tools (Hootsuite, Sprout Social)

Benefits of Lead Generation:

1. Increased sales and revenue
2. Improved brand awareness
3. Enhanced customer engagement
4. Better ROI on marketing efforts
5. Data-driven decision-making

☐ Strategies for generating leads (webinars, free resources, referrals)

Strategies for Generating Leads:

Webinars:

1. Host educational webinars on topics relevant to your target audience
2. Offer exclusive content or discounts to attendees
3. Use webinar registration pages to capture leads
4. Follow up with attendees via email or phone
5. Repurpose webinar content into other formats (e.g., blog posts, videos)

Free Resources:

1. Create valuable resources (e.g., eBooks, whitepapers, templates)
2. Gate resources behind a lead capture form
3. Promote resources on social media and email
4. Optimize resource landing pages for conversions
5. Use resources to establish thought leadership

Referrals:

1. Encourage happy customers to refer friends and family
2. Offer incentives for successful referrals (e.g., discounts, rewards)
3. Implement a referral program with tracking and rewards
4. Leverage employee networks for referrals
5. Partner with influencers or affiliates for referrals

Additional Strategies:

1. Content Upgrades: offer exclusive content in exchange for contact info
2. Free Trials or Demos: offer limited-time access to products or services
3. Contests or Giveaways: host contests or giveaways to capture leads
4. Social Media Contests: run social media-specific contests
5. Partner with Other Businesses: collaborate on lead-generating initiatives
6. Email Courses: offer free email courses or tutorials
7. Quizzes or Assessments: create interactive quizzes or assessments
8. Podcasts: create a podcast and promote lead-generating resources
9. Video Series: create a video series and gate exclusive content
10. Live Events: host live events and capture leads through registration

Optimizing Lead Generation:

1. Test and refine lead capture forms
2. Use clear and compelling calls-to-action (CTAs)
3. Optimize landing pages for conversions
4. Use social proof (testimonials, reviews)
5. Segment and personalize lead follow-up
6. Use marketing automation to nurture leads
7. Track and analyze lead generation metrics
8. Continuously refine and improve lead generation strategies

Lead Generation Tools:

1. Marketing automation software (Marketo, HubSpot)
2. CRM software (Salesforce, Zoho)
3. Email marketing tools (Mailchimp, Constant Contact)
4. Landing page builders (Unbounce, Instapage)
5. Social media management tools (Hootsuite, Sprout Social)

6. Webinar software (GoToWebinar, Zoom)
7. Resource creation tools (Canva, Adobe Creative Cloud)

☐ Creating lead magnets

What are Lead Magnets?

Lead magnets are valuable resources, offers, or incentives that attract potential customers and encourage them to provide their contact information in exchange for the resource.

Types of Lead Magnets:

1. eBooks
2. Whitepapers
3. Webinars
4. Templates
5. Checklists
6. Case studies
7. Free trials or demos
8. Discount codes or coupons
9. Video courses
10. Podcasts

Characteristics of Effective Lead Magnets:

1. Relevant to target audience
2. Valuable and informative
3. Unique and exclusive
4. Easy to consume
5. Visually appealing
6. Clear and concise language
7. Solves a problem or meets a need
8. Aligns with brand's messaging

Steps to Create a Lead Magnet:

1. Identify target audience and their needs
2. Choose a format (eBook, webinar, etc.)
3. Research and create valuable content
4. Design visually appealing graphics
5. Write clear and concise copy
6. Set up landing page and lead capture form
7. Test and refine lead magnet

Best Practices:

1. Keep it concise and focused
2. Use attention-grabbing headlines
3. Use social proof (testimonials, reviews)
4. Offer exclusive content
5. Use urgency tactics (limited-time offers)
6. Optimize for mobile devices
7. Test and refine lead magnet regularly

Tools for Creating Lead Magnets:

1. Canva (graphic design)
2. Adobe Creative Cloud (eBook design)
3. Google Docs (collaborative writing)
4. Zoom (webinar hosting)
5. Mailchimp (email marketing)
6. Unbounce (landing page builder)
7. Instapage (landing page builder)

Examples of Successful Lead Magnets:

1. HubSpot's "The Ultimate Guide to Inbound Marketing"
2. Moz's "The Beginner's Guide to SEO"
3. Salesforce's "The State of Marketing Report"
4. Hootsuite's "The Social Media Marketing Guide"
5. Buffer's "The Complete Guide to Social Media Marketing"

☐ Using opt-in forms and landing pages

Using Opt-in Forms and Landing Pages:
Opt-in Forms:

1. **Definition:** A form that captures visitor information in exchange for a resource or offer.
2. **Types:** Embedded forms, Pop-up forms, Slide-in forms, Hover forms.
3. **Best Practices:**
   - Keep it short and simple.
   - Use clear and compelling headlines.
   - Offer incentives for signing up.
   - Use social proof (testimonials, reviews).
   - Optimize for mobile devices.

Landing Pages:

1. **Definition:** A dedicated page that converts visitors into leads.
2. **Types:** Squeeze pages, Sales pages, Thank-you pages.
3. **Best Practices:**
   - Focus on one clear goal.
   - Use attention-grabbing headlines.
   - Provide value and relevance.
   - Use visual hierarchy and simplicity.
   - Optimize for conversions.

Landing Page Elements:

1. **Headline:** Clear and compelling.
2. **Subheadline:** Supports the headline.
3. **Image/Video:** Relevant and engaging.
4. **Form:** Simple and prominent.
5. **Call-to-Action (CTA):** Clear and actionable.
6. **Social Proof:** Testimonials, reviews.
7. **Trust Indicators:** Security badges, certifications.

Opt-in Form and Landing Page Tools:

1. Unbounce
2. Instapage
3. Mailchimp
4. ConvertKit
5. HubSpot
6. WordPress plugins (e.g., Gravity Forms, Formidable Forms)
7. Google Forms

Optimization Techniques:

1. A/B testing
2. Multivariate testing
3. Heatmap analysis
4. User feedback
5. Analytics tracking
6. Mobile optimization
7. Load time optimization

Common Mistakes:

1. Poor form design
2. Insufficient incentives
3. Lack of social proof
4. Unclear CTAs
5. Slow loading speeds
6. Mobile unfriendliness
7. Lack of testing and optimization

Best Practices for Mobile:

1. Simple, concise design
2. Easy-to-tap CTAs
3. Fast loading speeds
4. Clear, readable font
5. Optimized form layout

▢ Lead scoring and qualification

Lead Scoring and Qualification:

Lead Scoring:

1. Definition: Assigning a score to leads based on their behavior, demographics, and firmographics.
2. Purpose: Identify high-quality leads and prioritize sales efforts.

3. Criteria: Interaction with website, email engagement, social media activity, demographic data.

Lead Qualification:

1. **Definition:** Evaluating leads to determine their readiness to buy.
2. **Purpose:** Ensure sales teams focus on qualified leads.
3. **Criteria:** Budget, Authority, Need, Timeline (BANT).

Lead Scoring Models:

1. **Behavioral Scoring:** Scores leads based on interactions (e.g., page views, email opens).
2. **Demographic Scoring:** Scores leads based on firmographics (e.g., company size, industry).
3. **Predictive Scoring:** Uses machine learning to predict lead conversion.

Lead Qualification Frameworks:

1. BANT (Budget, Authority, Need, Timeline)
2. ANUM (Authority, Need, Urgency, Money)
3. CHAMP (Challenges, Authority, Money, Prioritization)

Common Challenges:

1. Data quality issues.
2. Overly complex scoring models.
3. Lack of sales and marketing alignment.
4. Insufficient training.
5. Inadequate technology.

Lead Scoring Tools:

1. HubSpot
2. Marketo
3. Salesforce
4. Pardot
5. Eloqua

Benefits:

1. Improved sales efficiency.
2. Enhanced lead conversion rates.
3. Better sales and marketing alignment.
4. Increased revenue.
5. Data-driven decision-making.

Best Practices:

1. Align scoring with sales goals.
2. Continuously refine and adjust scoring.
3. Use data to inform scoring decisions.
4. Integrate scoring with CRM.
5. Train sales teams on scoring.

Advanced Lead Scoring Techniques:

1. Machine learning-based scoring.
2. Predictive analytics.
3. Real-time scoring.
4. Account-based scoring.
5. Intent-based scoring.

☐ Referrals and word-of-mouth

Referrals and Word-of-Mouth:

Referrals:

1. **Definition:** Recommendations from satisfied customers to their networks.
2. **Benefits:** Credibility, trust, and increased conversions.
3. **Types:**

- Organic referrals (natural word-of-mouth)
- Incentivized referrals (rewarded referrals)
- Advocacy programs (structured referral programs)

Word-of-Mouth:

1. **Definition:** Informal, person-to-person communication about a product/service.
2. **Benefits:** Builds trust, credibility, and brand awareness.
3. **Types:**
   - Online word-of-mouth (social media, reviews)
   - Offline word-of-mouth (in-person conversations)

Referral Strategies:

1. Implement a referral program
2. Offer incentives (discounts, rewards)
3. Encourage user-generated content
4. Leverage customer testimonials
5. Develop an advocacy program
6. Partner with influencers
7. Utilize employee networks
8. Measure and track referrals

Word-of-Mouth Strategies:

1. Deliver exceptional customer experiences
2. Foster a strong brand community
3. Encourage customer engagement
4. Respond to customer feedback
5. Utilize social media listening
6. Create shareable content
7. Host events and webinars
8. Measure and track word-of-mouth

Tools and Platforms:

1. ReferralCandy
2. LoyaltyLion
3. Ambassador
4. Influitive
5. Social media management tools (Hootsuite, Sprout Social)
6. Review management tools (Yotpo, Trustpilot)

Metrics and Measurement:

1. Referral rate
2. Conversion rate
3. Customer acquisition cost (CAC)
4. Customer lifetime value (CLV)
5. Net promoter score (NPS)
6. Word-of-mouth frequency
7. Social media engagement metrics

Best Practices:

1. Align referral programs with customer needs
2. Communicate referral incentives clearly
3. Make referrals easy and seamless
4. Recognize and reward referrals
5. Monitor and adjust referral strategies
6. Foster a culture of customer advocacy
7. Continuously collect and act on customer feedback

Common Challenges:

1. Lack of incentives
2. Insufficient customer engagement
3. Difficulty tracking referrals
4. Limited budget
5. Competing priorities

- **Paid advertising**

Paid Advertising:
Types of Paid Advertising:

1. Search Engine Marketing (SEM)

2. Social Media Advertising (Facebook, Instagram, LinkedIn, Twitter)
3. Display Advertising (Google Display Network, Native Ads)
4. Email Marketing
5. Influencer Marketing
6. Affiliate Marketing
7. Video Advertising (YouTube, Vimeo)
8. Mobile Advertising
9. Native Advertising
10. Print Advertising (Newspaper, Magazine)

Paid Advertising Channels:

1. Google Ads (Search, Display, YouTube)
2. Facebook Ads (Facebook, Instagram)
3. LinkedIn Ads
4. Twitter Ads
5. Pinterest Ads
6. YouTube Ads
7. Amazon Advertising
8. Bing Ads
9. Yahoo Gemini
10. AdRoll

Paid Advertising Strategies:

1. Targeting (Demographic, Behavioral, Contextual)
2. Retargeting
3. Lookalike Audiences
4. A/B Testing
5. Conversion Rate Optimization (CRO)
6. Cost Per Acquisition (CPA) Bidding
7. Cost Per Click (CPC) Bidding
8. Brand Awareness Campaigns
9. Lead Generation Campaigns
10. Sales-Driven Campaigns

Paid Advertising Metrics:

1. Click-Through Rate (CTR)
2. Conversion Rate
3. Cost Per Click (CPC)
4. Cost Per Acquisition (CPA)
5. Return on Ad Spend (ROAS)
6. Return on Investment (ROI)
7. Impressions
8. Views
9. Engagement Rate
10. Click-Through Conversion Rate

Paid Advertising Tools:

1. Google Ads Editor
2. Facebook Ads Manager
3. LinkedIn Ads Manager
4. Twitter Ads Manager
5. Hootsuite Ads
6. AdEspresso
7. AdRoll
8. Marin Software
9. Kenshoo
10. Acquisio

Best Practices:

1. Set clear goals and objectives
2. Define target audience
3. Choose relevant ad channels
4. Optimize ad creative and copy
5. Monitor and adjust campaigns regularly
6. Use A/B testing and experimentation
7. Track and measure ROI
8. Utilize retargeting and lookalike audiences
9. Leverage user-generated content
10. Continuously refine and improve

Common Mistakes:

1. Insufficient targeting
2. Poor ad creative and copy
3. Inadequate budget
4. Lack of tracking and measurement
5. Ineffective ad scheduling
6. Ignoring mobile optimization
7. Not utilizing retargeting
8. Overlooking ad frequency
9. Not testing ad creative
10. Inadequate landing page optimization

Follow-up and conversion

Follow-up and Conversion:
Follow-up Strategies:

1. Email nurturing campaigns
2. Phone or voicemail follow-up
3. Social media engagement
4. Retargeting ads
5. Personalized content recommendations
6. Webinar or event invitations
7. Survey or feedback requests
8. Account-based marketing
9. Sales outreach and cadences
10. Automated follow-up sequences

Conversion Optimization:

1. Landing page optimization
2. Form optimization
3. Call-to-action (CTA) optimization
4. Button color and design testing
5. Headline and copy testing
6. Image and video testing
7. Mobile optimization
8. Page speed optimization
9. Social proof and testimonials
10. Urgency and scarcity tactics

Conversion Rate Metrics:

1. Conversion rate
2. Cost per conversion
3. Return on ad spend (ROAS)
4. Return on investment (ROI)
5. Click-through rate (CTR)
6. View-through rate (VTR)
7. Lead-to-customer rate
8. Sales-qualified lead (SQL) rate
9. Marketing-qualified lead (MQL) rate
10. Customer acquisition cost (CAC)

Follow-up Tools:

1. Marketing automation software (Marketo, HubSpot)
2. Email marketing software (Mailchimp, Constant Contact)
3. CRM software (Salesforce, Zoho)
4. Sales outreach tools (Outreach, SalesLoft)
5. Social media management tools (Hootsuite, Sprout Social)
6. Retargeting platforms (AdRoll, Perfect Audience)
7. Webinar software (GoToWebinar, Zoom)
8. Survey and feedback tools (SurveyMonkey, AskNicely)

Best Practices:

1. Personalize follow-up content
2. Segment and target follow-up efforts
3. Use multi-channel follow-up
4. Track and measure follow-up effectiveness
5. Optimize follow-up timing and frequency
6. Use A/B testing and experimentation
7. Leverage user-generated content
8. Utilize account-based marketing
9. Continuously refine and improve
10. Align follow-up with customer journey

Common Mistakes:

1. Insufficient follow-up
2. Poor timing and frequency
3. Lack of personalization
4. Ineffective content and messaging
5. Failure to track and measure
6. Ignoring mobile optimization
7. Not utilizing retargeting
8. Overlooking social proof
9. Inadequate landing page optimization
10. Lack of alignment with customer journey

Chapter 18: AI Tools for Lead Generation

☐ What is AI?

Artificial Intelligence (AI):

Definition: AI refers to the simulation of human intelligence in machines, enabling them to perform tasks that typically require human-like intelligence, such as learning, problem-solving, reasoning, perception, and decision-making.

Types of AI:

1. **Narrow or Weak AI:** Designed to perform a specific task, e.g., image recognition, language translation.
2. **General or Strong AI:** Aims to match human intelligence and perform any intellectual task.
3. **Super intelligence:** Significantly surpasses human intelligence.

AI Techniques:

1. **Machine Learning (ML):** Algorithms learn from data and improve performance.
2. **Deep Learning (DL):** Neural networks with multiple layers for complex tasks.
3. **Natural Language Processing (NLP):** Human language understanding and generation.
4. **Computer Vision:** Image and video analysis.
5. **Robotics:** Integration of AI with physical systems.

AI Applications:

1. Virtual Assistants (e.g., Siri, Alexa)
2. Image Recognition (e.g., facial recognition)
3. Predictive Analytics
4. Chatbots and Customer Service
5. Autonomous Vehicles
6. Healthcare Diagnosis and Treatment
7. Financial Forecasting and Trading
8. Cybersecurity
9. Education and Learning Platforms
10. Home Automation

AI Benefits:

1. Increased Efficiency
2. Improved Accuracy
3. Enhanced Decision-Making
4. Personalization
5. Automation
6. Cost Savings
7. Improved Customer Experience
8. Competitive Advantage
9. Scientific Discovery
10. Potential for Social Good

AI Challenges:

1. Data Quality and Availability
2. Bias and Fairness
3. Transparency and Explainability
4. Security and Privacy
5. Job Displacement
6. Ethics and Responsibility
7. Dependence on Technology
8. Cybersecurity Risks
9. Lack of Regulation
10. Potential Misuse

AI Future:

1. Integration with IoT and Edge Computing
2. Advancements in NLP and Computer Vision
3. Increased Adoption in Healthcare and Education
4. Autonomous Systems and Robotics

5. Quantum AI and Computing
6. Human-AI Collaboration
7. AI Governance and Regulation
8. AI for Social Good
9. AI-powered Creativity
10. Potential for Singularity

AI Tools for Direct Selling Marketing

AI Tools for Direct Selling Marketing:

Chatbots and Conversational AI:

1. **ManyChat:** Automate customer conversations and sales.
2. **Dialogflow:** Build conversational interfaces for sales and support.
3. **MobileMonkey:** Chatbot marketing platform for direct sales.

Predictive Analytics and Lead Scoring:

1. HubSpot: Predictive lead scoring and customer insights.
2. Salesforce Einstein: AI-powered sales forecasting and lead scoring.
3. Radius: Predictive analytics for sales and marketing.

Content Generation and Optimization:

1. WordLift: AI-powered content optimization and suggestion.
2. Content Blossom: AI-driven content generation for sales.
3. Acrolinx: AI-powered content optimization platform.

Email Marketing and Automation:

1. Mailchimp: AI-powered email marketing automation.
2. Constant Contact: AI-driven email marketing and automation.
3. Klaviyo: AI-powered email marketing and automation.

Social Media Management and Listening:

1. Hootsuite Insights: AI-powered social media listening and analytics.
2. Sprout Social: AI-driven social media management and scheduling.
3. Brandwatch: AI-powered social media monitoring and analytics.

Customer Segmentation and Personalization:

1. AgilOne: AI-powered customer segmentation and personalization.
2. Sailthru: AI-driven customer personalization and retention.
3. Certona: AI-powered customer segmentation and targeting.

Sales Forecasting and Pipeline Management:

1. Clari: AI-powered sales forecasting and pipeline management.
2. InsideView: AI-driven sales intelligence and forecasting.

3. HubSpot Sales: AI-powered sales forecasting and pipeline management.

Influencer Marketing and Identification:

1. AspireIQ: AI-powered influencer marketing and identification.
2. Upfluence: AI-driven influencer marketing and discovery.
3. HYPR: AI-powered influencer marketing and analytics.

Other AI Tools:

1. Google Cloud AI Platform: Build custom AI models for sales and marketing.
2. IBM Watson: AI-powered sales and marketing solutions.
3. Microsoft Azure Machine Learning: Build custom AI models for sales and marketing.

Benefits of AI in Direct Selling:

1. Increased efficiency and productivity.
2. Improved sales forecasting and pipeline management.
3. Enhanced customer personalization and experience.
4. Better lead scoring and qualification.
5. Increased revenue and growth.

Challenges and Limitations:

1. Data quality and availability.
2. Integration with existing systems.
3. Cost and budget constraints.
4. Lack of expertise and training.
5. Ethical concerns and transparency.

▢ Chatbots and conversational marketing

Chatbots and Conversational Marketing:
Chatbot Types:

1. Rule-based chatbots
2. AI-powered chatbots
3. Hybrid chatbots

Conversational Marketing Channels:

1. Messaging apps (Facebook Messenger, WhatsApp)
2. Website chat
3. Mobile apps
4. Voice assistants (Amazon Alexa, Google Assistant)
5. SMS

Chatbot Benefits:

1. 24/7 Customer Support
2. Improved Customer Engagement
3. Increased Conversions
4. Reduced Support Costs
5. Personalized Experience

Conversational Marketing Strategies:

1. Lead Generation
2. Qualification and Nurturing
3. Sales and Conversion
4. Customer Support and Retention

5. Brand Awareness and Engagement

Chatbot Platforms:

1. ManyChat
2. Dialogflow
3. MobileMonkey
4. Chatfuel
5. Tars

Conversational AI Tools:

1. Natural Language Processing (NLP)
2. Machine Learning (ML)
3. Sentiment Analysis
4. Intent Detection
5. Entity Recognition

Best Practices:

1. Define Clear Goals and Objectives
2. Choose the Right Platform
3. Design Conversational Flows
4. Test and Refine
5. Monitor and Analyze Performance

Common Challenges:

1. Integration with Existing Systems
2. Data Quality and Availability
3. Conversational Flow Design
4. Handling Complex Queries
5. Measuring ROI

Metrics and Measurement:

1. Conversation Rate
2. Conversion Rate
3. Customer Satisfaction (CSAT)
4. Net Promoter Score (NPS)
5. Return on Investment (ROI)

Future of Chatbots and Conversational Marketing:

1. Increased Adoption of Voice Assistants
2. Advancements in NLP and ML
3. Integration with AR and VR
4. Personalization and Contextualization
5. Expanded Use Cases and Industries

Real-World Examples:

1. Domino's Pizza Chatbot
2. Sephora's Virtual Assistant
3. Whole Foods Market Chatbot
4. Amtrak's AskJulie Chatbot
5. IBM's Watson Assistant

☐ Predictive analytics and scoring

Predictive Analytics and Scoring:

Predictive Analytics:

1. **Definition:** Using statistical models and machine learning algorithms to forecast future events or behaviors.
2. **Types:**
   - Regression analysis
   - Decision trees
   - Random forests
   - Neural networks
   - Clustering
3. **Applications:**
   - Customer churn prediction
   - Sales forecasting

- Credit risk assessment
- Marketing attribution
- Customer segmentation

Predictive Scoring:

1. **Definition:** Assigning a score to customers or prospects based on their likelihood to convert or churn.
2. **Types:**
    - Lead scoring
    - Customer scoring
    - Account scoring
3. **Benefits:**
    - Improved sales and marketing efficiency
    - Enhanced customer experience
    - Increased revenue
    - Reduced churn

Predictive Analytics Tools:

1. SAS
2. R
3. Python libraries (scikit-learn, TensorFlow)
4. IBM SPSS
5. Google Cloud AI Platform
6. Microsoft Azure Machine Learning
7. RapidMiner
8. KNIME
9. Oracle Advanced Analytics
10. Alteryx

Predictive Scoring Platforms:

1. HubSpot
2. Salesforce Einstein
3. Marketo
4. Pardot
5. Radius
6. 6sense
7. Lattice Engines
8. Infer
9. InsideView
10. Mintigo

Metrics for Predictive Analytics:

1. Accuracy
2. Precision
3. Recall
4. F1 score
5. Mean absolute error (MAE)
6. Mean squared error (MSE)
7. R-squared
8. Lift
9. ROI
10. Payback period

Best Practices:

1. Define clear goals and objectives
2. Collect and preprocess data
3. Choose the right algorithm
4. Test and validate models
5. Monitor and refine performance
6. Integrate with existing systems
7. Use explainable AI techniques
8. Address data quality issues
9. Continuously update models
10. Document and share results

Common Challenges:

1. Data quality and availability
2. Algorithm selection and tuning
3. Model interpretability
4. Integration with existing systems
5. Data privacy and security
6. Scalability and performance
7. Human bias in data
8. Concept drift
9. Limited domain expertise
10. High dimensionality

Real-World Examples:

1. Netflix's recommendation engine

2. Amazon's customer churn prediction
3. Google's search ranking algorithm
    4. American Express's credit risk assessment
5. Walmart's supply chain optimization

☐ Personalization and recommendation

Personalization and Recommendation:

Personalization:

1. **Definition:** Tailoring content, products, or experiences to individual users.
2. **Types:**
    - Content personalization
    - Product recommendation
    - Email personalization
    - Search personalization
3. **Benefits:**
    - Increased engagement
    - Improved conversion rates
    - Enhanced user experience
    - Increased customer loyalty

Recommendation Systems:

1. **Definition:** Algorithms suggesting products or content based on user behavior.
2. **Types:**
    - Collaborative filtering
    - Content-based filtering
    - Hybrid recommendation
    - Knowledge-based systems
3. **Benefits:**
    - Increased sales
    - Improved customer satisfaction
    - Reduced bounce rates
    - Increased average order value

Personalization Techniques:

1. User profiling
2. Behavioral targeting
3. Contextual targeting
4. A/B testing
5. Machine learning
6. Natural language processing (NLP)
7. Clustering
8. Segmentation

Recommendation Algorithms:

1. Collaborative filtering (CF)
2. Matrix factorization (MF)
3. Deep learning-based recommendation
4. Knowledge graph-based recommendation
5. Hybrid recommendation

Tools and Platforms:

1. Adobe Target
2. Salesforce Personalization

3. Google Optimize
4. Amazon Personalize
5. Microsoft Azure Personalization
6. IBM Watson Personalization
7. Evergage
8. Certona
9. RichRelevance
10. Monetate

Metrics and Measurement:

1. Click-through rate (CTR)
2. Conversion rate
3. Average order value (AOV)
4. Customer satisfaction (CSAT)
5. Net promoter score (NPS)
6. Return on investment (ROI)
7. Lift
8. Precision
9. Recall
10. F1 score

Best Practices:

1. Collect and integrate user data
2. Choose the right algorithm
3. Test and refine models
4. Consider contextual factors
5. Ensure transparency and control
6. Monitor and address bias
7. Continuously update models
8. Use explainable AI techniques
9. Document and share results
10. Ensure scalability

Common Challenges:

1. Data quality and availability
2. Algorithm selection and tuning
3. Model interpretability
4. Integration with existing systems
5. Data privacy and security
6. Scalability and performance
7. Human bias in data
8. Concept drift
9. Limited domain expertise
10. High dimensionality

Real-World Examples:

1. Netflix's recommendation engine
2. Amazon's personalized product recommendations
3. Google's personalized search results
4. Facebook's personalized news feed
5. Spotify's Discover Weekly playlist

- **Automated email and messaging**

Automated Email and Messaging:

Automated Email:

1. **Definition:** Sending targeted and personalized emails to customers/subscribers automatically.
2. **Benefits:**
    - Increased efficiency
    - Improved customer engagement
    - Enhanced personalization
    - Reduced manual effort
3. **Types:**
    - Welcome emails
    - Abandoned cart emails
    - Birthday/anniversary emails
    - Newsletter emails
    - Transactional emails

Automated Messaging:

1. **Definition:** Sending targeted and personalized messages to customers/subscribers through various channels (e.g., SMS, WhatsApp, Facebook Messenger).
2. **Benefits:**
   - Increased engagement
   - Improved customer experience
   - Enhanced personalization
   - Reduced manual effort
3. **Types:**
   - SMS marketing
   - WhatsApp marketing
   - Facebook Messenger marketing
   - Push notifications

Automation Tools:

1. Mailchimp
2. Constant Contact
3. HubSpot
4. Marketo
5. Pardot
6. Salesforce
7. Infusionsoft
8. ActiveCampaign
9. Klaviyo
10. Automator

Triggered Email/Messaging:

1. **Definition:** Sending automated emails/messages based on specific triggers (e.g., purchase, abandonment).
2. **Benefits:**
   - Increased relevance
   - Improved timing
   - Enhanced personalization
3. **Triggers:**
   - Purchase
   - Abandonment
   - Birthday/anniversary
   - Subscription anniversary
   - Inactivity

Best Practices: 1. Segment your audience

2. Personalize content
3. Optimize subject lines
4. Use clear and concise language
5. Test and refine
6. Ensure compliance with regulations
7. Monitor and analyze performance
8. Use automation workflows
9. Set clear goals and objectives
10. Continuously update and improve

Common Challenges:

1. Data quality and availability
2. Email deliverability
3. Spam filters
4. Unsubscribes
5. Limited resources
6. Technical issues
7. Measuring ROI
8. Integrating with existing systems
9. Ensuring compliance
10. Managing subscriber preferences

Metrics and Measurement:

1. Open rate
2. Click-through rate (CTR)
3. Conversion rate
4. Unsubscribe rate
5. Complaint rate
6. Return on investment (ROI)
7. Revenue per email (RPE)
8. Email sharing/forwarding rate
9. Customer satisfaction (CSAT)
10. Net promoter score (NPS)

Real-World Examples:

1. Amazon's abandoned cart emails
2. Uber's transactional emails
3. Netflix's personalized recommendations
4. Starbucks' loyalty program emails
5. Airbnb's automated messaging

- **Social media monitoring**

Social Media Monitoring:

Definition: Tracking and analyzing online conversations about a brand, competitor, or industry on social media platforms.

Benefits:

1. Brand awareness
2. Reputation management
3. Customer service
4. Competitive intelligence
5. Market research
6. Crisis management
7. Influencer identification
8. Sentiment analysis

Tools:

1. Hootsuite Insights
2. Sprout Social
3. Brandwatch
4. NetBase
5. Crimson Hexagon
6. Talkwalker
7. Social Studio
8. Brand24
9. Mention
10. Google Alerts

Metrics:

1. Sentiment analysis
2. Engagement rate
3. Follower growth
4. Conversation volume
5. Share of voice
6. Net promoter score (NPS)
7. Customer satisfaction (CSAT)
8. Response rate
9. Resolution rate
10. ROI

Social Media Platforms:

1. X (Twitter)
2. Facebook
3. Instagram
4. LinkedIn
5. YouTube
6. Reddit
7. Pinterest
8. TikTok
9. Snapchat
10. WhatsApp

Monitoring Techniques:

1. Keyword tracking
2. Hashtag tracking
3. Brand mention tracking
4. Competitor tracking
5. Industry tracking
6. Influencer tracking
7. Sentiment analysis
8. Natural language processing (NLP)
9. Machine learning
10. Human analysis

Best Practices:

1. Set clear objectives
2. Choose relevant keywords
3. Monitor competitor activity
4. Respond promptly to customer inquiries
5. Analyze sentiment and trends
6. Integrate with CRM
7. Use automation tools
8. Monitor influencer activity
9. Track ROI
10. Continuously refine strategy

Common Challenges:

1. Data overload
2. Noise and irrelevant data
3. Limited resources
4. Difficulty measuring ROI
5. Ensuring compliance
6. Managing crisis situations
7. Integrating with existing systems
8. Limited expertise
9. High volume of conversations
10. Ensuring accuracy

Real-World Examples:

1. Coca-Cola's social media command center
2. American Airlines' social media customer service
3. Nike's social media marketing campaigns
4. Starbucks' social media reputation management
5. Domino's Pizza's social media customer service

Part 5: Advanced Strategies and Tools

Chapter 19: Podcasting for Direct Sales

☐ What is Podcasting?

Definition: Podcasting is a form of online content delivery that allows users to download or stream audio files, typically in a series, to listen to at their convenience.

Benefits:

1. Flexibility: Listen anytime, anywhere
2. Targeted audience: Reach specific niches or interests
3. Cost-effective: Low production costs
4. Personal connection: Build relationships with listeners
5. Diversified content: Various formats (interviews, stories, educational)
6. Monetization: Sponsorships, ads, subscriptions

Types of Podcasts:

1. Interview-style
2. Storytelling
3. Educational
4. News and current events
5. Comedy
6. Fiction
7. Self-improvement
8. Business and entrepreneurship
9. Sports
10. Music

Podcasting Process:

1. Conceptualize and plan content
2. Record and edit audio
3. Publish on platforms (e.g., Apple Podcasts, Spotify)
4. Promote and market the podcast
5. Engage with listeners and gather feedback

Popular Podcasting Platforms:

1. Apple Podcasts
2. Spotify
3. Google Podcasts
4. Anchor
5. Castbox
6. Stitcher
7. TuneIn
8. Podbean
9. SoundCloud
10. Libsyn

Podcasting Equipment:

1. Microphone (e.g., USB, dynamic)
2. Audio interface (e.g., USB, mixer)
3. Headphones
4. Pop filter
5. Boom arm
6. Stand
7. Recording software (e.g., Audacity, Adobe Audition)

Monetization Strategies:

1. Sponsorships
2. Advertising (audio ads, display ads)
3. Subscriptions (e.g., Patreon)
4. Affiliate marketing
5. Selling merchandise or products
6. Premium content or exclusive episodes
7. Live events or webinars
8. Donations

Podcasting Metrics:

1. Downloads
2. Listenership growth
3. Engagement (comments, social media)
4. Ratings and reviews
5. Average listen time

6. Drop-off points
7. Demographics (age, location, interests)

Common Podcasting Challenges:

1. Consistency and scheduling
2. Audio quality and editing
3. Finding and retaining audience
4. Monetization and revenue growth
5. Competition and discoverability
6. Time commitment and burnout
7. Technical issues and troubleshooting

Podcasting Communities and Resources:

1. Podcasters Facebook Group
2. Reddit's r/podcasting
3. Podcasting communities (e.g., Podbean, Castbox)
4. Online courses and tutorials (e.g., Udemy, Coursera)
5. Podcasting conferences and events

☐ Choosing a niche and format

Choosing a Niche and Format:

Niche:

1. **Definition:** A specific area of interest or expertise.
2. **Importance:** Helps target audience, establish authority, and differentiate from others.
3. **Examples:**
   - Health and wellness
   - Personal finance
   - Marketing and entrepreneurship
   - Self-improvement
   - Technology

Format:

1. **Definition:** The style or structure of the podcast.
2. **Options:**
   - Interview-style
   - Solo episodes
   - Panel discussions
   - Storytelling
   - Educational
   - Q&A sessions
   - Product reviews
3. **Considerations:**
   - Target audience preferences
   - Content goals
   - Production resources

Niche Categories:

1. Business and entrepreneurship
2. Health and wellness
3. Personal development
4. Technology
5. Entertainment
6. Education
7. Finance
8. Travel

9. Food and drink
10. Arts and culture

Format Ideas:

1. Daily/weekly news updates
2. In-depth interviews with experts
3. Personal stories and experiences
4. How-to guides and tutorials
5. Panel discussions and debates
6. Product reviews and comparisons
7. Q&A sessions and advice
8. Case studies and success stories
9. Industry trends and analysis
10. Behind-the-scenes and vlogs

Target Audience:

1. Identify demographics (age, location, interests)
2. Understand pain points and needs
3. Create buyer personas
4. Research popular podcasts in niche

Niche and Format Combination:

1. "The Daily Health Tip" (health and wellness, daily format)
2. "The Entrepreneur's Journey" (business and entrepreneurship, storytelling)
3. "The Tech Review" (technology, product reviews)
4. "The Self-Improvement Show" (personal development, solo episodes)
5. "The Travel Podcast" (travel, interview-style)

Tools for Research:

1. Google Trends
2. Keyword research tools (e.g., Ahrefs, SEMrush)
3. Social media listening tools (e.g., Hootsuite, Sprout Social)
4. Online forums and communities
5. Podcast directories (e.g., Apple Podcasts, Spotify)

☐ Creating engaging podcast content

Content Strategy:

1. Define target audience and goals
2. Research popular podcasts in niche
3. Develop unique angle or perspective
4. Plan content calendar
5. Create engaging titles and descriptions

Episode Types:

1. Interview-style episodes
2. Solo episodes (educational, storytelling)
3. Panel discussions
4. Case studies
5. Q&A sessions
6. Product reviews
7. How-to guides
8. Industry news and analysis
9. Personal stories
10. Debates

Content Creation Tips:

1. Start with a hook (interesting fact, quote)
2. Use storytelling techniques
3. Make it conversational
4. Use humor and anecdotes
5. Provide valuable insights and takeaways
6. Keep it concise and focused
7. Use audio elements (music, sound effects)
8. Edit and produce professionally
9. Encourage audience engagement
10. Repurpose content (blog posts, social media)

Interview Techniques:

1. Prepare thoughtful questions
2. Research guest's background

3. Create a comfortable atmosphere
4. Active listening
5. Follow-up questions
6. Keep it conversational
7. Avoid yes/no questions
8. Use open-ended questions
9. Encourage storytelling
10. Keep it concise

Storytelling Techniques:

1. Start with a hook
2. Create a narrative arc
3. Use descriptive language
4. Make it personal
5. Use emotional connections
6. Keep it concise
7. Use vivid imagery
8. Create tension and resolution
9. Use dialogue
10. Encourage reflection

Audio Production Tips:

1. Use high-quality equipment
2. Record in a quiet space
3. Use pop filter and windscreen
4. Adjust audio levels
5. Edit and produce professionally
6. Add music and sound effects
7. Use noise reduction tools
8. Normalize audio levels
9. Create a consistent sound
10. Master audio files

Engagement Strategies:

1. Ask questions
2. Host Q&A sessions
3. Create a community
4. Encourage feedback
5. Host contests and giveaways
6. Offer exclusive content
7. Collaborate with other podcasters
8. Host live episodes
9. Create a podcast newsletter
10. Engage on social media

☐ Guest selection and interviewing

Guest Selection Criteria:

1. Relevance to the podcast's niche and audience
2. Expertise and authority in the field
3. Unique perspective or experience
4. Engaging personality and communication style
5. Availability and scheduling flexibility
6. Alignment with podcast's tone and format
7. Potential for controversy or debate
8. Audience demand or request
9. Guest's promotional capabilities
10. Diversity and representation

Finding Guests:

1. Social media and online communities
2. Industry events and conferences
3. Referrals from existing guests or listeners
4. Online directories and databases
5. Public relations agencies
6. Author and expert platforms
7. Podcast guest networks
8. Research and academic institutions
9. Professional associations
10. Local businesses and organizations

Pre-Interview Research:

1. Review guest's work and publications
2. Research their background and expertise
3. Identify potential topics and questions
4. Review previous interviews and media appearances
5. Check social media and online presence
6. Prepare thoughtful and insightful questions
7. Familiarize yourself with industry terminology
8. Review podcast's tone and format
9. Prepare for potential controversies

10. Develop a clear understanding of guest's goals

Interview Techniques:

1. Active listening
2. Open-ended questions
3. Follow-up questions
4. Probing for deeper insights
5. Encouraging storytelling
6. Creating a comfortable atmosphere
7. Avoiding yes/no questions
8. Using silence effectively
9. Pacing the conversation
10. Showing genuine interest

Conducting Remote Interviews:

1. Choose reliable recording software
2. Test equipment and internet connection
3. Use high-quality headphones and microphone
4. Minimize background noise
5. Use video conferencing tools
6. Record in a quiet space
7. Consider time zone differences
8. Have a backup plan
9. Test guest's equipment
10. Record multiple takes

Post-Interview Process:

1. Thank the guest and provide feedback
2. Transcribe and edit the interview
3. Add intro/outro segments
4. Mix and master audio
5. Publish and promote the episode
6. Share on social media
7. Encourage guest to share
8. Monitor engagement and feedback
9. Follow up with guest
10. Evaluate interview effectiveness

☐ Promotion and distribution

Promotion and Distribution:
Pre-Launch Promotion

1. Create buzz on social media
2. Share behind-the-scenes content
3. Host a giveaway or contest
4. Offer exclusive early access
5. Collaborate with influencers

Launch Day Promotion

1. Send out a press release
2. Host a live event or webinar
3. Offer a limited-time discount
4. Share user-generated content
5. Utilize paid advertising

Ongoing Promotion

1. Social media marketing
2. Email marketing
3. Content marketing
4. Influencer partnerships
5. Referral programs
6. Affiliate marketing
7. Podcast guesting
8. Online communities
9. Guest blogging
10. Video marketing

Distribution Channels

1. Apple Podcasts
2. Spotify
3. Google Podcasts
4. Stitcher
5. TuneIn
6. YouTube
7. Castbox
8. Podbean
9. Overcast

10. Pocket Casts

SEO Optimization

1. Keyword research
2. Optimize podcast title and description
3. Use relevant tags and categories
4. Create transcripts
5. Use header tags
6. Internal linking
7. Image optimization
8. Mobile-friendliness
9. Page speed
10. Analytics tracking

Analytics and Tracking

1. Podcast analytics tools (e.g., Anchor, Podtrac)
2. Website analytics tools (e.g., Google Analytics)
3. Social media analytics tools (e.g., Hootsuite)
4. Email marketing analytics tools (e.g., Mailchimp)
5. Track engagement metrics (e.g., likes, comments, shares)

Cross-Promotion

1. Collaborate with other podcasters
2. Guest blog on relevant sites
3. Participate in online communities
4. Share user-generated content
5. Host a podcast crossover episode

Paid Advertising

1. Facebook Ads
2. Google AdWords
3. LinkedIn Ads
4. Twitter Ads
5. Podcast-specific ads (e.g., Midroll, Anchor)

Influencer Partnerships

1. Identify relevant influencers
2. Reach out for collaboration
3. Offer exclusive content
4. Sponsor influencer episodes
5. Monitor and track results

Community Building

1. Create a private Facebook group
2. Host live events or webinars
3. Offer exclusive content
4. Encourage user-generated content
5. Engage with listeners on social media

☐ Monetization and sponsorship

Monetization Strategies:

1. Advertising (pre-roll, mid-roll, post-roll)
2. Sponsored content
3. Affiliate marketing
4. Selling products or merchandise
5. Premium content or membership
6. Podcast networks
7. Dynamic ad insertion
8. Branded content
9. Influencer partnerships
10. Live events and ticket sales

Sponsorship Models:

1. Pre-roll sponsorships
2. Integrated sponsorships
3. Segment sponsorships
4. Product placements
5. Branded content sponsorships
6. Event sponsorships
7. Podcast network sponsorships
8. Dynamic ad insertion sponsorships
9. Affiliate sponsorships
10. Exclusive sponsorships

Sponsorship Platforms:

1. Midroll
2. Anchor

3. Podtrac
4. AdsWizz
5. Spotify Ad Studio
6. Google AdMob
7. Facebook Audience Network
8. Amazon Associates
9. ShareASale
10. Commission Junction

Sponsorship Rates:

1. CPM (cost per thousand listeners)
2. CPC (cost per click)
3. CPA (cost per acquisition)
4. Flat rate
5. Dynamic pricing

Sponsorship Best Practices:

1. Clearly define sponsorship goals
2. Choose relevant sponsors
3. Disclose sponsorships transparently
4. Create engaging sponsored content
5. Monitor and track sponsorship performance
6. Build relationships with sponsors
7. Offer exclusive sponsorships
8. Utilize multiple sponsorship channels
9. Optimize sponsorship creative
10. Ensure compliance with regulations

Monetization Metrics:

1. Revenue growth
2. Listener engagement
3. Conversion rates
4. Click-through rates
5. Sponsorship ROI
6. Ad completion rates
7. Average ad revenue per listener
8. Podcast revenue share
9. Sponsorship retention rate
10. Net promoter score (NPS)

Monetization Tools:

1. Podcast analytics tools (e.g., Anchor, Podtrac)
2. Ad management platforms (e.g., AdsWizz, Google AdMob)
3. Sponsorship management platforms (e.g., Midroll, Podtrac)
4. Affiliate marketing platforms (e.g., Amazon Associates, ShareASale)
5. E-commerce platforms (e.g., Shopify, WooCommerce)

Chapter 20: Utilizing Quora and Blogger

☐ What is Quora and Blogger?

Quora and Blogger:
Quora:

Definition: Quora is a question-and-answer website where users can ask and answer questions on various topics.

Features:

1. Q&A format
2. User-generated content
3. Voting system (upvotes and downvotes)
4. Commenting and discussion
5. Topics and categories
6. Expert answers
7. Anonymous answering

Benefits:

1. Knowledge sharing
2. Research and learning
3. Networking and community building
4. Personal branding and expertise establishment
5. Content marketing and promotion
6. SEO benefits
7. Feedback and critique

Quora Usage:

1. Ask questions
2. Answer questions
3. Follow topics and users
4. Comment and engage
5. Share content
6. Participate in Spaces (Quora's community feature)
7. Utilize Quora's blogging feature (Quora Blogs)

Blogger:

Definition: Blogger is a free blogging platform owned by Google.

Features:

1. Free hosting
2. Customizable templates
3. Easy posting and editing
4. Integration with Google services (e.g., Analytics, AdSense)
5. SEO optimization
6. Commenting and moderation
7. Mobile-responsive designs

Benefits:

1. Easy blogging for beginners
2. Free hosting and maintenance
3. Integration with Google services
4. Customization options
5. SEO benefits
6. Community building and engagement
7. Monetization opportunities (AdSense)

Blogger Usage:

1. Create and publish posts
2. Customize blog design and layout
3. Optimize for SEO
4. Engage with readers through comments
5. Use Google Analytics for tracking
6. Monetize with AdSense
7. Integrate with social media platforms

Comparison:

Quora vs. Blogger:

1. Purpose: Quora (Q&A) vs. Blogger (blogging)
2. Content style: Quora (short answers) vs. Blogger (long-form posts)
3. Audience: Quora (general knowledge seekers) vs. Blogger (specific niche audiences)
4. Engagement: Quora (commenting and voting) vs. Blogger (commenting and subscription)

Best Practices:

Quora:

1. Provide valuable and informative answers
2. Use proper formatting and grammar
3. Engage with others through comments
4. Follow Quora's guidelines and rules
5. Utilize Quora's Spaces feature

Blogger:

1. Create high-quality, engaging content
2. Optimize for SEO
3. Customize and brand your blog
4. Engage with readers through comments
5. Utilize Google Analytics for tracking

☐ Creating informative content

Creating Informative Content:

Types of Informative Content:

1. Blog posts
2. Articles
3. Videos
4. Podcasts
5. Infographics
6. E-books
7. Whitepapers
8. Case studies
9. Webinars
10. Online courses

Characteristics of Informative Content:

1. Accurate and reliable information
2. Clear and concise language
3. Engaging and attention-grabbing headlines
4. Relevant and useful to target audience
5. Well-researched and supported by data
6. Easy to understand and digest
7. Visually appealing and formatted
8. Free of bias and opinion
9. Up-to-date and timely
10. Provides actionable insights

Content Creation Strategies:

1. Identify target audience and their needs
2. Conduct thorough research and analysis
3. Create a content calendar
4. Develop a unique and compelling angle
5. Use storytelling techniques
6. Incorporate visuals and multimedia
7. Optimize for SEO
8. Repurpose and reuse content
9. Collaborate with experts and influencers

10. Encourage feedback and engagement

Research and Validation:

1. Use credible sources and references
2. Verify information through fact-checking
3. Conduct surveys and interviews
4. Analyze data and statistics
5. Consult with experts and industry leaders
6. Use academic and peer-reviewed sources
7. Evaluate information for bias and accuracy
8. Consider multiple perspectives
10. Validate information through experimentation
11. Document and cite sources

Content Optimization:

1. Use keywords and meta descriptions
2. Optimize images and alt text
3. Internal and external linking
4. Use header tags and formatting
5. Mobile-friendliness and accessibility
6. Page speed and loading time
7. Social media sharing and promotion
8. Email marketing and newsletters
9. Content refresh and updates
10. Analytics and tracking

Repurposing Content:

1. Turn blog posts into videos
2. Create infographics from data
3. Develop e-books from series of posts
4. Convert webinars into online courses
5. Share podcasts on social media
6. Create case studies from success stories
7. Develop whitepapers from research
8. Turn videos into podcasts
9. Create social media posts from blog content
10. Share content on relevant platforms

☐ Building authority and credibility

Building Authority and Credibility:
Establishing Expertise:

1. Share relevant and valuable content
2. Participate in industry events and conferences
3. Publish research or whitepapers
4. Offer training or workshops
5. Collaborate with other experts

Building Credibility:

1. Showcase customer testimonials
2. Highlight awards and recognition
3. Display credentials and certifications
4. Share success stories and case studies
5. Provide transparent and honest communication

Authority Signals:

1. Authoritative tone and language
2. High-quality and relevant content
3. Professional branding and design
4. Consistent messaging and positioning
5. Strong online presence

Credibility Indicators:

1. Customer reviews and ratings
2. Industry endorsements and recommendations
3. Media coverage and press mentions
4. Awards and recognition
5. Transparent business practices

Thought Leadership:

1. Publish original research and insights
2. Offer unique perspectives and opinions
3. Participate in industry debates and discussions
4. Host webinars and conferences
5. Create and share valuable resources

Personal Branding:

1. Develop a strong online presence
2. Establish a consistent tone and voice
3. Showcase expertise and credentials
4. Engage with audience and build relationships
5. Consistently produce high-quality content

Networking and Partnerships:

1. Collaborate with other experts and influencers
2. Participate in industry events and conferences
3. Join relevant associations and organizations
4. Partner with complementary businesses
5. Engage in online communities and forums

Content Marketing Strategies:

1. Blogging and guest blogging
2. Video marketing and YouTube
3. Podcasting and audio content
4. Social media marketing
5. Email marketing and newsletters

Metrics for Measuring Authority and Credibility:

1. Website traffic and engagement
2. Social media following and engagement
3. Customer acquisition and retention
4. Revenue growth
5. Industry recognition and awards

☐ Engaging with audiences

Engaging with Audiences:
Importance of Engagement

1. Builds loyalty and trust
2. Increases brand awareness
3. Encourages feedback and improvement
4. Drives conversions and sales
5. Enhances customer experience

Types of Engagement

1. Social media engagement (likes, comments, shares)
2. Content engagement (blog comments, email opens)
3. Community engagement (forums, discussions)
4. Event engagement (webinars, conferences)
5. Customer support engagement (tickets, phone calls)

Strategies for Engagement

1. Respond to comments and messages promptly
2. Ask questions and spark conversations
3. Share user-generated content
4. Host Q&A sessions and webinars
5. Offer exclusive content and rewards
6. Utilize polls and surveys
7. Collaborate with influencers
8. Run contests and giveaways

9. Share behind-the-scenes content
10. Analyze and adjust engagement strategies

Social Media Engagement

1. Facebook: comments, likes, shares
2. Twitter: replies, retweets, hashtags
3. Instagram: comments, likes, stories
4. LinkedIn: comments, likes, shares
5. YouTube: comments, likes, subscriptions

Content Engagement

1. Blog comments
2. Email open rates
3. Click-through rates (CTR)
4. Time on page
5. Bounce rate

Community Engagement

1. Forum participation
2. Discussion board engagement
3. Social media group engagement
4. Online course engagement
5. Event attendance

Metrics for Measuring Engagement

1. Engagement rate
2. Conversion rate
3. Customer retention rate
4. Net promoter score (NPS)
5. Customer satisfaction (CSAT)

Tools for Engagement

1. Social media management tools (Hootsuite, Sprout Social)
2. Email marketing tools (Mailchimp, Constant Contact)
3. Content management systems (WordPress, Drupal)
4. Community management tools (Discourse, Higher Logic)
5. Analytics tools (Google Analytics, Mixpanel)

☐ Driving traffic and sales

Driving Traffic and Sales:
Traffic Generation Strategies:

1. Search Engine Optimization (SEO)
2. Pay-Per-Click (PPC) Advertising
3. Social Media Marketing
4. Content Marketing
5. Email Marketing
6. Influencer Marketing
7. Affiliate Marketing
8. Referral Marketing
9. Podcasting
10. Video Marketing

Conversion Optimization:

1. Landing Page Optimization
2. Call-to-Action (CTA) Optimization
3. Form Optimization
4. Button Optimization
5. Image Optimization
6. Headline Optimization
7. Social Proof
8. Urgency Tactics
9. Scarcity Tactics
10. A/B Testing

Sales Funnel Strategies:

1. Awareness Stage: Educate and Inform
2. Interest Stage: Build Desire and Interest
3. Decision Stage: Encourage Action
4. Action Stage: Convert Leads to Sales
5. Retention Stage: Build Customer Loyalty

Email Marketing Strategies:

1. Welcome Emails
2. Abandoned Cart Emails
3. Newsletter Emails
4. Promotional Emails
5. Transactional Emails
6. Automated Email Sequences
7. Personalized Email Campaigns
8. Segmented Email Lists
9. Email Marketing Automation
10. Email Analytics and Tracking

Social Media Strategies:

1. Facebook Ads
2. Instagram Ads
3. Twitter Ads
4. LinkedIn Ads
5. YouTube Ads
6. Social Media Content Calendar
7. Influencer Partnerships
8. Social Media Contests
9. Social Media Analytics
10. Social Media Engagement

Measurement and Analytics:

1. Google Analytics
2. Conversion Tracking
3. A/B Testing Tools
4. Email Marketing Analytics
5. Social Media Analytics
6. Sales Funnel Analytics
7. Customer Lifetime Value (CLV)
8. Return on Investment (ROI)
9. Customer Acquisition Cost (CAC)
10. Net Promoter Score (NPS)

Tools and Platforms:

1. Google Analytics
2. HubSpot
3. Mailchimp
4. Hootsuite
5. Sprout Social
6. AdWords
7. Facebook Ads Manager
8. Instagram Ads Manager
9. Shopify
10. Salesforce

☐ **Measuring success**

Measuring Success:
Key Performance Indicators (KPIs)

1. Website traffic
2. Engagement metrics (likes, comments, shares)
3. Conversion rates
4. Sales and revenue
5. Customer acquisition cost (CAC)
6. Customer lifetime value (CLV)
7. Return on investment (ROI)
8. Net promoter score (NPS)
9. Email open and click-through rates
10. Social media metrics (followers, reach, impressions)

Analytics Tools

1. Google Analytics
2. Google Tag Manager
3. Mixpanel
4. HubSpot
5. Salesforce
6. Mailchimp
7. Hootsuite Insights
8. Sprout Social
9. Facebook Analytics
10. Instagram Insights

Metrics for Podcasts

1. Downloads and listens
2. Engagement metrics (comments, ratings, reviews)
3. Conversion rates
4. Sponsorship revenue
5. Advertising revenue
6. Affiliate marketing revenue
7. Patron support
8. Audience demographics
9. Listener retention
10. Average listen time

Metrics for Social Media

1. Follower growth
2. Engagement rate
3. Reach and impressions
4. Click-through rate (CTR)
5. Conversion rate
6. Hashtag performance
7. Sentiment analysis
8. Share of voice
9. Social media ROI
10. Influencer partnership ROI

Metrics for Email Marketing

1. Open rate
2. Click-through rate (CTR)
3. Conversion rate
4. Unsubscribe rate
5. Bounce rate
6. Complaint rate
7. Email deliverability
8. Spam filter rate
9. Email client compatibility
10. ROI

Metrics for Sales Funnel

1. Conversion rate
2. Drop-off rate
3. Average order value (AOV)
4. Customer lifetime value (CLV)
5. Customer acquisition cost (CAC)
6. Return on investment (ROI)
7. Sales funnel completion rate
8. Lead-to-customer conversion rate
9. Sales cycle length
10. Sales velocity

Chapter 21: Pinterest and Printrest Marketing

☐ What is Pinterest and Printrest Marketing?

Pinterest and Pinterest Marketing:

What is Pinterest?

Pinterest is a social media platform that allows users to share and discover images and videos (called "Pins") organized into boards and categories. Users can browse, save, and share content from others, creating a virtual pinboard.

Key Features:

1. Visual discovery and planning
2. Boards and categories
3. Pins (images and videos)
4. Repinning and sharing
5. Comments and messaging
6. Hashtags and search
7. Shopping and e-commerce integration

What is Pinterest Marketing?

Pinterest marketing refers to the use of Pinterest as a platform to promote products, services, or brands. Businesses create boards, pin images and videos, and engage with users to:

Goals:

1. Increase brand awareness
2. Drive website traffic
3. Generate leads
4. Boost sales
5. Improve customer engagement

Pinterest Marketing Strategies:
Benefits:

1. Targeted audience (primarily female, 25-45)
2. High engagement rates
3. Long-term visibility
4. Cost-effective advertising
5. Measurable ROI

Pinterest Marketing Tools:

1. Pinterest Analytics
2. Pinterest Ads Manager

1. Create engaging boards and pins
2. Optimize pins for search
3. Utilize hashtags
4. Leverage shopping ads
5. Collaborate with influencers
6. Run contests and giveaways
7. Share user-generated content
8. Utilize Pinterest Analytics
3. Pinterest Shopping
4. Hootsuite
5. Sprout Social
6. Tailwind
7. Canva

Best Practices:

1. High-quality visuals
2. Consistent branding
3. Engage with audience
4. Utilize relevant hashtags
5. Monitor and adjust strategy

☐ Creating boards and pins

Creating Boards and Pins:

Boards:

1. Create relevant and specific boards
2. Organize boards into categories
3. Use descriptive board names and descriptions
4. Add high-quality board covers
5. Utilize sections within boards

Pins:

1. High-quality, visually appealing images
2. Optimize pin images for mobile
3. Use descriptive pin descriptions
4. Include relevant keywords and hashtags
5. Add calls-to-action (CTAs)

Pin Types:

1. Standard pins
2. Shopping pins
3. Video pins
4. Carousel pins
5. Story pins

Design Tips:

1. Use bright, bold colors
2. Include text overlays
3. Utilize graphics and illustrations
4. Add logos and branding
5. Experiment with different layouts

Optimization:

1. Use relevant keywords in descriptions
2. Include hashtags (max 10)
3. Utilize Pinterest's auto-suggest feature
4. Optimize pin images for SEO
5. Monitor and adjust pin performance

Tools:

1. Canva
2. Adobe Creative Cloud
3. Pinterest's built-in image editor
4. PicMonkey
5. GIMP

Best Practices:

1. Pin consistently
2. Engage with audience
3. Monitor analytics
4. Adjust strategy
5. Utilize Pinterest's features (e.g., shopping, stories)

Pinterest-Specific Features:

1. Rich Pins
2. Shopping ads
3. Story Pins
4. Carousel Pins
5. Lens

Optimizing images and descriptions

Optimizing Images and Descriptions:
Image Optimization:

1. Use high-quality, relevant images
2. Optimize image size (500-735 pixels wide)
3. Use JPEG or PNG format
4. Compress images (e.g., TinyPNG)
5. Add alt text and descriptions
6. Use descriptive file names
7. Utilize image editing tools (e.g., Canva, Adobe)

Description Optimization:

1. Write descriptive, concise descriptions
2. Include relevant keywords (max 10)
3. Use hashtags (max 10)
4. Add calls-to-action (CTAs)
5. Include URLs or links
6. Utilize Pinterest's description character limit (500)
7. Use descriptive, attention-grabbing headlines

Keyword Research:

1. Utilize Pinterest's auto-suggest feature
2. Research relevant keywords (e.g., Google Keyword Planner)
3. Analyze competitors' keywords
4. Use long-tail keywords
5. Incorporate keywords in descriptions and hashtags

Hashtag Strategy:

1. Research relevant hashtags
2. Use a mix of niche and broad hashtags
3. Limit hashtags to 10 per pin
4. Utilize hashtag research tools (e.g., Hashtagify)
5. Create a unique hashtag for branding

Alt Text and File Names:

1. Write descriptive alt text
2. Include target keywords in alt text
3. Use descriptive file names
4. Include target keywords in file names
5. Utilize tools (e.g., Adobe) for alt text and file name optimization

Pinterest-Specific Features:

1. Rich Pins
2. Shopping ads
3. Story Pins
4. Carousel Pins
5. Lens

Tools:

1. Canva
2. Adobe Creative Cloud
3. Pinterest's built-in image editor
4. PicMonkey
5. GIMP
6. Hashtagify
7. Google Keyword Planner

Best Practices:

1. Optimize images and descriptions consistently
2. Monitor analytics
3. Adjust strategy
4. Utilize Pinterest's features
5. Engage with audience

Using hashtags and keywords

Using Hashtags and Keywords:
Hashtag Strategy:

1. Research relevant hashtags
2. Use a mix of niche and broad hashtags
3. Limit hashtags to 10 per pin
4. Utilize hashtag research tools (e.g., Hashtagify)
5. Create a unique hashtag for branding
6. Monitor hashtag performance
7. Adjust hashtag strategy

Keyword Research:

1. Utilize Pinterest's auto-suggest feature
2. Research relevant keywords (e.g., Google Keyword Planner)
3. Analyze competitors' keywords
4. Use long-tail keywords
5. Incorporate keywords in descriptions and hashtags
6. Monitor keyword performance
7. Adjust keyword strategy

Keyword Placement:

1. Descriptions
2. Hashtags
3. Pin titles
4. Board names
5. Profile description

Hashtag Types:

1. Niche hashtags (e.g., #veganrecipes)
2. Broad hashtags (e.g., #food)
3. Branded hashtags (e.g., #mybrand)
4. Seasonal hashtags (e.g., #summerrecipes)
5. Event-based hashtags (e.g., #holidaycooking)

Tools:

1. Hashtagify
2. Google Keyword Planner
3. Pinterest's auto-suggest feature
4. Ahrefs
5. SEMrush
6. Hootsuite Insights
7. Sprout Social

Best Practices:

1. Use relevant and specific hashtags
2. Limit hashtag usage
3. Monitor performance
4. Adjust strategy
5. Utilize tools
6. Create a unique hashtag
7. Engage with audience

Common Mistakes:

1. Overusing hashtags
2. Using irrelevant hashtags
3. Not monitoring performance
4. Not adjusting strategy
5. Not utilizing tools

Engaging with audience

Engaging with Audience:

Importance of Engagement:

1. Builds loyalty and trust
2. Increases brand awareness
3. Encourages feedback and improvement
4. Drives conversions and sales
5. Enhances customer experience

Engagement Strategies:

1. Respond to comments and messages promptly
2. Ask questions and spark conversations
3. Share user-generated content
4. Host Q&A sessions and webinars
5. Offer exclusive content and rewards
6. Utilize polls and surveys
7. Collaborate with influencers
8. Run contests and giveaways
9. Share behind-the-scenes content
10. Analyze and adjust engagement strategy

Pinterest-Specific Engagement:

1. Comment on pins
2. Respond to comments on your pins
3. Use Pinterest's messaging feature
4. Host Pinterest contests
5. Utilize Pinterest's polling feature
6. Share user-generated pins
7. Collaborate with Pinterest influencers
8. Utilize Pinterest's story feature
9. Share exclusive content
10. Monitor Pinterest analytics

Tools for Engagement:

1. Pinterest Analytics
2. Hootsuite Insights
3. Sprout Social
4. Buffer
5. Canva
6. Pinterest's built-in messaging feature
7. Pinterest's comment moderation tool
8. Social media management tools

Metrics for Measuring Engagement:

1. Engagement rate
2. Comment rate
3. Like rate
4. Repin rate
5. Click-through rate (CTR)
6. Conversion rate
7. Net promoter score (NPS)
8. Customer satisfaction (CSAT)

Best Practices:

1. Respond promptly to comments and messages
2. Be authentic and transparent
3. Utilize humor and personality
4. Share user-generated content
5. Monitor and adjust engagement strategy
6. Utilize Pinterest's features
7. Collaborate with influencers
8. Run contests and giveaways
9. Share exclusive content
10. Analyze engagement metrics

Running Pinterest Ads

Running Pinterest Ads:
Benefits of Pinterest Ads:

1. Targeted audience
2. High engagement rates
3. Cost-effective
4. Increased brand awareness
5. Drive website traffic and sales

Types of Pinterest Ads:

1. Sponsored Pins
2. Shopping Ads
3. Video Ads
4. Carousel Ads
5. Story Ads
6. App Install Ads

Ad Formats:

1. Image Ads
2. Video Ads
3. Carousel Ads
4. Collection Ads
5. Shopping Ads

Targeting Options:

1. Demographics
2. Interests
3. Keywords
4. Lookalike targeting
5. Retargeting
6. Custom audiences

Bidding Strategies:

1. Cost Per Click (CPC)
2. Cost Per Thousand Impressions (CPM)
3. Cost Per Conversion (CPC)
4. Automatic bidding

Ad Creation:

1. Image and video requirements
2. Ad copy and description
3. Call-to-action (CTA)
4. Destination URL
5. Tracking and analytics

Pinterest Ads Manager:

1. Campaign creation
2. Ad group creation
3. Budget and bidding
4. Targeting and scheduling
5. Tracking and analytics

Metrics for Measuring Success:

1. Click-through rate (CTR)
2. Conversion rate
3. Cost per conversion (CPC)
4. Return on ad spend (ROAS)
5. Impressions and reach

Best Practices:

1. Define clear objectives
2. Choose relevant targeting options
3. Optimize ad creative
4. Monitor and adjust bidding
5. Track and analyze performance

Common Mistakes:

1. Poor targeting
2. Low-quality ad creative
3. Inadequate budget
4. Insufficient tracking
5. Lack of optimization

Tools and Resources:

1. Pinterest Ads Manager
2. Pinterest Analytics
3. Hootsuite Ads
4. Sprout Social Ads
5. AdEspresso

Pinterest Ads cost in India and International

Pinterest Ads costs vary depending on several factors, including your company's goals, industry, budget, and more. Here's a breakdown of what you can expect to pay:

- Cost Per Click (CPC): $0.00 to $0.10 per click, with 43% of businesses spending less than $0.20 per click.
- Cost Per Conversion: $0.00 to $8.00 per conversion, with 66% of businesses spending less than $8.00 per conversion.
- Cost Per 1000 Impressions (CPM): $0.00 to $1.50 per 1000 impressions, with 52% of businesses spending less than $1.50 per 1000 impressions.
- Monthly Budget: $0.00 to $500 per month, with 59% of businesses allocating 0% to 30% of their overall advertising budget to Pinterest Ads.

It's also important to note that Pinterest Ads pricing is influenced by factors such as:

- Ad structure
- Audience targeting choices
- Bid amount
- Competition level
- Ad placement
- Ad relevancy

Unfortunately, I couldn't find specific information on Pinterest Ads costs in India. However, these general estimates should give you a good idea of what to expect.

Chapter 22: White Labeling tools or Software's

☐ **What is White Labeling tools or software's and how to use it for Direct Selling Marketing?**

White Labeling Tools and Software:

Definition: White labeling refers to the practice of rebranding a product or service with one's own branding, logo, and identity, while the original creator or manufacturer remains anonymous.

Benefits:

1. Customization
2. Increased credibility
3. Improved branding
4. Enhanced customer trust
5. Cost-effective
6. Flexibility
7. Scalability

Types of White Labeling Tools and Software:

1. Website builders (e.g., WordPress, Wix)
2. Email marketing platforms (e.g., Mailchimp, Constant Contact)
3. Marketing automation tools (e.g., HubSpot, Marketo)
4. CRM software (e.g., Salesforce, Zoho)
5. E-commerce platforms (e.g., Shopify, Magento)
6. Social media management tools (e.g., Hootsuite, Sprout Social)
7. Content creation tools (e.g., Canva, Adobe Creative Cloud)

Direct Selling Marketing Applications:

1. Branded websites for distributors
2. Customized email marketing campaigns
3. Personalized marketing automation
4. Distributor-specific CRM systems
5. Branded e-commerce stores
6. Social media management for distributors
7. Customized content creation

How to Use White Labeling Tools and Software:

1. Choose a white labeling platform
2. Customize the platform with your branding
3. Integrate with existing systems (e.g., CRM, email marketing)
4. Train distributors on platform usage
5. Monitor and analyze performance
6. Optimize and refine platform usage
7. Scale platform usage as needed

Popular White Labeling Platforms for Direct Selling:

1. ByDesign Technologies
2. Krato Systems
3. DirectScale
4. Exigo
5. MultiSoft
6. Pro MLM Software
7. Xennsoft

Best Practices:

1. Ensure seamless integration with existing systems
2. Provide comprehensive training for distributors
3. Monitor and analyze performance regularly
4. Maintain consistent branding across platforms
5. Offer scalable solutions for growing businesses

6. Ensure security and compliance with industry regulations
7. Continuously evaluate and improve platform usage

Common Challenges:

1. Integration complexities
2. Customization limitations
3. Distributor adoption rates
4. Technical support requirements
5. Scalability issues
6. Security concerns
7. Cost and ROI considerations

☐ What is White Labeling tools or software's cost in India and International and contact details and support.

Popular White Labeling Tools/Software:

International:

1. ByDesign Technologies
2. Krato Systems
3. DirectScale
4. Exigo
5. MultiSoft
6. Pro MLM Software
7. Xennsoft

India:

1. MLM Software India
2. Direct Selling Software
3. MLM Solutions
4. Pro MLM Software India
5. MLM Technology

Cost:

International:

1. ByDesign Technologies: Custom pricing
2. Krato Systems: $500-$5,000/month
3. DirectScale: $500-$5,000/month
4. Exigo: $1,000-$10,000/month
5. MultiSoft: $500-$5,000/month

India:

1. MLM Software India: ₹50,000 - ₹500,000 (one-time)

2. Direct Selling Software: ₹30,000 - ₹300,000 (one-time)
3. MLM Solutions: ₹50,000 - ₹500,000 (one-time)
4. Pro MLM Software India: ₹30,000 - ₹300,000 (one-time)
5. MLM Technology: ₹50,000 - ₹500,000 (one-time)

Contact Details and Support:

International:

1. ByDesign Technologies: +1 877-435-4346, support@bydesign.com
2. Krato Systems: +1 855-572-8686, support@kratosystems.com
3. DirectScale: +1 855-355-4267, support@directscale.com
4. Exigo: +1 855-392-4469, support@exigo.com
5. MultiSoft: +1 800-284-0616, support@multisoft.com

India:

1. MLM Software India: +91 98844 44444, support@mlmsoftwareindia.com
2. Direct Selling Software: +91 99999 99999, support@directsellingsoftware.com
3. MLM Solutions: +91 98888 88888, support@mlmsolutions.in
4. Pro MLM Software India: +91 99999 99999, support@promlmsoftwareindia.com
5. MLM Technology: +91 98844 44444, support@mlmtechnology.com

Support Options:

1. Phone support
2. Email support
3. Live chat support
4. Online documentation
5. Training and onboarding

Key Features:

1. Customizable branding
2. Multi-level marketing (MLM) support
3. E-commerce integration
4. Payment gateway integration
5. Reporting and analytics
6. Mobile app support
7. Security and compliance

Chapter 23: Measuring Success and Tracking Performance

☐ **Measuring Success and Tracking Performance of direct selling marketing**

Measuring Success and Tracking Performance of Direct Selling Marketing:

Key Performance Indicators (KPIs):

1. Sales Revenue
2. Conversion Rate
3. Customer Acquisition Cost (CAC)
4. Customer Lifetime Value (CLV)
5. Return on Investment (ROI)
6. Return on Ad Spend (ROAS)
7. Website Traffic
8. Social Media Engagement
9. Lead Generation
10. Customer Retention Rate

Metrics for Direct Selling:

1. Sales per Representative
2. Average Order Value (AOV)
3. Number of Customers
4. Customer Retention Rate
5. Sales Growth Rate
6. Productivity per Representative
7. Conversion Rate of Leads
8. Lead Response Time
9. Sales Cycle Length
10. Customer Satisfaction (CSAT)

Tools for Tracking Performance:

1. Google Analytics
2. CRM Software (e.g., Salesforce)
3. Marketing Automation Tools (e.g., HubSpot)
4. Social Media Analytics Tools (e.g., Hootsuite)
5. Email Marketing Tools (e.g., Mailchimp)
6. Sales Tracking Software (e.g., Zoho)
7. Customer Feedback Tools (e.g., SurveyMonkey)
1. Direct Selling Platform Analytics (e.g., Shopify)
2. Mobile App Analytics (e.g., Firebase)
3. Call Tracking Software (e.g., CallRail)

Direct Selling Platforms with Built-in Analytics:

1. Shopify
2. Amazon Associates
3. eBay Partner Network
4. Rakuten
5. ShareASale
6. ClickBank
7. Commission Junction
8. AvantLink
9. Refersion
10. Impact

Best Practices for Measuring Success:

1. Set clear goals and objectives
2. Track relevant KPIs and metrics
3. Use analytics tools to monitor performance
4. Regularly review and adjust strategy
5. Conduct A/B testing and experimentation
6. Monitor customer feedback and satisfaction
7. Analyze sales funnel and conversion rates
8. Optimize marketing campaigns for better ROI
9. Use data to inform product development
10. Continuously evaluate and improve performance

Common Challenges in Measuring Success:

1. Lack of clear goals and objectives
2. Insufficient data and analytics

3. Difficulty tracking customer journey
4. Limited resources and budget
5. Inaccurate or incomplete data
6. Complexity of multi-channel sales
7. Difficulty measuring ROI
8. Limited visibility into sales funnel
9. Inadequate training and support
10. Inconsistent reporting and analysis

☐ Key metrics for digital direct selling (website traffic, social media engagement, lead generation)

Key Metrics for Digital Direct Selling:
Website Traffic:

1. Unique Visitors
2. Page Views
3. Bounce Rate
4. Average Session Duration
5. Conversion Rate
6. Traffic Sources (organic, paid, referral)
7. Landing Page Conversion Rate
8. Exit Pages
9. Time on Site
10. Scroll Depth

Social Media Engagement:

1. Follower Growth Rate
2. Engagement Rate (likes, comments, shares)
3. Reach (impressions)
4. Social Media Conversion Rate
5. Social Media ROI
6. Top-Performing Content
7. Social Media Sentiment Analysis
8. Response Rate and Time
9. Social Media Share of Voice
10. Influencer Engagement

Lead Generation:

1. Lead Volume
2. Lead Quality (conversion rate)
3. Cost Per Lead (CPL)
4. Lead Source (email, social, paid ads)
5. Lead Conversion Rate
6. Sales Qualified Leads (SQLs)
7. Lead Response Time
8. Lead Nurturing Conversion Rate
9. Lead Scoring

10. Return on Lead Generation Investment (ROLG)

Additional Metrics:

1. Customer Acquisition Cost (CAC)
2. Customer Lifetime Value (CLV)
3. Return on Investment (ROI)
4. Return on Ad Spend (ROAS)
5. Email Open and Click-Through Rates
6. Mobile App Downloads and Engagement
7. Customer Retention Rate
8. Net Promoter Score (NPS)
9. Sales Funnel Conversion Rates
10. Average Order Value (AOV)

Tools for Tracking:

1. Google Analytics
2. Google Tag Manager
3. Mixpanel
4. HubSpot
5. Salesforce
6. Hootsuite Insights
7. Sprout Social
8. Mailchimp
9. Ahrefs
10. SEMrush

Best Practices:

1. Set clear goals and objectives
2. Track relevant metrics
3. Use analytics tools
4. Regularly review and adjust strategy
5. Conduct A/B testing
6. Monitor customer feedback
7. Analyze sales funnel
8. Optimize marketing campaigns

9. Use data to inform product development
10. Continuously evaluate and improve performance

- **Tools for tracking (Google Analytics, social media insights, Email marketing metrics, Sales funnel analysis)**

Tools for Tracking:

Google Analytics:

1. Website traffic analysis
2. Conversion tracking
3. Goal setting and tracking
4. Audience insights (demographics, interests)
5. Behavior analysis (bounce rate, session duration)
6. Acquisition analysis (traffic sources)
7. E-commerce tracking

Social Media Insights:

1. Hootsuite Insights
2. Sprout Social
3. Facebook Insights
4. Twitter Analytics
5. Instagram Insights
6. LinkedIn Analytics
7. Social media listening tools (e.g., Brand24)

Email Marketing Metrics:

1. Mailchimp
2. Constant Contact
3. Klaviyo
4. HubSpot Email
5. Campaign Monitor
6. Sendinblue
7. Email open and click-through rates

Sales Funnel Analysis:

1. HubSpot Sales
2. Salesforce
3. Zoho CRM
4. Pipedrive
5. Google Analytics (goal tracking)
6. Mixpanel (funnel analysis)
7. ChartMogul (revenue analytics)

Additional Tools:

1. Mixpanel (product analytics)
2. Hotjar (heat maps, user behavior)
3. Crazy Egg (A/B testing, heat maps)
4. Unbounce (landing page optimization)
5. CallRail (call tracking)
6. Ahrefs (SEO analysis)
7. SEMrush (SEO and competitor analysis)

All-in-One Tools:

1. HubSpot (marketing, sales, customer service)
2. Salesforce (sales, marketing, customer service)
3. Zoho One (marketing, sales, customer service)
4. Infusionsoft (marketing automation)

5. Marketo (marketing automation)

Free Tools:

1. Google Analytics
2. Google Tag Manager
3. Facebook Insights
4. Twitter Analytics
5. Instagram Insights
6. LinkedIn Analytics

7. Mailchimp (free plan)

Premium Tools:

1. HubSpot (starting at $50/month)
2. Salesforce (starting at $75/month)
3. Zoho One (starting at $30/month)
4. Mixpanel (starting at $25/month)
5. Hootsuite Insights (starting at $19/month)

☐ CRM software and sales funnel analysis (Sales Revenue)

CRM Software and Sales Funnel Analysis:
CRM Software:

1. Salesforce
2. HubSpot CRM
3. Zoho CRM
4. Pipedrive
5. Freshsales
6. Microsoft Dynamics 365
7. Oracle CX Sales
8. SAP Sales Cloud
9. Copper CRM
10. Insightly CRM

Sales Funnel Analysis:

1. Lead Generation
2. Lead Qualification
3. Opportunity Creation
4. Conversion Rate
5. Sales Revenue
6. Customer Acquisition Cost (CAC)
7. Customer Lifetime Value (CLV)
8. Sales Cycle Length
9. Sales Velocity
10. Funnel Drop-Off Points

Sales Funnel Stages:

1. Awareness
2. Interest
3. Desire
4. Action
5. Conversion
6. Retention
7. Advocacy

Sales Revenue Metrics:

1. Total Revenue
2. Average Sale Price (ASP)
3. Revenue Growth Rate
4. Sales Conversion Rate
5. Revenue per Sales Representative
6. Sales Cycle Length
7. Deal Size
8. Sales Velocity
9. Customer Retention Rate
10. Upsell/Cross-Sell Revenue

CRM Features for Sales Funnel Analysis:

1. Lead tracking
2. Opportunity management
3. Sales forecasting
4. Pipeline management
5. Sales analytics
6. Reporting and dashboards
7. Automation and workflows

8. Integration with marketing tools
9. Mobile access
10. Customization and scalability

Benefits of CRM Software:

1. Improved sales productivity
2. Enhanced customer engagement
3. Increased sales revenue
4. Better sales forecasting
5. Improved customer retention
6. Streamlined sales processes
7. Enhanced collaboration
8. Data-driven decision-making
9. Scalability and flexibility

10. Integration with other tools

Best Practices for Sales Funnel Analysis:

1. Define clear sales stages
2. Track key metrics
3. Identify funnel drop-off points
4. Analyze sales cycle length
5. Optimize sales processes
6. Use data to inform decisions
7. Continuously monitor and adjust
8. Align sales and marketing efforts
9. Use CRM software to streamline processes
10. Provide regular training and coaching

☐ Adjusting strategies based on data

Adjusting Strategies Based on Data:
Why Adjust Strategies:

1. Improve performance
2. Increase efficiency
3. Enhance customer experience
4. Stay competitive
5. Maximize ROI

Data-Driven Decision Making:

1. Analyze key metrics
2. Identify trends and patterns
3. Set data-driven goals
4. Test hypotheses
5. Refine strategies

Types of Data to Analyze:

1. Website analytics (Google Analytics)
2. Social media metrics (engagement, reach)
3. Email marketing metrics (open rates, click-through)
4. Sales funnel metrics (conversion rates, drop-off)
5. Customer feedback (surveys, reviews)

6. Market research (trends, competitor analysis)
7. CRM data (customer behavior, interactions)
8. Financial data (revenue, expenses)

Adjusting Strategies:

1. Content marketing
2. Social media advertising
3. Email marketing campaigns
4. Sales funnel optimization
5. Customer segmentation
6. Pricing strategies
7. Product development
8. Customer service improvements

Tools for Data Analysis:

1. Google Analytics
2. Google Data Studio
3. Mixpanel
4. HubSpot
5. Salesforce
6. Excel
7. Tableau

8. Power BI

Best Practices:

1. Set clear goals and objectives
2. Use relevant data metrics
3. Analyze data regularly
4. Test and refine strategies
5. Collaborate with teams
6. Stay up-to-date with industry trends
7. Use data visualization tools
8. Document and track changes

Common Challenges:

1. Data quality issues
2. Lack of resources
3. Insufficient data
4. Difficulty interpreting data
5. Resistance to change
6. Limited budget
7. Complexity of data analysis
8. Ensuring data-driven culture

Benefits of Data-Driven Strategies:

1. Improved decision making
2. Enhanced customer experience
3. Increased efficiency
4. Better ROI
5. Competitive advantage
6. Improved collaboration
7. Data-driven innovation
8. Reduced risk

Chapter 24: Overview of video editing software's and keyword research tools and techniques

☐ Overview of video editing software's

Video Editing Software for Beginners:

1. iMovie (Free, Mac)
2. Adobe Premiere Elements ($99.99, Windows, Mac)
3. DaVinci Resolve (Free, Windows, Mac)
4. Shotcut (Free, Windows, Mac, Linux)
5. CyberLink PowerDirector ($99.99, Windows)

Professional Video Editing Software:

1. Adobe Premiere Pro ($20.99/month, Windows, Mac)
2. Avid Media Composer ($23.99/month, Windows, Mac)
3. Final Cut Pro X ($299.99, Mac)
4. Blackmagic Design DaVinci Resolve Studio ($299, Windows, Mac)
5. Sony Vegas Pro ($599, Windows)

Free Video Editing Software:

1. Shotcut (Windows, Mac, Linux)
2. Lightworks (Windows)
3. VSDC Free Video Editor (Windows)
4. OpenShot (Windows, Mac, Linux)
5. Hitfilm Express (Windows, Mac)

Online Video Editing Tools:

1. Canva Video Editor (Web-based)
2. WeVideo (Web-based)
3. Clipchamp (Web-based)
4. Kizoa (Web-based)
5. Wideo (Web-based)

Mobile Video Editing Apps:

1. Adobe Premiere Rush (iOS, Android)
2. InShot (iOS, Android)
3. PowerDirector (iOS, Android)
4. Filmic Pro (iOS)
5. Quik (iOS, Android)

Video Editing Software for Specific Industries:

1. Filmmaking: Avid Media Composer, Blackmagic Design DaVinci Resolve Studio
2. Broadcasting: Adobe Premiere Pro, Avid Media Composer
3. Social Media: Adobe Premiere Rush, Canva Video Editor
4. Education: WeVideo, Kizoa

Video Editing Software Comparisons:

1. Adobe Premiere Pro vs. Final Cut Pro X
2. DaVinci Resolve vs. Adobe Premiere Pro
3. Avid Media Composer vs. Blackmagic Design DaVinci Resolve Studio
4. iMovie vs. Adobe Premiere Elements

System Requirements for Video Editing Software:

1. Processor: Intel Core i5 or AMD equivalent
2. RAM: 8 GB or more
3. Storage: 256 GB or more
4. Graphics Card: NVIDIA GeForce or AMD Radeon
5. Operating System: Windows 10 or macOS High Sierra or later

Video Editing Tutorials and Resources:

1. YouTube tutorials
2. Udemy courses
3. Skillshare courses
4. Adobe Creative Cloud tutorials
5. Video editing blogs (e.g., PremiumBeat, Video Editing Pro)

1. AI-powered video editing
2. Cloud-based video editing
3. 360-degree video editing
4. Virtual reality (VR) video editing
5. Augmented reality (AR) video editing

Video Editing Trends and Future Developments:

☐ Overview of keyword research tools and techniques

Keyword Research Tools:

1. Google Keyword Planner (Free)
2. Ahrefs Keyword Explorer ($99-$999/month)
3. SEMrush Keyword Magic Tool ($99-$449/month)
4. Moz Keyword Explorer ($99-$599/month)
5. Long Tail Pro ($27-$97/month)
6. KWFinder ($29-$99/month)
7. Ubersuggest (Free)
8. AnswerThePublic (Free)
9. Keyword Tool ($29-$99/month)
10. SECockpit ($29-$99/month)

Advanced Keyword Research Techniques:

1. Keyword clustering
2. Topic modeling
3. Entity-based keyword research
4. Intent-based keyword research
5. Long-tail keyword research
6. Keyword gap analysis
7. Competitor keyword analysis
8. Keyword research for featured snippets
9. Keyword research for voice search
10. Keyword research for international markets

Keyword Research for YouTube:

1. TubeBuddy (Free-$9.99/month)
2. VidIQ (Free-$39.99/month)
3. Keyword Tool for YouTube (Free)
4. YouTube Keyword Research Tool (Free)
5. Ahrefs YouTube Keyword Research ($99-$999/month)

Keyword Research for E-commerce:

1. Google Shopping Keyword Research (Free)
2. Amazon Keyword Research Tool (Free)
3. eBay Keyword Research Tool (Free)
4. SEMrush E-commerce Keyword Research ($99-$449/month)
5. Ahrefs E-commerce Keyword Research ($99-$999/month)

Keyword Research for Local SEO:

1. Google My Business Keyword Research (Free)
2. Moz Local Keyword Research ($99-$599/month)
3. Ahrefs Local Keyword Research ($99-$999/month)
4. BrightLocal Keyword Research ($29-$99/month)
5. Whitespark Keyword Research ($20-$100/month)

Keyword Research Tools Comparison:

1. Ahrefs vs. SEMrush
2. Moz vs. Ahrefs
3. Long Tail Pro vs. KWFinder

4. Google Keyword Planner vs. Ahrefs
5. Ubersuggest vs. AnswerThePublic

Keyword Research Best Practices:

1. Conduct thorough keyword research
2. Analyze competitor keywords
3. Use long-tail keywords
4. Optimize for intent-based keywords
5. Use keyword research tools
6. Monitor keyword performance
7. Adjust keyword strategy
8. Use keyword clustering
9. Use entity-based keyword research
10. Stay up-to-date with keyword trends

Common Keyword Research Mistakes:

1. Targeting overly broad keywords
2. Ignoring long-tail keywords
3. Not analyzing competitor keywords
4. Not optimizing for intent-based keywords
5. Not using keyword research tools
6. Not monitoring keyword performance
7. Not adjusting keyword strategy
8. Using outdated keyword research methods
9. Not considering keyword cannibalization
10. Not using keyword clustering

Keyword Research Certifications and Courses:

1. HubSpot Keyword Research Certification (Free)
2. Moz Keyword Research Certification ($599)
3. Ahrefs Keyword Research Certification ($999)
4. SEMrush Keyword Research Certification ($449)
5. Coursera Keyword Research Course ($39-$79)

Keyword Research for Voice Search:

1. Optimize for natural language keywords
2. Use long-tail keywords
3. Target featured snippets
4. Use entity-based keyword research
5. Analyze competitor voice search keywords

Keyword Research for International Markets:

1. Use country-specific keyword research tools
2. Analyze local competitor keywords
3. Optimize for language and cultural differences
4. Use international keyword research databases
5. Consider geo-targeting and language targeting

www.ingramcontent.com/pod-product-compliance
Lightning Source LLC
Chambersburg PA
CBHW082244220526
45469CB00009B/2874